SUMMIT
COOKING IN COLOUR

SUMMIT
COOKING
IN COLOUR

Compiled by Tess Mallos

SUMMIT BOOKS
Published by Paul Hamlyn Pty Limited
Sydney·Auckland·London·New York

Summit Books
Published by Paul Hamlyn Pty Limited
176 South Creek Road, Dee Why West, NSW, 2099
First published 1977
© Copyright Paul Hamlyn Pty Limited 1977
Typeset by G.T. Setters Pty Limited
Printed in Hong Kong by
Leefung-Asco Printers Ltd.

ISBN 0 7271 0142 0.

CONTENTS

Introduction 6

Soups 8

Sauces 16

Entrées 20

Fish & Shellfish 30

Eggs & Cheese 40

Pasta & Rice 50

Vegetables 56

Salads 64

Meat Main Dishes

    Family Fare 74

    Quick Meat Dishes 86

    Outdoor Meat Dishes 92

    Special Occasion Meat Dishes 96

Poultry & Game 106

Puddings & Desserts

    Hot Puddings 118

    Cold Desserts 126

    Pies & Tarts 134

Cakes & Biscuits

    Cakes & Tortes 140

    Small Cakes & Biscuits 150

Scones & Quick Breads 160

Yeast Breads 168

Glossary 173

Index 174

INTRODUCTION

It is said that experience is the best teacher. Many years of experience in working with cooks, both male and female, has taught me just what is expected of a cookbook if it is to perform its function adequately. This book is planned to incorporate all of these criteria.

First and foremost, recipe directions should be easy to follow so that even a novice cook will be tempted to try them. The recipes here give an indication of the yield or number of serves and the total cooking time where applicable. Preparation time has not been given, however, as no two cooks can perform a certain task in the same time. Cup and spoon measures are used as much as possible as it is a far more efficient means of meal preparation than constantly grappling with scales. Please read the section on Weights and Measures before attempting any recipe.

The ingredients required for a particular recipe should be readily obtainable — not so difficult as we are fortunate in that we have such a wealth of fine foods available almost all year round. The selection of recipes is such that, whatever the occasion or the season, you will find an ample range of dishes from which to choose.

A special feature of the book is that every recipe has a photographic illustration of the finished dish. In a few instances a preparation detail or the basic ingredients have been illustrated for art's sake as well as the cook's. Whether planning family meals or a sumptuous dinner party, you will be better able to visualise your final result with the aid of the illustrations; they will assist you in the presentation of a dish and its garnish. I hope too, they will inspire you to be adventurous in the kitchen and to try out new or unfamiliar recipes.

So here it is, your *Summit Cooking in Colour* for all occasions, compiled with your needs in mind. Successful cooking and enjoyable eating to you and yours!

TESS MALLOS

GUIDE TO WEIGHTS & MEASURES

Both metric and imperial weights are given for each recipe in this book; fluid measures are given in cups and spoons as set out below. A good set of scales, a graduated measuring cup and a set of measuring spoons will be most helpful.

Note: For successful cooking use either metric weights and measures **or** imperial weights and measures — do **not** use a mixture of the two.

1 cup = 250 ml = 9 fl oz (an average breakfast cup)
½ cup = 125 ml
¼ cup = 63 ml
1 tablespoon = 20 ml (a generous B.S.I. tablespoon)
1 teaspoon = 5 ml

Weight, volume & liquid measures

In all recipes, imperial equivalents of metric measures are shown in parentheses, e.g. 500 g (1 lb). Although the metric yield of cup or weighed measures is approximately 10% greater, the proportions remain the same.

Important points

Although accurate measuring is not crucial for many recipes, it is important that standard measures be used for baked goods. The baked goods recipes in this book have been tested with the 250 ml cup. Use 60 g (2 oz) eggs. If smaller eggs are used it may be necessary to add a little more of the liquid used in the recipe to get the correct consistency.

Oven temperature guide

Description of oven	Celsius °C	Farenheit °F	Gas mark
Cool	100	200	¼
Very slow	120	250	½
Slow	150-160	300-325	2-3
Moderately slow	160-170	325-350	3-4
Moderate	180-190	350-375	4-5
Moderately hot	190-200	375-400	5-6
Hot	200-230	400-450	6-8
Very hot	230-250	450-500	8-9

Note: Where two temperatures are given, the lower temperature relates to gas ovens, the higher to electric ovens. These temperatures are meant as a guide only as stoves vary. Follow the manufacturer's guide for your particular oven.

Substitutions

cooking chocolate: 30 g (1 oz)	=	3 tablespoons cocoa + 30 g (1 oz) butter
cream, sour: 1 cup	=	1 tablespoon lemon juice or white vinegar + cream to make 1 cup (*see* sour milk)
garlic, fresh: 1 clove	=	¼ teaspoon powdered or to taste
ginger, fresh green root	=	Use preserved ginger with syrup washed off, or ¼-½ teaspoon ground ginger to 1 tablespoon grated fresh ginger root
herbs, fresh chopped: 1 tablespoon	=	1 teaspoon dried or ½ teaspoon powdered
milk, fresh: 1 cup	=	½ cup evaporated milk + ½ cup water
milk, sour: 1 cup	=	1 tablespoon lemon juice or white vinegar + milk to make 1 cup with similar flavour and reaction in cooking. To get the true, thick consistency, warm slightly
self raising flour: 1 cup	=	1 cup plain flour + 2 teaspoons baking powder
yeast, compressed: 30 g (1 oz)	=	2 teaspoons (1 sachet – 7 g or ¼ oz) active dry yeast

Equivalents

Key — t — teaspoon (5 ml)
       T — tablespoon (20 ml)
       C — 250 ml metric cup in conjunction with metric weight, or 8 fl oz cup in conjunction with imperial weight

Ingredient	30g / 1 oz	125g / 4 oz	250g / 8 oz
almonds, ground	¼C	1¼C	2¼C
slivered	¼C	1C	2¼C
whole	¼C	¾C	1½C
apricots, dried, chopped	¼C	1C	2C
whole	3T	1C	1¾C
arrowroot	2T	⅔C	1⅓C
barley	2T	⅔C	1¼C
breadcrumbs, dry	¼C	1C	2C
soft	½C	2C	4¼C
biscuit crumbs	¼C	1¼C	2¼C
butter, margarine or fat	6t	½C	1C
cheese, grated, lightly packed			
natural Cheddar	¼C	1C	2C
processed Cheddar	2T	¾C	1⅔C
Parmesan, Romano (i.e. hard grating cheese)	¼C	1C	2¼C
cherries, glacé, chopped	2T	¾C	1½C
whole	2T	⅔C	1⅓C
cocoa	¼C	1¼C	2¼C
coconut, desiccated	⅓C	1⅓C	2⅔C
shredded	⅔C	2½C	5C
cornflour, custard powder	3T	1C	2C
cornflakes	1C	4½C	8⅓C
currants	2T	¾C	1⅔C
dates, chopped	2T	¾C	1⅔C
whole, pitted	2T	¾C	1½C
figs, dried, chopped	2T	¾C	1½C
flour, plain or self-raising	¼C	1C	2C
wholemeal	3T	1C	1¾C
fruit, mixed dried	2T	¾C	1½C
haricot beans	2T	⅔C	1¼C
milk powder, full cream	¼C	1¼C	2¼C
non-fat	⅓C	1½C	3¼C
nuts *see under names*			
oatmeal	2T	¾C	1⅔C
pasta, short (e.g. macaroni)	2T	¾C	1⅔C
peanuts, shelled, raw, whole	2T	¾C	1½C
roasted, whole	2T	¾C	1⅔C
chopped	¼C	1C	2C
peas, split	2T	⅔C	1¼C
peel, mixed	2T	¾C	1½C
prunes, whole, pitted	2T	¾C	1¼C
raisins	¼C	¾C	1½C
rice, short grain, raw	2T	⅔C	1¼C
long grain, raw	2T	¾C	1½C
rolled oats	2T	1⅓C	2¾C
semolina	2T	¾C	1½C
sugar, white crystalline	6t	½C	1C
caster	5t	½C	1¼C
icing	2T	¾C	1½C
brown, firmly packed	2T	¾C	1½C
sultanas	2T	¾C	1½C
walnuts, chopped	¼C	1C	2C
halved	⅓C	1¼C	2½C
yeast, active dried	8t	—	—
compressed	6t	—	—

SOUPS

A soup can be a marvellous prelude to a meal. Many recipes are simple to prepare; all you need is the basic stock on hand, or stock tablets and water. Some soups are a meal in themselves—served with crusty bread, toast or crackers they are great for fire-side winter meals or a weekend lunch, brunch or supper.

Pumpkin Soup

Serves: 4
Cooking time: 20-30 minutes

500 g (1 lb) pumpkin, cut into pieces
1 onion, chopped
¼ teaspoon salt
6 peppercorns
1 tablespoon butter
2 tablespoons plain flour
pinch nutmeg
125 g (4 oz) processed Cheddar cheese, shredded

Cover pumpkin, onion, salt and peppercorns with water. Simmer until vegetables are cooked. Drain and reserve pumpkin liquid, make up to 2 cups with water if necessary. Mash pumpkin and onion or purée in blender.

Melt butter in a saucepan, blend in flour and cook 1 minute. Gradually add pumpkin liquid and stir until boiling. Add mashed vegetables, nutmeg and adjust seasonings. Just before serving add shredded cheese, and stir until melted. Do not reboil.

Beef Stock

Yield: 2½ litres (4 pints)
Cooking time: 3 hours

2 kg (4 lb) meaty soup bones
500 g (1 lb) shin of beef
1 onion, quartered
1 stalk celery, chopped
1 large carrot, quartered
1 turnip, quartered
bouquet garni
½ teaspoon whole peppercorns
salt

Rinse bones in cold water, and dice shin beef. Place bones and meat in a large boiler and add cold water to almost cover meat and bones. Bring slowly to the boil, skimming when necessary. Add remaining ingredients, cover and simmer gently for 3 hours. Strain through a fine sieve into a basin, cover and chill. When fat sets on top, remove it and store stock in refrigerator or freezer until required.

Chicken stock: Substitute 1 large boiling fowl weighing about 2 kg (4 lb) for soup bones and shin beef. Rinse fowl, place in boiler and proceed as above. Reserve chicken fat for pâtés if desired. (Carcases from roast chicken may be added to pot for a richer stock.) Yields 1½ to 2 litres (2½ to 3 pints).

Cooking tip: For a rich, brown beef stock, place bones, meat and chopped vegetables in a large baking dish with 3 to 4 tablespoons good beef dripping or trimmed fat from beef. Cook in a hot oven for 30 minutes until browned. Place in boiler, add water, bouquet garni and seasonings and cook as above.

Cream of Lettuce Soup

Serves: 6-8
Cooking time: 1¼ hours

2 medium-sized young lettuces
5 cups milk
1 small white onion, quartered
3 parsley stalks
1 clove
1 bay leaf
90 g (3 oz) butter
2 teaspoons plain flour
pinch of ground nutmeg
salt and pepper to taste
2 egg yolks
½ cup cream
chopped parsley for garnish
croutons

Discard coarse outer leaves of lettuce. Shred lettuce finely, rinse under running cold water and dry thoroughly.

Heat milk slowly to scalding point with onion, parsley, clove and bay leaf (about 20 minutes). Strain and discard flavourings. Melt half the butter in a large, heavy-based saucepan, stir in flour, cook for about 1 minute. Add scalded milk gradually, stirring all the time over moderate heat until just below boiling point. Add shredded lettuce and simmer gently over very low heat for 30 minutes. Stand soup on an asbestos mat to avoid burning. Add nutmeg, salt and pepper.

Rub soup through a sieve or purée in an electric blender. Return purée to clean saucepan, place over moderate heat and bring almost to the boil. Simmer 10 minutes, stirring occasionally

Beat egg yolks with cream. Add with remaining butter to simmering puree, stirring continuously. Adjust seasoning. Garnish with chopped parsley and serve croutons separately.

Cream of celery soup: Use 750 g (1½ lb) celery, well washed and chopped, instead of lettuce.

Cream of cauliflower soup: Use 750 g (1½ lb) cauliflower, well washed and broken into small flowerets, instead of lettuce.

Pea Soup

Serves: 8
Cooking time: 3 hours

500 g (1 lb) split dried peas
1 kg (2 lb) bacon or ham bones
1 onion, finely chopped
8 cups water
salt
freshly ground pepper
croutons for garnish

Wash peas well and place in a large saucepan with bones and water. Bring to the boil, skimming when necessary. Add onion, cover and simmer very gently for 2½ hours. Remove bones and scrape off meat. Rub soup through sieve. Return meat to soup. Season to taste with salt and pepper and stir in a little more water if too thick.

Reheat soup and serve with croutons or toast.

Dutch pea soup: Simmer 1 Rookwurst sausage in water for 30 minutes—do not boil. Slice into soup tureen and add hot soup.

Cooking tip: To prevent split peas sticking to base of saucepan, do not stir during cooking.

Cream of Mushroom Soup

Serves: 8
Cooking time: 15 minutes

375 g (12 oz) mushrooms
125 g (4 oz) butter
freshly ground pepper to taste
½ teaspoon salt
1 garlic clove, crushed
5 cups chicken stock
few drops Tabasco sauce
½ cup cream, warmed
croutons for serving

Before cooking mushrooms, select some of the smallest ones and take a slice from the centre of each so that you have the outline of the mushroom. Put aside for garnish.

Wash mushrooms only if they are field mushrooms; if cultivated, wipe with a damp cloth. Do not peel, and only trim off discoloured section of stalks. Chop mushrooms and fry in sizzling butter with a good grind of fresh pepper and salt. Add garlic towards end of frying. Press through a sieve or purée in an electric blender with 1 cup of stock. Add purée to remaining stock in a large saucepan and bring to simmering point. Add Tabasco sauce and reserved mushroom slices and simmer 5 minutes. Stir in warm cream. Taste and adjust seasoning if necessary. Serve hot with croutons.

Cream of Carrot Soup

Serves: 8
Cooking time: 30 minutes

500 g (1 lb) young carrots
1 onion, chopped
2 tablespoons butter
2 garlic cloves, crushed
5 cups chicken stock or water and chicken stock cubes
4 parsley stalks
salt and pepper to taste
½ cup cream
finely chopped parsley for garnish

Buy very young carrots with smooth skins. Cut off carrot tops if green and remove any rough bumps on skin. Wash carrots well but do not scrape as the skin gives both colour and flavour to the soup. Cut carrots into 1 cm (½ inch) slices and sauté with onions in butter until onion is transparent. Add garlic, cook 1 minute then add chicken stock, parsley stalks, salt and pepper. Bring to the boil, reduce heat, cover and simmer 20 minutes. Remove parsley stalks and discard. Rub soup through a sieve or purée in an electric blender. Reheat, stir a cup of warm soup into cream and combine with remaining soup. Bring to simmering point. Avoid boiling as cream may curdle. Adjust seasoning.

Serve hot, sprinkled with chopped parsley.

Gazpacho

Serves: 8

1 large ripe tomato, skinned
1 small cucumber, peeled
1 medium-sized green capsicum
¼ cup olive oil
¼ cup white vinegar
salt
freshly ground pepper
4 spring onions
1 x 430 g (15 oz) can beef consommé
1 soup can water
1½ cups tomato juice
Croutons
4 slices white bread
vegetable oil for frying
2 garlic cloves, crushed (optional)
salt

Remove seeds from tomato and cucumber, cut into 5 mm (¼ inch) cubes. Remove seeds and white membrane from green capsicum and cut into 5 mm (¼-inch) cubes.

Mix oil and vinegar with salt and pepper to taste and combine with tomato, cucumber, green capsicum and sliced spring onions. Allow to stand for 1 hour, stirring occasionally so that vegetables absorb dressing.

Heat consommé with water just long enough to combine, stir in tomato juice and add vegetables. Adjust seasoning.

Chill thoroughly and serve with garlic-flavoured croutons.

Croutons: Slice bread 1 cm (½ inch) thick, remove crusts and cut bread into cubes. Fry in hot oil with garlic (if used) until golden. Drain well on paper towels and sprinkle lightly with salt before serving.

Egg and Prawn Chowder

Serves: 4-6
Cooking time: 30 minutes

2 tablespoons butter
1 onion, chopped
500 g (1 lb) potatoes, peeled and diced
1¼ cups boiling water
salt and pepper
6 hard-boiled eggs, sliced
1 x 310 g (10 oz) can Lima beans, drained
375 g (12 oz) small prawns, shelled and deveined
1¼ cups milk
chopped parsley for garnish

Melt butter in a large saucepan over a low heat and sauté onion until soft but not brown. Add potatoes and water, season well with salt and pepper and bring to the boil. Cover and simmer until potatoes are cooked. Add eggs, beans, prawns and milk. Heat through slowly but do not allow soup to boil. Adjust seasoning, pour into a warmed soup tureen, bowl or deep casserole. Garnish with chopped parsley and serve immediately with buttered pumpernickel or crispbread.

French Onion Soup Gratinée

Serves: 8
Cooking time: 1½ hours
Oven temperature: 180-190° C (350-375° F)

750 g (1½ lb) white onions
3 tablespoons butter
½ teaspoon sugar
6 cups well-flavoured beef stock
½ cup dry white wine or dry vermouth
salt and pepper to taste
8 rounds of French bread
2 cups freshly grated Gruyère cheese

Peel onions and slice thinly. Melt butter in a saucepan, add onion rings and sugar and cook gently over a low heat until onion becomes soft and golden brown. Stir occasionally with a wooden spoon to prevent catching as there must be no hint of burning. Add stock, wine or vermouth, salt and pepper to taste. Cover and simmer gently for 1 hour.

Toast bread in moderate oven until crisp and lightly coloured. Place toast in base of deep casserole or individual ovenproof bowls. Sprinkle half the freshly grated cheese over toast. Pour soup carefully into casserole or bowls so that the cheese covered toast floats gently to the surface. Sprinkle remaining cheese over soup. Place in a moderate oven for 10 minutes or until cheese turns to a deep golden crust without burning.

Serve piping hot.

Fish and Spinach Soup

Serves: 6-8
Cooking time: 2¼ hours

⅔ cup split peas
3 garlic cloves
1 large onion, finely chopped
1 carrot, diced
250 g (8 oz) smoked cod
bouquet garni
2 tomatoes, skinned and chopped
2½ cups chicken stock
1 bunch spinach, chopped and cooked
salt and pepper
2 hard-boiled eggs for garnish

Wash split peas well. Place in a large saucepan, cover with cold water and bring to the boil. Crush 1 garlic clove and add to peas with onion, carrot, cod and bouquet garni. Cover and simmer gently for 2 hours. After 1 hour crush remaining 2 garlic cloves into another large saucepan, add tomatoes and stock and simmer this mixture for 45 minutes. Add cooked spinach. When pea mixture is cooked remove bouquet garni, cool and press through a sieve or purée in an electric blender. Pour purée into spinach and tomato mixture. Season to taste with salt and pepper and heat through. Garnish with finely chopped hard-boiled eggs and serve hot with hot bread rolls and butter or crisp savoury crackers.

Scallop Chowder

Serves: 8
Cooking time: 25 minutes

2 fish heads
2 cups water
1 onion, chopped
salt and pepper
500 g (1 lb) scallops
125 g (4 oz) butter
3 tablespoons plain flour
2 cups milk
½ cup cream
salt and pepper
paprika
chopped parsley
cracker biscuits for serving

Simmer fish heads in a large covered saucepan with water, onion, salt and pepper. Reduce slowly until there are 1½ cups fish stock after straining. Keep aside.

Separate coral from white meat of scallops. Melt butter in a large saucepan until bubbling gently and add both coral and white of scallops. Fry scallops, turning over gently for 5 minutes. Remove and keep aside leaving butter in pan. Blend flour into butter and cook 2 minutes, stir in milk and reserved fish stock. Stir continuously until bubbling. Reduce heat and simmer gently for 10 minutes. Add scallops and simmer for 2 to 3 minutes. Blend a little of the hot soup with cream and stir into remaining soup in pan. Adjust seasoning with salt and pepper. Serve in a tureen, sprinkled with paprika and chopped parsley, accompanied by cracker biscuits. The biscuits are broken up over the chowder.

Oyster Soup Vert

Serves: 4
Cooking time: 10-12 minutes

12 fresh oysters
¼ cup cooked spinach
1½ cups milk
1 cup cream
½ teaspoon monosodium glutamate
1 garlic clove, crushed
½ cup dry white wine
salt and pepper to taste
1 tablespoon butter
sour cream for serving

Place oysters and spinach in blender jar. Cover and purée. Combine milk and cream in a saucepan and bring to simmering point. Add oyster purée, monosodium glutamate and garlic. Simmer for 3 minutes, stirring continuously, add wine and return to simmering point. Season to taste with salt and pepper.

Before serving, stir in butter until melted. Pour soup into bowls and float a spoonful of sour cream on top of each bowl.

Note: Soup must be stirred continuously once ingredients are added to heated milk and cream. Do not bring soup to the boil at any stage.

Venetian Chicken Soup

Serves: 6
Cooking time: 20-25 minutes

1 tablespoon olive oil
2 bacon rashers, chopped
3 spring onions, chopped
2 tablespoons flour
4 cups Chicken Stock (page 8)
¼ cup dry vermouth
2 tablespoons chopped parsley
2 cups diced, cooked chicken (left from making chicken
   stock)
salt
freshly ground pepper
chopped parsley for garnish
grated Parmesan cheese for serving

Heat oil in a large saucepan, add diced bacon and cook until
lightly browned. Add spring onions and sauté until soft. Stir
in flour and cook 2 minutes. Add half the stock and stir until
liquid thickens and bubbles. Add remainder of stock,
vermouth, parsley and diced chicken. Season to taste with
salt and pepper, cover and simmer for 10 minutes. Ladle into
a tureen or individual bowls, sprinkle with a little parsley and
serve with Parmesan cheese.

Bortsch

Serves: 8
Cooking time: 3 hours

2 large brown onions, sliced
3 tablespoons beef dripping or butter
2 kg (4 lb) gravy beef
salt and pepper
pinch mixed herbs
1 bay leaf
1 sprig thyme
3 tablespoons butter
2 large carrots
1 leek
1 turnip
1 medium-sized cabbage, coarsely shredded
2 cups chopped, peeled tomatoes
3 large fresh raw beetroots
sour cream

Brown sliced onion in beef dripping, in a large saucepan. Cut
beef into small cubes discarding as much fat as possible. Add
beef to browned onion and quickly sear on all sides. Add
salt, pepper, mixed herbs, bay leaf and sprig of thyme. Cover
with water to about 1 cm (½ inch) above meat. Simmer for 2
hours or until meat is tender.

Melt butter in a large saucepan. Dice carrots, leek and
turnip and add to sizzling butter. Stir with a wooden spoon
for 2 minutes and then add cabbage and tomatoes Lift the
cooked meat out of the stock and add to fried vegetables.
Skim fat from stock, strain and add to meat and vegetables.
Cover and simmer for 1 hour.

Peel beetroot and shred with a coarse grater or cut into
julienne strips. Add 10 minutes before end of cooking time.
Adjust seasoning. Stir in ½ cup sour cream and serve hot
with additional sour cream.

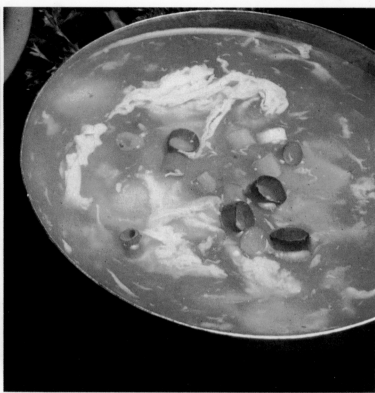

Mulligatawny

Serves: 6
Cooking time: 3 hours

1 kg (2 lb) lamb neck chops
2 tablespoons butter
2 onions, chopped
2 carrots, diced
2 green apples, peeled and diced
1 parsnip or turnip, diced
1 tablespoon curry powder
2 tablespoons flour
1 bay leaf, 1 leafy celery stalk and 3 parsley sprigs tied
    together
2 tablespoons lemon juice
salt to taste
boiled rice to serve

Rinse meat in cold water, place in a soup pot or large saucepan and cover with cold water. Bring slowly to the boil, removing any scum as it rises. Cover and simmer over low heat for 1 hour.

In another saucepan melt the butter and gently fry onion, carrot, apple, parsnip or turnip for 15 minutes. Stir in curry powder and cook for 2 minutes, then add flour and cook for a further 2 minutes. Strain some of the stock and add to this mixture, stirring until thickened and bubbling. Then pour it into the soup pot with the rest of the stock, the bunch of flavouring herbs and the meat. Cover and simmer gently for 1½ hours or until meat is very tender. Remove meat from bones and chop finely. Remove bunch of flavouring herbs from soup and discard. Return chopped, cooked meat to soup and reheat. Add lemon juice and salt and ladle soup into bowls. Serve with boiled rice.

Chinese Egg Noodle Soup

Serves: 4-6
Cooking time: 20 minutes

5 cups chicken stock or water and chicken stock cubes
8 slices root ginger
salt and pepper
1½ cups egg noodles
2 eggs
chopped spring onion for garnish

Pour stock into a saucepan, add ginger and bring slowly to boil to extract the ginger flavour.

Season with salt and pepper. Add noodles, cover saucepan and simmer for 10 minutes or until noodles are cooked. Remove the ginger slices. Lightly beat eggs and pour into the boiling soup, stirring slowly with a fork or whisk to form shreds. Serve at once, garnished with chopped spring onions. Serve with crisp crackers or shrimp crackers.

SAUCES

Many cooks are timid about tackling a sauce recipe. If lumpy or curdled sauces are your problem, use a balloon whisk instead of a wooden spoon. For lighter coloured sauces, avoid using the whisk in an aluminium saucepan as the sauce discolours.

Basic equipment, ideally, should be a double boiler made of heatproof glass, or with the insert made of china; a wooden spoon; a whisk (even good sauciers need them) and a fine sieve or strainer. A heatproof bowl which fits over a saucepan can be used instead of a double boiler. Once you are set up, give it a go and try that Béarnaise or Hollandaise Sauce which will lift your food to the gourmet class.

Mayonnaise
Yield: 1¼ cups

2 egg yolks
salt and white pepper
½ teaspoon dry mustard
2 teaspoons white wine vinegar or lemon juice
1 cup olive oil

Place egg yolks in a heavy mixing bowl and whisk in salt and pepper, mustard and vinegar. Using a tablespoon or a measuring jug, carefully add the oil, drop by drop, mixing it in well. (If you add the oil too quickly, the mayonnaise will curdle. If the mayonnaise curdles, add a little more vinegar and mix well). Once the mixture begins to thicken the oil may be added in a slow stream. When all the oil is beaten in the mayonnaise is ready. It should take only about 5 minutes to add all the oil. Store covered in refrigerator.

Cucumber mayonnaise: Add ¼ cup finely chopped cucumber and 1 teaspoon finely chopped fresh mint.

Garlic mayonnaise (Aioli): Crush 2 garlic cloves in a bowl with salt, add egg yolks and proceed as above. Serve with summer salads.

Béchamel Sauce

1¼ cups milk
1 onion, quartered
1 stalk celery, chopped
1 carrot, chopped
6 peppercorns
1 blade of mace
1 bay leaf
2 cloves
2 tablespoons butter
2 tablespoons plain flour
salt

Place the milk, onion, celery, carrot, peppercorns, mace, bay leaf and cloves into the top half of a double boiler over gently boiling water, cover the pan and heat very slowly for 30 minutes. Strain the milk.

Melt the butter in a heavy-based saucepan, stir in flour and cook 1 minute over a moderate heat. Add the milk, and heat, stirring constantly until boiling, then reduce heat to low and cook for 2 minutes. Season to taste with salt.

White sauce: Use 1 cup milk and do not infuse with the flavouring ingredients. Melt butter, stir in flour and finish as above.

Cooking tip: If sauce becomes lumpy, stir briskly with a wire balloon whisk.

16

Tomato Sauce

Yield: 2-2½ cups

¼ cup oil
1 onion, very finely chopped
2 bacon rashers, diced
1 garlic clove, finely chopped
1 small carrot, finely chopped
2 tablespoons flour
1½ cups chopped, peeled tomatoes
¼ cup tomato paste
1 cup stock or water
1 bay leaf
1 small onion, studded with 2 cloves
pinch of dried basil
2 teaspoons brown sugar
salt to taste
freshly ground pepper
5 cm (2 inch) strip lemon peel
2 teaspoons lemon juice

Heat oil in large, heavy-based saucepan. Add onion, bacon, garlic and carrot. Sauté gently for 10 minutes. Stir in flour, cook 1 minute, then add tomatoes and tomato paste. Gradually blend in stock or water. Cook, stirring constantly until sauce boils and thickens. Add all remaining ingredients and simmer gently for 45 minutes, stirring frequently.

Remove bay leaf, clove-studded onion and lemon peel. Adjust seasoning and serve as it is, or strain through a sieve if a smooth sauce is required. Serve with pasta, meat balls, Beef Fondue and barbecued meats.

Cooking tip: Make a double quantity of sauce, store in a screw-topped jar in refrigerator.

Hollandaise Sauce

125 g (4 oz) butter
4 egg yolks
1 tablespoon lemon juice
salt and white pepper

Divide butter into 4 equal pieces, and leave until quite soft. Place 1 portion of the butter and the egg yolks in a bowl or in the top of a double boiler (see cooking tip). Place over hot, but not boiling water, stir quickly and constantly with a wire balloon whisk until butter and eggs are well combined. Add remaining butter, one piece at a time, whisking the mixture constantly until sauce is well mixed and thickened. Remove bowl or top of double boiler from heat and beat sauce for 2 minutes. Add lemon juice, salt and pepper to taste, replace over hot water and beat for a further 2 minutes. Serve with cauliflower, asparagus and broccoli, grilled steak and chicken, poached or grilled fish and poached eggs.

Blender hollandaise: Melt butter and heat gently until just bubbling. Place egg yolks, lemon juice, salt and pepper in blender jar. Cover and blend for a few seconds only. Have butter ready and pour immediately in a steady stream onto yolk mixture. Stop blender as soon as the butter is added.

Cooking tip: If using the stove-top method, do not use a metal double boiler. Either use a double boiler with a china insert, one of heat-proof glass, or a heat-proof bowl over simmering water. Metal can become too hot and cause sauce to curdle.

Espagnole Sauce

Cooking time: 1¼ hours
Yield: 2 cups

60 g (2 oz) butter
2 bacon rashers, chopped
1 carrot, chopped
1 stalk celery, chopped
1 onion, sliced
4 tablespoons plain flour
3 cups Beef Stock (page 8)
4 mushrooms, sliced
2 tablespoons tomato paste
bouquet garni
salt and pepper
2-3 tablespoons sherry

Heat butter in a heavy saucepan, add bacon, carrot, celery and onion and cook gently until vegetables are golden brown—they must not burn. Add flour and stir well. Cook over gentle heat until the roux is a deep golden brown (12 to 15 minutes). Do not allow to burn. Add stock and bring to boil, stirring continuously. Add mushrooms, tomato paste, bouquet garni, salt and pepper and simmer gently, uncovered, for at least 1 hour, stirring fequently and skimming if necessary. Strain through a fine pointed strainer. Add sherry, taste and adjust flavour if necessary before serving.

Mushroom Sauce

125 g (4 oz) button mushrooms
2 spring onions, chopped
2 tablespoons butter
¼ cup dry white wine
1 cup Espagnole Sauce
salt
freshly ground pepper
chopped parsley

Wipe mushroom caps and slice thinly. Sauté spring onions in butter until soft, add mushrooms and cook until lightly browned. Stir in wine and espagnole sauce and cook until bubbling. Adjust seasoning with salt and pepper. Pour into sauce boat and sprinkle with a little chopped parsley. Serve with roast or grilled beef and Beef Fondue.

Creamy mushroom sauce: Replace espagnole sauce with equal quantity of Béchamel Sauce. Serve with veal, chicken, brains and sweetbreads.

Sweet and Sour Sauce

Yield: 2½ cups

1½ cups cold water
½ cup carrots, cut in julienne strips
½ cup fresh pineapple, chopped
½ cup sugar
4 tablespoons vinegar
2 tablespoons soy sauce
1 tablespoon oil
½ cup red or green capsicum, cut in julienne strips
½ cup finely chopped spring onions
3 thin slices fresh root ginger, chopped, or ½ teaspoon
  ground ginger
1 tablespoon cornflour
salt and pepper

Bring water to the boil in a saucepan and cook carrot strips until just tender. Add pineapple pieces and cook for 1 minute. Stir in sugar, vinegar and soy sauce. Cover and simmer for 2 minutes.

Heat oil in a separate pan, and gently fry capsicum strips for 1 minute. Add spring onions, chopped or powdered ginger and fry for a further 2 minutes. Add fried mixture to carrot mixture in saucepan. Blend cornflour to a smooth paste with a little cold water and stir into mixture. Bring to the boil, stirring continuously, until sauce thickens. Simmer for 2 minutes. Season to taste with salt and pepper and serve hot. Serve with grilled fish, lamb and pork, or meat balls.

Béarnaise Sauce

¾ cup white wine
1 tablespoon tarragon vinegar
2 tablespoons finely chopped spring onions
½ teaspoon dried tarragon
1 teaspoon finely chopped parsley
2 peppercorns, crushed
3 egg yolks
250 g (8 oz) butter, melted
salt and pepper

Combine white wine, vinegar, spring onions, tarragon, parsley and peppercorns in a small saucepan and boil until reduced to one-third its original quantity, strain and cool liquid. Mix egg yolks in the top of a double boiler, place over gently simmering water and add strained liquid, stirring constantly.

Gradually add melted butter, stirring continuously until the sauce has the consistency of whipped cream. Add salt and pepper to taste.

Note: Should the sauce curdle add 1 to 2 tablespoons cold water and beat to re-emulsify (the sauce becomes smooth).

Cooking tip: It is not necessary to serve this sauce piping hot. If making sauce a while before using, cover and keep warm over a pan of fairly hot water at side of stove.

ENTRÉES

Appetisers, entreés, starters, hors d'oeuvres, call them what you will. Their purpose is to whet the appetite for what is to come, not to satisfy it.

You will find recipes here for hot, cold, fish, vegetable and fruit starters. To extend your selection of entrées, look through the chapters on Eggs and Cheese, Vegetables, Fish and Shellfish, Pasta and Rice for more recipes.

Smoked Ham with Fruit
Serves: 5

250 g (8 oz) Parma or proscuitto ham
1 small pawpaw
8 ripe figs

Ask your delicatessen to slice the smoked ham wafer thin.

Peel, slice and seed the pawpaw. Peel the figs just before serving, cut each into quarters from the top without cutting through the base. Open out slightly to give a petalled effect. Arrange one pawpaw slice and a fig on each plate and place rolls of ham on one side. If desired fruit and ham may be arranged on a large platter. Serve with a chilled fruity dry white wine.

Variation: Rockmelon or honey dew melon and pears may be used instead of pawpaw and figs.

Stuffed Eggplants
Serves: 4
Cooking time: 45 minutes
Oven temperature: 180-190° C (350-375° F)

4 small eggplants
2 tablespoons butter
1 onion, finely chopped
500 g (1 lb) minced steak
1 tablespoon finely chopped parsley
½ teaspoon mixed spice
salt and pepper
1 tomato, peeled and chopped
¼ cup water
1 egg
¼ cup milk
½ cup grated Cheddar cheese

Cut eggplants in halves lengthways, scoop out centres and chop. Melt half the butter in a saucepan, add onion, chopped eggplant, minced steak, parsley and seasonings. Cook for 10 to 15 minutes, stirring occasionally. Remove from heat and divide mixture between halved eggplants.

Melt remaining butter, mix with tomato and water and season to taste. Pour into a large shallow ovenproof dish. Arrange halved eggplants in a single layer in dish. Bake in a moderate oven for 30 minutes.

Meanwhile, beat egg and milk together, add cheese and season to taste with salt and pepper. Remove dish from oven and place some cheese mixture on top of each eggplant. Return to oven for approximately 15 minutes or until eggplants are tender and cheese is golden brown on top. Serve immediately.

Chicken and Mushroom Vols-au-Vent

Serves: 4
Cooking time: 15-20 minutes
Oven temperature: 180-190° C (350-375° F)

2 chicken stock cubes
¼ cup sour cream
2 tablespoons butter
2 tablespoons plain flour
1 cup milk
2 cups chopped cooked chicken
1 x 250 g (8 oz) can champignons
salt and pepper
4 individual, ready baked vol-au-vent cases

Crumble chicken stock cubes and mix with sour cream.

Melt butter and stir in flour until smooth, cook 1 to 2 minutes over gentle heat. Add milk and, stirring continuously, bring to the boil. Add sour cream mixture, chopped chicken and drained champignons. Season to taste with salt and pepper.

Fill vol-au-vent cases with mixture and place on a baking tray. Bake in a moderate oven for 15 to 20 minutes.

Serve piping hot.

Russian Oysters

For each serving:

12 oysters in the shell
3 tablespoons finely chopped onion or chives
1 hard-boiled egg
1 x 56 g (2 oz) jar black caviare

Oysters must be absolutely fresh. Arrange oysters on a bed of ice. Sprinkle with chopped onion or chives. Separate egg white from egg yolk. Finely chop egg white, sieve egg yolk and sprinkle both over oysters.

Top oysters with black caviare and serve immediately.
Note: It is worthwhile buying genuine caviare for this delectable hors d'oeuvre. You can use less on each oyster than amount stated and your guests would be quite happy to have only 6 or 8 oysters topped with this delicacy, rather than 12 topped with the less expensive lumpfish caviare.

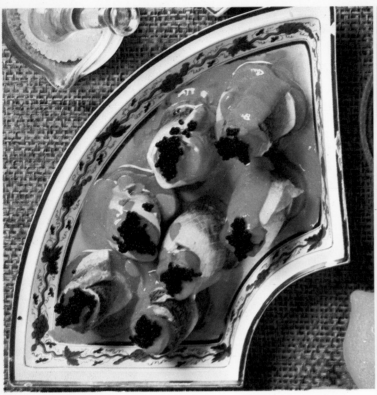 

Russian Herrings
Serves: 4

8 fillets pickled herring or mullet
4 tablespoons finely chopped onion
1 large dill pickle
1 cup Mayonnaise (page 16)
4 tablespoons lemon juice
1 tablespoon tomato paste
1 x 50 g (1¾ oz) jar black caviare

Place fillets of pickled herring on a board with skin side down. Put ½ tablespoon chopped onion on each fillet and roll up tightly. Slice dill pickle into 8 thick slices. Place a rolled fillet of herring on each slice of dill pickle and place on a serving dish. Blend mayonnaise with lemon juice and tomato paste and spoon over each rolled fillet.

Top with caviare and chill before serving.

Chicken Liver Pâté
Serves: 6

2 medium-sized onions, finely chopped
2 garlic cloves, crushed
250 g (8 oz) butter
500 g (1 lb) chicken livers
3 hard-boiled eggs, chopped
2 tablespoons cognac or brandy
salt to taste
freshly ground pepper
¼ teaspoon ground cloves
½ cup Mayonnaise (page 16)
½ teaspoon ground mace
2-3 tablespoons melted butter or chicken fat for topping pâté

Fry onion and garlic in half the butter until soft. Trim chicken livers of threads and gall and chop into small pieces. Add to the cooked onion and sauté gently until firm but still pink inside. Tip into jar of blender. Pour cognac or brandy into pan, stir to lift browned sediment and add to liver with eggs and blend until smooth. Add remaining butter, seasonings and spices and blend again. Taste and adjust seasoning if necessary.

Place in earthenware pot, smooth top and cover with melted butter or chicken fat. Chill for several hours at least, and serve with hot toast or crusty bread.

Stuffed Lemons
Serves: 4

4 large lemons
1 cup flaked canned salmon or tuna
2 tablespoons finely chopped celery
¼ cup Mayonnaise (page 16)
salt and pepper to taste
2 hard-boiled eggs, finely chopped
crisp lettuce leaves
fresh bread and butter for serving

Cut lemons in halves, squeeze out juice and remove pulp, reserve lemon juice. Cut a small slice from the base of each half so they stand upright.

Combine flaked fish with celery, mayonnaise and a teaspoon of the reserved lemon juice. Season to taste with salt and pepper. Fill lemon halves with fish mixture and sprinkle tops with chopped hard-boiled egg.

Serve on a bed of crisp lettuce leaves with fresh brown bread and butter.

Brandied Tomatoes
Serves: 4-6

4-6 firm, ripe tomatoes
½ cup olive oil
½ teaspoon salt
½ teaspoon caster sugar
1 tablespoon finely chopped parsley
1 tablespoon finely chopped fresh basil
1 teaspoon grated lemon rind
3 tablespoons brandy

Place tomatoes in a bowl and cover with boiling water. Leave for 30 seconds, drain, and cover with cold water. Drain again and peel off skins. Thinly slice the tomatoes and arrange in a shallow serving dish.

Combine remaining ingredients and pour over tomatoes. Cover and stand for 30 minutes at room temperature before serving.

Serve with crusty bread or bread rolls and butter.

Cooking tip: If fresh basil is not available, soak 1 teaspoon dried basil in 1 tablespoon of the brandy for 10 minutes.

Stuffed Eggs with Mushrooms

Serves: 6

14 eggs
250 g (8 oz) button mushrooms
½ cup Mayonnaise (page 16)
6 anchovy fillets, chopped
1 tablespoon finely chopped spring onion
salt and pepper
60 g (2 oz) red caviare for garnish (optional)

Boil eggs for 15 minutes, stirring occasionally to set the yolks in the centre. Plunge into cold water, shell when cold. Poach mushrooms in salted water for 5 minutes. Drain and cool. Select 12 good shaped mushrooms for decoration. Chop remaining mushrooms finely. Cut 12 eggs in halves lengthways and carefully remove yolks. Chop the 2 remaining eggs finely. Mix egg yolks, chopped eggs, mayonnaise, anchovies, spring onion, chopped mushrooms, salt and pepper to taste. Spoon mixture into the egg halves. Place stuffed eggs on a serving platter and top with reserved mushrooms. Garnish with red caviare if desired and serve.
Note: Canned champignons may be used instead of fresh button mushrooms.

Crab Crêpes

Serves: 6
Cooking time: 20 minutes
Oven temperature: 180-190° C (350-375° F)

12 crêpes (page 41)
¼ cup grated Parmesan cheese
2 tablespoons butter
Filling
1 × 185 g (6½ oz) can crab meat
3 hard-boiled eggs, chopped
1 tablespoon tomato purée
1 cup Béchamel Sauce (page 16)

Make crêpes as directed.
Prepare filling, spread some over each crêpe and roll up like cigars or fold into quarters. When all crêpes are filled, place in a well-greased, shallow ovenproof casserole in a single layer if rolled, or slightly overlapping if folded. Sprinkle with Parmesan cheese and dot with butter.
Cover with aluminium foil and place in a moderate oven for approximately 20 minutes or until hot. If a crisp finish to the crêpes is preferred, uncover for last 10 minutes of cooking time. Serve immediately.

Filling: Mix drained crab meat, chopped hard-boiled egg, tomato purée and béchamel sauce together.

Variation: Substitute shelled prawns or chopped lobster for crab meat.

Antipasto

Serves: 6-8

250 g (8 oz) button mushrooms
1 x 430 g (15 oz) can artichoke hearts
bottled French or Italian dressing
1 bunch radishes
crisp celery stalks
4 firm tomatoes, sliced
2 pickled beetroot, sliced
12 gherkins
250 g (8 oz) black and green olives
1 x 120 g (4 oz) can pimientos, sliced
6 hard-boiled eggs, halved or sliced
500 g (1 lb) Italian salami of various types, thinly sliced
250 g (8 oz) prosciutto ham, thinly sliced
500 g (1 lb) cheese, sliced (2 varieties)
Mayonnaise (page 16)

Place cleaned and trimmed mushrooms and drained artichoke hearts in separate bowls, cover with French or Italian dressing and leave to marinate for 2 hours, stirring occasionally. Drain and chill.

Wash radishes, trim and cut partly through skin to make 'roses'. Soak in iced water for 2 hours. Cut celery in 8 cm (3 inch) lengths, make into 'curls' if desired.

Arrange ingredients in an attractive pattern on a large serving tray. Serve a bowl of mayonnaise and a cruet of French or Italian dressing separately. Serve Antipasto with slices of fresh crusty bread.

Garlic Prawns

Serves: 12 as an appetiser, 8 as an entrée
Cooking time: 15-22 minutes
Oven temperature: 200-230° C (400-450° F)

1 cup olive oil, preferably Spanish
4 large garlic cloves, peeled and sliced
½ teaspoon salt
1 dried chilli, sliced
1 kg (2 lb) small green prawns, peeled and deveined
chopped parsley

In an earthenware casserole or ovenproof dish, place olive oil, garlic cloves, salt and dried chilli. Place in a hot oven for 10 to 15 minutes until the oil is very hot. Do not overheat as the garlic will burn readily.

Add prawns and cook a further 5 to 7 minutes, just long enough for them to turn pink and heat through.

Serve as an appetiser on small cocktail sticks or as an entrée in small ovenproof or earthenware dishes.
Note: If serving as an entrée, divide all ingredients equally into 8 small dishes before cooking. Sprinkle with chopped parsley, if desired, just before serving.

Chicken and Orange Kebabs
Serves: 4

250 g (8 oz) small mushroom caps
2 tablespoons butter
4 oranges
3 bacon rashers
500 g (1 lb) cooked chicken
¼ cup melted butter

Sauté mushroom caps in butter.

Peel 3 oranges, remove pith and cut into segments. Remove rind from bacon, fry gently and cut into 2.5 cm (1 inch) squares. Remove skin and membrane from chicken and cut into 2.5 cm (1 inch) cubes.

Thread 4 skewers alternately with orange segments, chicken, mushroom caps and bacon. Squeeze juice from remaining orange and combine with melted butter. Brush kebabs and grill over hot coals, turning once or twice until lightly browned on all sides. Serve immediately.
Note: The kebabs may be cooked under a hot grill.

Mushrooms à la Grecque
Serves: 4-6
Cooking time: 25 minutes

500 g (1 lb) mushrooms
1 onion, finely chopped
½ cup olive oil
1 garlic clove, crushed
1 tablespoon lemon juice
1 cup chopped, peeled tomatoes
bouquet garni
1 teaspoon coriander seeds, crushed
salt
freshly ground pepper
chopped parsley for serving

Choose plump, fresh mushrooms. Wipe with damp cloth, trim stalks if long. Slice mushrooms if large, otherwise leave whole. Sauté onion in oil until transparent, add garlic and cook a few seconds longer. Add lemon juice, tomatoes, bouquet garni, coriander and season to taste with salt and pepper. Cover and simmer gently for 10 minutes. Add prepared mushrooms and simmer uncovered for 10 to 15 minutes. Remove bouquet garni, cool, place in serving dish and chill. Sprinkle with chopped parsley and serve cold.
Cooking Tip: Only high quality olive oil should be used if this dish is to be served chilled, as most oils coagulate when chilled. If another oil is preferred, chill for a short time only.

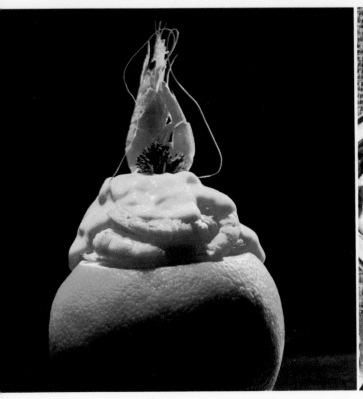 

Grapefruit Prawns
Serves: 6

3 grapefruit
250 g (8 oz) small cooked prawns
salt and pepper
½ cup Mayonnaise (page 16)
6 medium-sized prawns for garnish
parsley sprigs for garnish

Place grapefruit in refrigerator for 1 to 2 hours before required. Cut grapefruit in halves. Remove flesh, divide into segments and replace in grapefruit skins. Shell and devein prawns and season lightly with salt and pepper. Arrange on top of grapefruit and coat with mayonnaise. Garnish each serving with an unshelled prawn and a parsley sprig and serve immediately.

Sardine Hors d'Oeuvre
Serves: 4

2 x 125 g (4 oz) cans sardines
2 small onions
white vinegar
salt
2 hard-boiled eggs
2 teaspoons capers
lemon wedges for serving

Drain sardines and arrange in a shallow serving dish. Slice onions in thin rings. Place onion rings in a bowl, cover with vinegar and stir in a good pinch of salt. Leave for 10 minutes then drain.

Chop hard-boiled eggs coarsely. Sprinkle onion rings, chopped eggs and capers over sardines.

Serve with wedges of lemon.

Cheese and Pineapple Refresher

Serves: 6

7 slices canned pineapple
crisp lettuce leaves
250 g (8 oz) cottage or cream cheese
1 tablespoon honey
3 tablespoons chopped cucumber
⅓ cup chopped walnuts or almonds
chopped parsley or nuts for garnish

Chill pineapple and arrange 6 slices on lettuce leaves. Chop remaining pineapple and mix with cottage cheese, honey, cucumber and nuts. A little pineapple juice may be added if desired. Mix well and pile onto pineapple slices. Garnish with chopped parsley or nuts.

Note: If using a processed creamed cheese that is very rich, serve smaller quantities on the pineapple slices.

Variation: This flavoured cottage cheese may be used to stuff prunes, canned pears or peaches as an hors d'oeuvre.

Vegetable Hors d'Oeuvre

Serves: 4

1 small cucumber, grated
3 carrots, coarsely grated
1 cup sliced tender celery
250 g (8 oz) button mushrooms, sliced
375 g (12 oz) zucchini, sliced and blanched
2-3 small leeks, halved and cooked
2 small cooked beetroot, sliced
250 g (8 oz) small new potatoes, boiled
375 g (12 oz) green beans, cooked

To add
¾ cup sour cream
French dressing (see below)
chopped spring onions, parsley, mint, chives, crushed
   coriander seed, crushed garlic, thinly sliced onion rings
chopped hard-boiled egg
salt and pepper

Salt grated cucumber, stand 10 minutes and drain. Add 1 teaspoon chopped mint, a little garlic and blend into sour cream. Mix grated carrot with chopped spring onions and French dressing to moisten. Toss celery with French dressing and sprinkle with coriander. Marinate mushrooms in ½ cup dressing, add onion rings and parsley. Marinate zucchini in ¼ cup dressing, add chives and parsley. Sprinkle dressing on leeks while hot. Marinate beetroot in French dressing. Sprinkle dressing and chopped egg over potatoes. Marinate beans in dressing.

Chill thoroughly in separate bowls. Just before serving, arrange on platters and/or individual bowls.

French dressing: In a screw top jar, combine 1½ cups olive oil with ½ cup lemon juice, 2 teaspoons salt, 1 teaspoon each dry mustard and sugar and freshly ground black pepper. Seal and shake well.

Seafood Cocktail
Serves: 6

1 dozen oysters, shelled
½ cup prawns, shelled and deveined
125 g (4 oz) crab meat
125 g (4 oz) lobster meat
lettuce leaves for serving
sliced lemon for garnish
Cocktail sauce
4 tablespoons Mayonnaise (page 16)
3 tablespoons tomato paste
1 teaspoon Worcestershire sauce
1 teaspoon lemon juice
dash Tabasco sauce
pinch paprika
4 tablespoons cream

Mix seafood lightly with cocktail sauce. Shred lettuce very finely and put into cocktail glasses. Pile seafood on lettuce. Garnish with slices of lemon. Serve immediately.

Cocktail sauce: Mix mayonnaise, tomato paste, Worcestershire sauce, lemon juice, Tabasco sauce and paprika together. Whip cream lightly and fold into sauce.

Avocado Pears with Orange
Serves: 6

3 avocado pears
French dressing (see below)
3 oranges
lettuce for serving

Cut avocado pears in halves lengthways, remove stones. Keeping the skin intact, remove the flesh with a melon-ball scoop or cut into dice. Coat with French dressing to prevent discolouration.

Peel oranges and cut into segments, removing all the skin and pith. Mix avocado balls and orange segments together with enough French dressing to moisten. Pile into avocado skins. Place lettuce leaves on a serving plate and arrange filled avocado pears on top.

French dressing: In a screw top jar combine 2 tablespoons white vinegar with 6 tablespoons olive oil, a pinch of sugar, salt and finely ground white pepper to taste. Screw lid on tightly and shake vigorously until combined.

FISH & SHELLFISH

Fish is a delicate food and should be handled properly both in its storage and cooking. It is at its best when fresh, so learn to recognise quality. If the fish is whole when purchased, make sure that the eyes are bright and clear, the gills bright red and the skin brilliant. Fish fillets should be pinky white with a translucent appearance. If fish is not to be prepared within two days of purchase (or when caught), it is advisable to wrap it well in foil or place it in a high density plastic freezer bag, extract air, seal, label and store in the freezer. Thaw fish in the refrigerator, not at room temperature. If whole, it can be thawed quickly and safely under running cold water.

Lobster and lobster tails are often purchased frozen. Slowly thaw in the refrigerator, or, if whole, place in a sinkful of cold water with a large handful of salt added. This applies to both green and cooked lobsters.

Island Tuna

Serves: 4-6
Cooking time: 30-35 minutes
Oven temperature: 180-190° C (350-375° F)

185 g (6 oz) noodles or macaroni shells
1 × 425 g (15 oz) can tomato soup
1 x 425 g (15 oz) can pineapple pieces
½ cup sliced green capsicum
1 x 454 g (16 oz) can tuna, drained

Cook noodles or macaroni as directed on packet. Drain. While noodles are cooking, heat tomato soup and liquid from the pineapple pieces in a saucepan. Add green capsicum and pineapple pieces and stir gently till boiling.

Place tuna in an ovenproof dish, spread cooked noodles or macaroni on top. Pour hot contents in saucepan over the noodles or macaroni, spreading the capsicum and pineapple pieces evenly over the casserole contents.

Cover and bake in a moderate oven for 30 to 35 minutes. Serve with potato straws or crisps and buttered vegetables.

Lobster Tails Marinière

Serves: 6
Cooking time: 8 minutes

6 small green lobster tails
3 tablespoons butter
¼ cup chopped spring onions
1 tablespoon finely chopped parsley
¾ cup dry white wine
pinch dried thyme
salt
freshly ground pepper

Brush lobster tails lightly with oil, place under a medium grill and cook 1 minute each side, just long enough for shells to turn red. Remove and when cool enough to handle, cut through each side of the soft shell on the underside of the tails. Remove this and carefully lift out meat in one piece. Keep hard tail shells aside. Slice meat into 1 cm (½ inch) medallions (i.e. round slices).

Heat butter over moderate heat until foaming, add spring onions and cook 1 minute. Add lobster medallions and sauté gently on each side until flesh turns white, about 4 to 5 minutes in all. Do not overcook. Lift out and arrange in reserved tail shells. Keep warm.

Add wine to pan with parsley, thyme, salt and a good grind of pepper. Boil briskly until reduced by one-third and spoon sauce over medallions. Serve immediately.

Sweet and Sour Fish

Serves: 4
Cooking time: 20-25 minutes

1 snapper, about 1 kg (2 lb)
seasoned flour for coating
1 tablespoon dry sherry
oil for frying
small piece fresh root ginger
1 red capsicum, seeded and sliced
1 green capsicum, seeded and sliced
½ cup sliced mushrooms
2 tablespoons sliced bamboo shoots
1 tablespoon sliced fresh root ginger
1 cup fish or chicken stock
2 tablespoons vinegar
2 tablespoons sugar
1 tablespoon soy sauce
1 tablespoon cornflour
¼ cup water
2 tablespoons hot oil

Clean and scale fish and cut deeply in 3 or 4 places on each side. Coat with seasoned flour.

Heat oil, add piece of ginger and fry fish for 10 to 15 minutes or until cooked golden and crisp. Drain on absorbent paper and place on platter. Sprinkle with sherry and keep warm.

In a saucepan heat 2 tablespoons oil and stir-fry sliced capsicum, mushrooms, bamboo shoots and ginger for 3 to 4 minutes. Keep aside.

Heat stock and vinegar together, add sugar and bring to the boil. Add soy sauce and stirring continuously, add cornflour, previously mixed to a smooth paste with water. When sauce comes to the boil, add vegetables and bring back to the boil. Add hot oil to give the sauce a glaze. Pour sauce over fish and serve immediately. If desired sauce may be served separately.

Oven Poached Fish

Serves: 3-4
Cooking time: 45 minutes
Oven temperature: 180-190° C (350-375° F)

½ cup dry white wine
2 cups water
1 onion, sliced
1 carrot, sliced
bouquet garni
2 teaspoons salt
½ teaspoon black peppercorns
3-4 small whole fish, each about 375 g (12 oz)
90 g (3 oz) butter
1 tablespoon finely chopped spring onions
1 teaspoon finely chopped parsley
1 small garlic clove, crushed
lemon slices, parsley sprigs and olives for garnish

Combine wine, water, onion, carrot, bouquet garni, salt and peppercorns in a saucepan, bring to the boil. Cover and simmer gently for 30 minutes.

Clean and scale fish if necessary, and place side by side in an ovenproof dish just large enough to contain them. Strain prepared liquid over fish, cover with greased aluminium foil and cook in a moderate oven for 12 to 15 minutes or until flesh is white. Carefully drain off liquid and keep fish hot. Melt butter in a saucepan and sauté spring onions until soft. Add garlic and parsley and cook 1 minute. Pour over fish, garnish with lemon slices, parsley sprigs and olives and serve immediately.

Lobster en Brochette
Serves: 6
Cooking time: 7-10 minutes

1 lobster, about 1 kg (2 lb)
6 large mushrooms
4 bacon rashers
dry breadcrumbs
lemon slices and parsley sprigs for garnish
French dressing
½ cup olive oil
2 tablespoons lemon juice
salt
freshly ground pepper
1 garlic clove (optional)

Remove meat from the lobster tail and take out the intestine. Cut meat into 3 cm (1¼ inch) pieces. Marinate for 1 hour in French dressing (see below). Wipe mushrooms and cut into quarters. Remove rind from bacon and cut into squares.

On 6 skewers thread lobster pieces alternately with mushrooms and bacon, brush well with French dressing. Cook under a moderately hot grill for 5 to 8 minutes, turning frequently and basting during cooking. When cooked, roll in breadcrumbs, baste again and brown lightly. Place on a heated platter, garnish with lemon slices and parsley and serve as an entrée.

French dressing: Place ingredients in a screw top jar, seal and shake well to combine. Add a cut clove of garlic if desired, let stand for 1 hour, remove garlic and shake again before using.
Note: Substitute 500 g (1 lb) green lobster tails for whole lobster. If frozen, thaw in refrigerator.

Whiting with Almonds
Serves: 4
Cooking time: 15-20 minutes

4 whole whiting
2 tablespoons plain flour
½ teaspoon salt
freshly ground pepper
125 g (4 oz) butter
3 tablespoons slivered almonds
¼ cup lemon juice

Wash and dry fish thoroughly. Combine flour, salt and pepper, roll fish in seasoned flour. Heat half of the butter in a frying pan, add fish and fry 15 to 20 minutes until fish flakes easily with a fork. Turn once during cooking.

Heat remaining butter in a small saucepan, add almonds, stir occasionally until almonds are golden brown. Add lemon juice and stir well.

Place fried fish on a warm serving plate and pour sauce over.
Note: Whiting may also be cooked in a heavy-based frying pan or skillet over barbecue.

Prawn Créole

Serves: 4
Cooking time: 30-40 minutes

3 tablespoons butter
1 large onion, finely chopped
1 small capsicum, seeded and finely chopped
1 garlic clove, crushed
1 × 430 g (15 oz) can peeled tomatoes
3 tablespoons tomato paste
1 tablespoon Worcestershire sauce
1 teaspoon paprika
pinch of sugar
salt
freshly ground pepper
2 teaspoons cornflour
750 g (1½ lb) cooked prawns, shelled and deveined
boiled rice for serving

Melt butter in a heavy-based saucepan or frying pan with lid to fit, sauté onion gently until transparent, add capsicum and garlic and cook a few minutes longer. Add tomatoes, tomato paste, Worcestershire sauce and seasonings. Cover and simmer gently for 20 to 30 minutes. Blend cornflour with a little cold water and thicken sauce. Add prawns, mix well and adjust seasonings if necessary. Cook over very low heat for a further 10 minutes or until prawns are hot. Do not let mixture boil. Serve with boiled rice.

Note: When using raw prawns, add to thickened sauce and simmer, stirring often, until prawns turn pink.

West Coast Lobster

Serves: 2
Cooking time: 10-12 minutes
Oven temperature: 180-190° C (350-375° F)

1 small cooked lobster
2 tablespoons butter
1 garlic clove, crushed
½ cup sliced button mushrooms
1 teaspoon chopped parsley
1 tablespoon prepared mustard (French, American or German)
1 teaspoon Worcestershire sauce
1 tablespoon dry sherry
salt and pepper
1 tablespoon lemon juice
4 tablespoons grated tasty cheese

Cut lobster in half lengthways, remove bag in the head and intestine. Lift meat from shell, cut into cubes. Heat butter in a frying pan and sauté lobster meat with garlic, mushrooms and parsley for 2 minutes. Add mustard, Worcestershire sauce, sherry and salt and pepper to taste. Simmer gently, stirring occasionally, for 4 or 5 minutes. Do not boil.

Spoon mixture into lobster shells, sprinkle with lemon juice and cover with grated cheese. Place under a pre-heated grill until top is golden brown.

Serve immediately.

Tuna Almond Sauté

Serves: 4
Cooking time: 20 minutes

3 tablespoons butter
½ cup blanched almonds
1 cup finely chopped onion
1 x 425 g (15 oz) can chunk-style tuna, drained
1 × 285 g (10 oz) can whole kernel sweet corn, drained
2 teaspoons lemon juice
1 teaspoon soy sauce
¼ cup chopped parsley
freshly ground pepper
boiled rice for serving

Melt 1 tablespoon butter in a large frying pan, add almonds and stir over moderate heat until golden. Remove and keep aside.

Add remaining butter to pan and sauté onion until transparent. Stir in drained tuna and corn, lemon juice, soy sauce, salt to taste and a generous grind of pepper. Toss gently over heat until heated thoroughly, stir in almonds and serve immediately with boiled rice.

Egg and Tuna Croquettes

Serves: 4
Cooking time: 2-3 minutes per batch

1 small onion
2 tablespoons butter
1 x 185 g (6½ oz) can tuna, drained
4 hard-boiled eggs, chopped
1 cup mashed potato
1 teaspoon lemon juice
1 tablespoon chopped parsley
salt and pepper to taste
1 egg, beaten
flour
1 egg, beaten with 1 tablespoon water
dry breadcrumbs for coating
oil for frying
lemon wedges for garnish

Chop onion and fry in butter until soft. Mix with tuna, chopped eggs, potato, lemon juice, parsley, salt and pepper and bind with beaten egg. Divide into 12 portions, shape into cylinder shapes and roll in flour. Coat croquettes with egg and water mixture then roll in breadcrumbs. Deep fry in hot oil, six at a time, until golden brown. Serve immediately with lemon wedges.

Poached Trout

Serves: 6
Cooking time: 25-30 minutes

1½ cups warm vinegar
6 freshwater trout
2 cloves
2 black peppercorns
1 small onion, sliced
1 bay leaf
Caviare butter
90 g (3 oz) butter
1 x 45 g (1½ oz) jar black caviare
1 tablespoon chopped parsley
lemon juice to taste
salt and pepper

Pour warm vinegar over trout and stand aside for 20 minutes. Add cloves, peppercorns, onion and bay leaf to fish kettle or a large pan of boiling salted water. Simmer for 15 minutes. Add prepared trout and simmer over a gentle heat for 10 to 15 minutes, according to size. Drain.

Arrange trout on a serving plate and serve immediately with Caviare Butter.

Caviare butter: Beat butter with a wooden spoon until soft. Blend in caviare, parsley, lemon juice and salt to taste and a good grind of black pepper. Roll into balls with butter pats or wet hands. Chill until firm.

Cooking tip: A fish kettle has an inner perforated tray on which to place fish so that, when cooked, the tray can be lifted out without breaking fish. If such a utensil is not available, place fish on a large piece of muslin, tie ends, and lower into a large saucepan. The fish can then be easily removed when cooked.

Fish'n'Chips

Serves: 4
Cooking time: 10-15 minutes

4 white fish fillets, about 750 g (1½ lb) in all
seasoned flour
4 medium-sized potatoes
oil for frying
Batter
1 cup plain flour
½ teaspoon salt
2 eggs
1¼ cups milk

Wipe fish fillets with a damp cloth, remove skin and bones. Peel potatoes and cut into neat strips 1 cm (½ inch) thick. Soak in iced water for 15 minutes, drain and dry well. Place potatoes in a frying basket and fry in deep, hot oil for 2 to 3 minutes, take out and put aside.

Make fritter batter (see below). Dip fish into seasoned flour, then into batter and deep fry in hot oil until cooked and golden, about 5 minutes. Drain well and keep hot. Return 'blanched' chips to hot oil and fry for a further 2 to 3 minutes until golden and crisp. Drain well and serve immediately with fried fish garnished with lemon wedges (or wrap in greaseproof paper and newspaper for a special treat!).

Batter: Sift flour and salt into a bowl. Drop eggs into the centre, add half the milk gradually and mix to a smooth batter, gradually working in remainder of milk. Beat until surface is bubbly. Rest for 30 minutes before using if possible.

Scallops en Brochette

Serves: 4
Cooking time: 5 minutes

40 scallops
¼ cup melted butter
1 tablespoon lemon juice
salt and pepper to taste
boiled rice and lemon wedges for serving

Thread scallops on to 4 skewers. Brush with melted butter and sprinkle with lemon juice.

Grill under a pre-heated grill or over a hot charcoal fire for approximately 5 minutes, turning often. Baste with a little more melted butter while cooking. Season to taste with salt and pepper.

Serve immediately with boiled rice and lemon wedges.

Cooking tip: If bamboo skewers are used, soak them for several hours in cold water beforehand to prevent them from burning

Mussels Marinière

Serves: 4-6
Cooking time: 20 minutes

2 kg (4 lb) mussels
4 spring onions, finely chopped
1 garlic clove, chopped
1 tablespoon butter
3 cups dry white wine
2 tablespoons finely chopped parsley
2 fresh thyme sprigs or pinch dried thyme
1 bay leaf
ground black pepper
extra chopped parsley and crusty French bread for serving

Wash mussels under running water. Remove all traces of mud, seaweed and barnacles with a brush or knife. Remove beards. If mussels have cracked or broken shells discard them. If any are slightly open, tap sharply and if they do not close, discard.

Sauté spring onions and garlic in butter until transparent but not coloured. Add wine, parsley, thyme, bay leaf and pepper. Simmer for 10 minutes. Add mussels, cover saucepan and steam over a high heat for about 5 minutes, shaking pan constantly. The shells will open as the mussels cook. Lift mussels out of pan and keep in half shell. Place in a large serving bowl and keep warm.

Boil cooking liquid until reduced to half the original quantity. Taste and adjust seasonings if necessary. Pour over mussels. Sprinkle with extra chopped parsley and serve immediately with crusty French bread.

Crunchy Cod Fingers

Serves: 4
Cooking time: 4-6 minutes

750 g (1½ lb) fish fillets
½ teaspoon curry powder
¼ teaspoon celery salt
¼ teaspoon onion or garlic salt
1 teaspoon water
1 egg
4 tablespoons plain flour
1 cup fine dry breadcrumbs
tartare sauce for serving (see below)

Cut the fish fillets into finger length pieces about 8 × 1 × 1 cm (3 × ½ × ½ inches) removing any bones. Mix seasonings with water. Add egg and beat to mix well. Coat the fish pieces with flour, then egg, then breadcrumbs. Shallow fry for 2 to 3 minutes on each side in hot fat until golden brown. Do not overcook. Drain well on absorbent paper and serve immediately with tartare sauce.

Tartare sauce: Blend ½ cup mayonnaise with 1 tablespoon each chopped gherkin, green olives and capers.

Cooking tip: Coating becomes firmer on standing. Fish may be coated, covered and refrigerated for several hours before cooking.

Salmon Mousse

Serves: 6-8

3 spring onions, finely chopped
2 teaspoons butter
2 x 220 g (7¾ oz) cans red salmon
2 tablespoons lemon juice
1 tablespoon gelatine
¼ cup hot water
salt
dash of Tabasco sauce
pinch of ground nutmeg
¾ cup cream, whipped
¼ cup Mayonnaise (page 16)
1 egg white
Cucumber Mayonnaise for serving (page 16)

Sauté spring onions in butter until soft. Remove skin and bones from salmon and place salmon with its liquid, spring onion and lemon juice in the jar of an electric blender, and pureé. Alternatively, pass ingredients through a food mill. Place in a large bowl. Dissolve gelatine in hot water, cool and add to salmon with salt, Tabasco sauce and nutmeg to taste. Fold in whipped cream and mayonnaise. Beat egg white until stiff and fold into salmon mixture with a metal spoon or spatula. Lightly oil a mould and pour in mousse. Cover and leave in refrigerator for several hours until set. Unmould onto serving platter and garnish with salad vegetables. Serve with Cucumber Mayonnaise.
Note: Canned tuna may be used instead of salmon.

Stuffed Baked Fish

Serves: 4-6
Cooking time: 40-60 minutes
Oven temperature: 190-200° C (375-400° F)

1 whole snapper, about 1.5 kg (3 lb)
2 tablespoons lemon juice
salt
freshly ground pepper
90 g (3 oz) butter
125 g (4 oz) mushrooms, sliced
4 shallots, chopped
½ cup white breadcrumbs
10-12 fresh or bottled oysters

Clean and scale fish if necessary, rinse and dry with paper towels. Rub each side of fish with 1 tablespoon lemon juice and lightly season with salt and freshly ground pepper.

Meanwhile melt half the butter in a pan and gently sauté the mushrooms and shallots. Add breadcrumbs and cook a further 2 minutes. Remove from heat and add drained oysters and remaining lemon juice. Season to taste with salt and pepper. Stuff the fish with the mixture and sew up the opening with cotton or fine string.

Place fish on a well-buttered piece of aluminium foil, dot with remaining butter and wrap fish, sealing package with double folds. Place in a roasting dish and cook in a moderately hot oven for 40 minutes or until cooked. Time will depend on thickness of fish.

Salmon Koulibiaka

Serves: 6
Cooking time: 30-35 minutes
Oven temperature: 200-230° C (400-450° F)

500 g (1 lb) salmon, fresh poached or canned
3 hard-boiled eggs, chopped
125 g (4 oz) butter, melted
1 tablespoon chopped parsley
1 small onion, chopped
250 g (8 oz) mushrooms, sliced
1 cup boiled rice
salt
freshly ground pepper
1 x 340 g (12 oz) packet commercial puff pastry
beaten egg to glaze

Flake salmon and if using canned salmon, drain off any liquid. Add hard-boiled egg, half the melted butter and chopped parsley. Sauté onion and mushrooms in remaining butter. Add to mixture with boiled rice. Mix thoroughly and season to taste with salt and pepper.

Roll out pastry on a lightly floured board until approximately 5 mm (¼ inch) thick. Cut in half. Place filling on half the pastry, brush edges of pastry with beaten egg. Cover with remaining half of pastry and press edges firmly together. Brush with remaining beaten egg and make 2 or 3 slits on top to allow steam to escape.

Place on a baking tray and cook in a hot oven for approximately 30 to 35 minutes or until golden brown. Cut into wedges to serve.

Old-Fashioned Fish Pie

Serves: 4
Cooking time: 30-35 minutes
Oven temperature: 190-200° C (375-400° F)

375 g (12 oz) smoked cod
1 cup milk
2 hard-boiled eggs, sliced
3 tablespoons butter
2 tablespoons plain flour
salt
freshly ground pepper
500 g (1 lb) old potatoes
2 tablespoons hot milk
2 tablespoons grated Parmesan cheese

Place fish in a greased ovenproof dish, add half the milk, cover and poach in a moderately hot oven for 10 to 15 minutes. Remove fish from casserole, drain and reserve milk. Bone and flake fish, replace in casserole with hard-boiled eggs.

In a saucepan melt half the butter and blend in flour until smooth. Add remaining milk and milk from poached fish. Stirring continuously, bring to the boil. Season to taste with salt and pepper, pour over fish.

Peel potatoes and cook in boiling salted water until tender. Drain thoroughly and mash. Add remaining butter, milk and salt and pepper to taste. Spread potato evenly over fish and sprinkle with Parmesan cheese.

Cook in a hot oven for approximately 20 minutes or until heated through and top is crisp and golden brown. Serve immediately.

Cooking tip: Shallow ovenproof dishes seldom have a lid to fit. Either cover with foil or place a baking tray on top when poaching.

Scallops with Cream (Coquilles St Jacques)

Serves: 4
Cooking time: 10-12 minutes

2 tablespoons butter
1 tablespoon finely chopped spring onion
2 tablespoons button mushrooms, sliced
½ cup dry white wine
250 g (8 oz) scallops with coral
½ cup cream
dash of cayenne pepper
salt and pepper
½ cup soft breadcrumbs
extra 2 tablespoons melted butter
2 tablespoons grated Parmesan cheese
lemon slices and parsley sprigs for garnish

Melt butter in a saucepan and sauté spring onion and mushrooms until soft. Add wine and cook until wine is reduced to half the original quantity. Add scallops and simmer for 2 minutes. Add cream, cayenne pepper, salt and pepper to taste. Re-heat gently and place in scallop shells. Toss breadcrumbs with melted butter and sprinkle over scallops with Parmesan cheese. Place under a hot grill until golden brown. Serve immediately as an entrée, garnished with lemon slices and parsley sprigs.

EGGS & CHEESE

With eggs and cheese on hand, you can always whip up a satisfying snack, entrée or main meal.

Eggs should be stored in the refrigerator with the pointed end down. Remove 30 minutes before required to bring them to room temperature, or place them in warm water for 5 minutes.

Cheese should be purchased in quantities that can be used within a week. Wrap in a moisture and vapour-proof material and store in refrigerator. Cheese can be frozen, but as it becomes crumbly in texture on thawing, it is only suitable for cooking uses. But then that is what this chapter is all about!

Scrambled Cheese Eggs

Serves: 4
Cooking time: 1-2 minutes

1 cup grated cheese
6 eggs
6 tablespoons milk or cream
salt
freshly ground pepper
3 tablespoons butter

Choose a good melting cheese with a flavour to your taste—Gruyère (or Swiss), Emmenthal, or a Cheddar. Grate coarsely and pack loosely into cup measure.

Break eggs into a bowl, add milk or cream (or a mixture) a little salt and freshly ground pepper. Beat with a fork until whites and yolks are blended and egg will run smoothly through a fork without being foamy. Stir in cheese.

Place butter in a heavy-based saucepan, one with a non-stick surface is ideal. Melt over moderate heat until gently foaming. Add egg mixture and stir with a wooden spoon until eggs are set but still creamy. Serve immediately with hot buttered toast.

Swiss Bread Rosti

Serves: 4
Cooking time: 10-12 minutes

440 g (14 oz) stale white bread
250 g (8 oz) Swiss cheese
¾ cup milk
¾ cup water
125 g (4 oz) butter
1 onion, finely grated
freshly ground pepper

Leave crust on bread, only removing any burnt crust. Cut bread and cheese into thin slices and place in a bowl. Heat milk and water together until scalding hot but not boiling, and pour over bread and cheese. Allow to stand for 30 minutes until liquid is absorbed. Stir now and then.

Melt butter in a large frying pan and sauté onion for 5 minutes. Add bread and cheese mixture and fry on a low heat, turning continually, until golden brown. Season with freshly ground pepper and serve as a luncheon or light supper dish.

Pancakes (Crêpes)

Yield: 12-15 small pancakes or crêpes

1 cup plain flour
pinch salt
1 egg
1 egg yolk
1 tablespoon oil
1¼ cups milk
oil or clarified butter for cooking

Sift flour and salt into a mixing bowl. Make a well in the centre and drop in the whole egg, egg yolk and add oil. Using a wooden spoon, stir rapidly from the centre to blend egg etc. with a little flour. As this mixture thickens, add the milk by degrees, stirring from the centre, and making bigger circular movements as more flour is incorporated. When all the flour is blended, beat well and add remaining milk. The resulting batter should be the consistency of thin cream. Strain, cover, and allow to stand for at least 30 minutes, to enable the starch cells in the flour to swell and soften.

Heat pan a little, add sufficient oil or butter to cover bottom, tilt to coat sides and pour off excess. Pour in sufficient batter to coat base thinly, tilting pan if necessary. Return to medium heat and cook until upper surface is bubbly. Turn and cook other side. Place cooked pancakes on a napkin-lined plate if to be used in a sweet or savoury recipe; if to be eaten immediately, stack on a plate over simmering water and cover with a lid.

Cooking tip: Keep a special pan just for making pancakes. Do not wash after use; wipe clean with a piece of oiled or buttered paper.

Chicken and Ham Pancakes

Serves: 4
Cooking time: 25-30 minutes
Oven temperature: 150-160° C (300-325° F)

1 cup chopped cooked chicken
½ cup chopped cooked ham
1 teaspoon chopped parsley
1 teaspoon chopped chives
salt and pepper
1 tablespoon butter
1½ tablespoons plain flour
1 cup chicken stock
1 tablespoon sherry
12 pancakes
tomato and toasted slivered almonds for garnish
melted butter

Mix chicken, ham, parsley, chives and season lightly with salt and pepper. Melt butter in a saucepan, add flour, and working off the heat, mix to a smooth paste. Warm stock and add gradually. Blend well, return to heat and bring to boiling point, stirring continuously. Add sherry. Blend sauce with chicken mixture.

Spread filling over pancakes, roll up and arrange in an ovenproof dish. Brush pancakes with melted butter and heat in a moderately slow oven for 15 to 20 minutes.

Serve hot, garnished with skinned, lightly cooked tomato segments and sprinkled with toasted almonds.

Mushroom Fondue

Serves: 6

60 g (2 oz) butter
375 g (12 oz) mushrooms, finely sliced
1 medium-sized onion, peeled and chopped
3 tablespoons flour
1 cup milk
¾ cup Cheddar cheese, grated
½ cup cream
salt and pepper
2 tablespoons chopped parsley
Curried bread cubes
1 small white, unsliced loaf
60 g (2 oz) butter
2 tablespoons oil
4 teaspoons curry powder

Melt butter in fondue pot and gently fry mushrooms and onion for 10 minutes. Sprinkle in flour and add milk. Bring to the boil, stirring, until thickened. Cook for 2 minutes. Add cheese, stir over a low heat until melted. Stir in cream, add seasonings to taste. Sprinkle with chopped parsley. Serve curried bread cubes for dipping.

Curried bread cubes: Remove crusts from loaf and cut into 2 cm (¾ inch) cubes. Heat butter and oil together in frying pan, stir in curry powder. Fry bread cubes until golden brown and crisp. Drain well before serving.

Smoked Salmon Flan

Serves: 4-6
Cooking time: 40-45 minutes
Oven temperature: 190-200° C (375-400° F)

Pastry case
1½ cups plain flour
½ teaspoon salt
pinch cayenne pepper
90 g (3 oz) butter
1 egg yolk
2 teaspoons lemon juice
1-1½ tablespoons water
Filling
2 x 90 g (3½ oz) jars smoked salmon
4 eggs
1 tablespoon plain flour
¼ teaspoon ground white pepper
½ cup cream
1 tablespoon melted butter

Pastry case: Sift dry ingredients into a bowl. Rub butter into flour with fingertips until mixture is crumbly. Mix egg yolk, lemon juice and water, add to flour and mix to a dough with a round-bladed knife. Wrap in plastic film and refrigerate for 30 minutes.

Roll out and line a 23 cm (9 inch) flan ring. Prick base of flan, line inside with a circle of greased greaseproof paper and fill with dried beans. Bake on the middle shelf of a moderately hot oven for 15 minutes. Remove paper and beans.

Filling: Cover base of partly cooked pastry case with smoked salmon. Beat eggs together with flour and pepper. Add cream and melted butter, mix thoroughly. Pour custard mixture gently over salmon in pastry case.

Cook in a moderately hot oven for 25 to 30 minutes until mixture is set and golden brown. Serve hot.

Eggs Florentine

Serves: 4
Cooking time: 15 minutes

4 cups cooked spinach
4 tablespoons butter
4 tablespoons flour
2 cups milk
1 cup Cheddar cheese, grated
salt and pepper
nutmeg
8 eggs
grated Parmesan cheese

Place cooked spinach in a shallow casserole or 4 individual ovenproof dishes and keep hot.

Melt butter in a saucepan, add flour and cook over a low heat for 2 to 3 minutes, gradually add milk, stirring continuously. Bring to the boil, stirring continuously, add cheese and seasonings. Keep warm.

Poach eggs. Arrange on top of spinach and pour cheese sauce on top. Sprinkle with a little Parmesan cheese, place under heated grill until lightly browned and serve immediately.

Spinach Pancakes

Serves: 4
Cooking time: 15-20 minutes
Oven temperature: 150-160° C (300-325° F)

2 x 315 g (10 oz) packets frozen chopped spinach
salt and pepper
lemon juice
1 teaspoon butter
1 quantity Béchamel Sauce (page 16)
3 tablespoons cream
½ cup grated tasty cheese
250 g (8 oz) bacon rashers
10 pancakes (page 41)
1 tablespoon grated Parmesan cheese

Cook spinach as directed on packet. Drain very thoroughly, season with salt, black pepper and lemon juice. Add butter and heat gently. Heat Béchamel Sauce, stir in cream and grated tasty cheese and blend well. Blend 2 tablespoons of this sauce into prepared spinach and set aside.

Remove rind from bacon, dice and fry until crisp. Drain on paper towels. Place a pancake on a round ovenproof serving dish and spread with a little spinach mixture. Sprinkle with a little bacon. Cover with second pancake and continue to layer in this fashion to form a 'cake'. Coat with remaining sauce, sprinkle with grated Parmesan cheese and heat in a moderately slow oven for 15 to 20 minutes. Brown under a hot grill before serving, if desired.

Ham and Corn Omelette

Serves: 4-6
Cooking time: 5-8 minutes

2 teaspoons butter
1 teaspoon oil
1 medium-sized onion, chopped
6 eggs, lightly beaten
1 tablespoon water
1 cup grated tasty Cheddar cheese
1½ cups whole kernel sweet corn, drained
60 g (2 oz) ham, cut into strips
salt
freshly ground pepper
2 tablespoons chopped parsley
¼ red capsicum, cut into strips

Heat butter and oil together in a pan and lightly fry onion until transparent. Combine eggs, water, ¾ cup of cheese, 1 cup corn and the ham, and season to taste with salt and pepper. Pour the mixture over the cooked onion. As egg mixture starts to set around edges, lift with a spatula, tilt pan if necessary and allow uncooked egg to flow underneath. When egg mixture is almost cooked top with remaining cheese and corn, parsley, and red capsicum strips. Place under a hot grill until cheese melts.

Cut into wedges and serve with hot crusty bread.

Cheese Fondue

Serves: 4-6

1 garlic clove
1½ cups dry white wine
2 cups grated Gruyère cheese
2 cups grated Emmenthal cheese
freshly grated nutmeg
freshly ground white pepper
1 tablespoon cornflour
2 tablespoons kirsch
crusty French bread for serving

Rub inside of fondue pot with cut clove of garlic. Pour in wine and heat. Add grated cheese gradually and stirring in a figure of eight, cook over a low heat until cheese has dissolved into wine. Add nutmeg and pepper to taste. Blend cornflour with kirsch until smooth and add to mixture. Continue to stir over a low heat until mixture thickens. Do not allow fondue to boil. If it thickens too much, add a little warmed wine. If too thin, add more grated cheese.

Cut bread into 2.5 cm (1 inch) cubes and place in a bread basket. (Bread should be 1 day old).

Each guest spears a piece of bread on to a fondue fork, dips it into the fondue and quickly swirls it around.

Ham and Mushroom Flan

Serves: 4-6
Cooking time: 30-35 minutes
Oven temperature: 190-200° C (375-400° F)

1 × 23 cm (9 inch) pastry case (page 42)
3 large white onions, thinly sliced
2 cups finely sliced mushrooms
1 tablespoon butter
1 tablespoon plain flour
½ cup milk
½ cup cream
3 eggs, lightly beaten
salt
freshly ground black pepper
freshly grated nutmeg
185 g (6 oz) cooked ham, sliced
¼ cup grated Gruyère cheese
4 medium-sized mushrooms for garnish
extra butter

Prepare and partly cook pastry case as directed in Smoked Salmon Flan recipe.

Sauté onions and mushrooms in butter in a covered saucepan until soft. Add flour and stir over medium heat for 1 or 2 minutes until golden brown. Add milk and stir continuously until the mixture boils, simmer 5 minutes. Remove from heat and stir in cream, eggs, and salt, pepper and nutmeg to taste. Place ham in bottom of flan case, reserving 4 small slices. Pour onion and mushroom mixture over. Sprinkle with cheese and bake on middle shelf of a moderately hot oven for 15 to 20 minutes, or until the filling is set. Sauté whole mushrooms in a little butter and arrange on top of cooked flan with reserved ham (rolled). Serve immediately.

Dutch Egg Casserole

Serves: 4
Cooking time: 15-20 minutes
Oven temperature: 190-200° C (375-400° F)

500 g (1 lb) potatoes
60 g (2 oz) butter
6 hard-boiled eggs, chopped
1 tablespoon finely chopped chives
2 teaspoons finely chopped parsley
½ teaspoon French mustard
salt
freshly ground pepper
½ cup chopped ham
1 cup sour cream
2 tablespoons grated tasty cheese

Peel potatoes, cook until just tender in boiling, salted water and slice thickly. Heat butter in a frying pan and fry potatoes until golden on both sides.

Arrange potato slices in a greased ovenproof dish and cover with egg, chives, parsley, mustard, salt and pepper to taste and ham. Pour sour cream over and sprinkle with cheese.

Bake in a moderately hot oven for 15 to 20 minutes or until hot and golden brown on top. Serve immediately.

Eggs and Cheese en Cocotte

Serves: 4
Cooking time: 15 minutes
Oven temperature: 180-190° C (350-375° F)

125 g (4 oz) Cheddar cheese
1 tablespoon butter
4 eggs
salt
freshly ground pepper
4 tablespoons cream or top of milk
hot butter toast for serving

Grate a quarter of the cheese and thinly slice remainder.

Grease the bases of four small cocotte dishes with butter and cover with slices of cheese. Break eggs carefully on to cheese, making sure yolks do not break. Season with salt and pepper, pour a spoonful of cream on top of each egg and sprinkle with grated cheese. Place dishes in a dish of hot water and bake uncovered in a moderate oven for 10 to 15 minutes until eggs are set. Serve immediately with hot buttered toast.

Tarte Nicoise

Serves: 4-6
Cooking time: 45-50 minutes
Oven temperature: 190-200° C (375-400° F)
   reducing to 150-160° C (300-325° F)

1 × 23 cm (9 inch) pastry case (page 42)
6 small tomatoes
½ cup grated tasty cheese
¼ cup fresh white breadcrumbs
1 tablespoon chopped fresh basil
salt and pepper
grated nutmeg
cayenne pepper
2 tablespoons butter
6 black olives
Custard
2 eggs
½ cup cream
¼ cup milk
pinch grated nutmeg
salt and pepper

Prepare and partly cook pastry case as directed in Smoked Salmon Flan recipe.

Cut tomatoes in half and using a teaspoon and squeezing gently, remove all seeds and juice. Mix cheese, breadcrumbs, basil, salt and pepper, nutmeg and cayenne pepper together and press into the tomato halves. Place in cooked flan case and dot with butter. Make custard by beating all ingredients together and seasoning lightly with salt and pepper. Pour custard into flan case around the tomatoes and arrange olives in custard. Bake on middle shelf of a moderately hot oven for 30 to 35 minutes or until the custard is set, reducing the heat if necessary to moderately slow. Serve hot.

Rice Omelette

Serves: 3-4
Cooking time: 7-10 minutes

6 eggs
6 tablespoons milk
pinch of powdered saffron
salt and pepper
1 cup boiled rice
1 tablespoon butter
watercress sprigs for garnish

Separate eggs. Add milk and saffron to egg yolks and season to taste with salt and pepper. Beat well with a rotary beater. Add rice and gently fold in stiffly beaten egg whites.

Heat omelette pan, add butter and tip so that bottom and sides of pan are well coated. Pour in mixture and cook over a gentle heat until omelette starts to rise and set.

Place under a hot grill until puffed and golden brown on top. Garnish with watercress sprigs and serve immediately with a tossed salad. A good luncheon or supper dish.

Cheese Soufflé

Serves: 4
Cooking time: 35-40 minutes
Oven temperature: 190-200° C (375-400° F)

3 tablespoons butter
1 tablespoon fresh white breadcrumbs
½ cup grated Parmesan cheese
3 tablespoons plain flour
1 cup milk
4 egg yolks
¾ teaspoon salt
¼ teaspoon ground black pepper
pinch cayenne pepper
30 g (1 oz) Gruyère cheese, grated
5 egg whites

Grease a 5 to 6 cup soufflé dish with ½ tablespoon of the butter, then sprinkle with breadcrumbs and 1 tablespoon Parmesan cheese. Place a collar of buttered greaseproof paper around the soufflé dish and secure with string.

Melt remaining butter in a saucepan, stir in flour and cook over a gentle heat for about 1 minute. Add milk and stir continuously over a moderate heat until mixture thickens and boils. Simmer for 5 seconds. Remove from heat, add egg yolks one at a time, beating well. Add seasonings, grated Parmesan and Gruyère cheeses.

Whisk egg whites until stiff, firm peaks are formed. Stir a heaped tablespoon of whisked egg white into the sauce to lighten it, then with a spatula, lightly fold in the remaining egg whites. Gently pour soufflé mixture into prepared soufflé dish. Bake on middle shelf of a moderately hot oven, for 30 to 40 minutes. Serve immediately.

Asparagus Flan

Serves: 4-6
Cooking time: 40 minutes
Oven temperature: 200-220° C (400-425° F)
  reducing to 180-190° C (350-375° F)

1 × 20 cm (8 inch) pastry case (page 42)
1 medium-sized onion, finely chopped or grated
2 eggs, lightly beaten
½ cup cream
1 cup grated tasty Cheddar cheese
salt
freshly ground pepper
12 canned asparagus spears, drained
2 small tomatoes

Prepare pastry as directed in recipe for Smoked Salmon Flan. Line a 20 cm (8 inch) pie plate or flan ring but do not prick or cook.

Combine onion, eggs, cream and grated cheese, add salt and pepper to taste. Pour into flan case. Arrange asparagus spears over the filling. Bake in a hot oven for 10 minutes, reduce heat to moderate and cook for a further 30 minutes or until set.

Cut tomatoes into wedges and garnish flan before serving either hot or cold.

Onion and Cheese Flan

Serves: 6
Cooking time: 45-50 minutes
Oven temperature: 190-200° C (375-400° F)

1 × 23 cm (9 inch) pastry case (page 42)
250 g (8 oz) Swiss cheese, grated
2 tablespoons flour
1 large onion, finely sliced
1 tablespoon butter
4 eggs
1 cup cream
1 cup milk
¼ teaspoon nutmeg
2 drops Tabasco sauce
freshly ground pepper

Prepare and partly cook pastry case as directed for Smoked Salmon Flan.

Mix cheese and flour together and sprinkle into partly baked flan case. Sauté onion in butter until transparent and arrange over cheese mixture. Beat eggs lightly and add cream, milk, nutmeg, Tabasco sauce and salt and pepper to taste. Pour carefully over onion rings, place flan in a moderately hot oven and cook for 30 to 35 minutes or until filling is set and top is golden brown.

Serve hot or cold.

Belgian Parmesan Cakes

Yield: 30-35
Cooking time: 30 minutes

90 g (3 oz) butter
$^2/_3$ cup plain flour
2½ cups milk
salt and pepper
ground nutmeg
5 egg yolks
¾ cup grated Parmesan cheese
extra butter
extra flour
egg and fine white breadcrumbs for coating
oil for frying
cayenne pepper (optional)

Melt butter in a heavy-based saucepan, add flour and stir over a low heat for 2 or 3 minutes—do not allow the roux to brown. Add milk and bring to the boil, stirring constantly. Season with salt and pepper, add nutmeg to taste. Simmer very gently for 25 minutes. Remove from heat and take skin off top of sauce. Mix the egg yolks and cheese together and stir into hot sauce. Spoon onto a greased plate, spread a little butter on top and leave to cool.

Press out mixture till 1 cm (½ inch) thick on a floured board. Cut into rounds 4 cm (1½ inches) in diameter. Dip into flour then into beaten egg and coat with breadcrumbs. Fry in deep hot oil. Drain and sprinkle lightly with cayenne pepper if desired.

Serve hot as an hors d'oeuvre or as a savoury.

Cooking tip: To make fine white breadcrumbs quickly, break some crustless stale white bread into blender jar, switch on for 30 seconds. Tip out and repeat until sufficient bread is crumbed. Shake through a coarse sieve to separate larger crumbs.

Cider Cheese Casserole

Serves: 4-6
Cooking time: 1¼ hours
Oven temperature: 160-170° C (325-350° F)

1 cup milk
1 small onion, chopped
1 cup cider
½ cup grated apple
salt to taste
½ teaspoon dry mustard
3 cups grated Cheddar cheese
2½ cups diced white bread
4 eggs, separated
2 tablespoons butter
2 teaspoons cinnamon

Place milk and onion in a saucepan. Heat to just below boiling point. Add the cider, apple, seasonings, cheese and 2 cups diced bread. Stir until cheese has melted and remove from heat. Beat egg yolks and blend in. Whisk egg whites until stiff and fold into mixture. Pour into a greased casserole dish, dot with butter and sprinkle with cinnamon and remaining bread cubes. Bake in a moderately slow oven for 1¼ hours or until golden brown.

Serve as a luncheon or supper dish with a salad.

Cooking tip: Care must be taken not to overheat cheese in the saucepan as it could go 'stringy'.

PASTA & RICE

The variety of pastas available is as fascinating as it is extensive. Always boil briskly in plenty of salted water to the 'al dente' stage, that is, firm to the bite. Add a tablespoon of oil to the water to prevent it boiling over, and stir well during early part of cooking to prevent strands or pieces sticking together.

For perfectly cooked, dry rice, cook in a copious amount of boiling, salted water for about 12 minutes, then press a grain between the fingers. If there is a tiny gritty piece in the centre, the rice is ready. Pour into a large sieve and run hot water through the grains. Make 3 to 4 holes in the rice with the end of a spoon, cover with a lid and place over a pan. The rice will complete cooking in its own heat and the grains separate and dry.

The alternative absorption method of cooking rice is covered in the recipes. If substituting brown rice for the white rice used, increase water to 4½ cups for each cup of rice and cook for 1 to 1¼ hours.

Fried Rice
Serves: 4-6
Cooking time: 8-10 minutes

1 cup chopped cooked chicken
½ cup chopped cooked pork or ham
6 dried mushrooms, soaked in warm water for 20 minutes
5 tablespoons oil
2 eggs, lightly beaten
small piece fresh root ginger
1 cup chopped spring onions
6 cups cold boiled rice
½ cup cooked green peas
½ cup cooked shelled prawns
1 tablespoon dry sherry
¼ cup chicken stock
1 tablespoon soy sauce

Remove skin from chicken and trim pork or ham before chopping into small pieces. Drain and squeeze mushrooms dry and chop.

Beat eggs lightly with a pinch of salt. Heat 1 tablespoon of the oil in a large frying pan or wok and pour in eggs. Fry lightly on each side, remove and cut into small pieces. Heat remaining oil in pan and stir-fry chicken, pork or ham, mushrooms, ginger and spring onions for 2 to 3 minutes. Remove ginger. Add rice and stir constantly until rice is well coated with oil and heated through. Season lightly with salt and add chopped egg, peas and prawns.

Mix sherry, stock and soy sauce together and sprinkle over rice. Mix thoroughly and serve hot.

Pasta with Red Clam Sauce
Serves: 4-6
Cooking time: 15-20 minutes

250 g (8 oz) noodles
¼ cup olive oil
2 garlic cloves, crushed
¼ cup water
2 teaspoons chopped parsley
¼ teaspoon oregano
1 x 250 g (8 oz) can whole clams, drained
salt and pepper
¾ cup smooth Tomato Sauce (page 17)

Cook noodles in boiling, salted water until just tender. While they are cooking, heat oil in frying pan, add garlic and cook till golden. Slowly stir in water. Add parsley, oregano and clams. Season to taste with salt and pepper and mix well. Add tomato sauce and bring to the boil.

Drain noodles and place in warm serving dish. Spoon clam sauce on top and serve immediately.
Note: Other shellfish may be used with the clams.

Stuffed Cannelloni

Serves: 4-6
Cooking time: 50 minutes
Oven temperature: 180-190° C (350-375° F)

12 cannelloni tubes
3 cups ricotta cheese
2 eggs
¾ cup grated Parmesan cheese
salt and pepper
pinch ground nutmeg
2 tablespoons butter
Tomato sauce
1 small onion, chopped
3 tablespoons olive oil
2 cups chopped, peeled tomatoes
1 tablespoon tomato paste
1 bay leaf
salt and pepper to taste
pinch sugar

Cook cannelloni in plenty of boiling, salted water and while still a little firm, add 2 cups cold water. Set aside until ready to fill. Mix thoroughly ricotta cheese, eggs and ¼ cup of the Parmesan cheese. Season to taste with salt and pepper, add nutmeg.

Drain cannelloni and fill with ricotta cheese mixture. Place side by side in a single layer in a buttered shallow ovenproof casserole. Pour tomato sauce around the cannelloni, sprinkle with remaining Parmesan cheese and dot with butter. Bake in a moderate oven until bubbling, approximately 20 minutes. Serve at once.

Tomato sauce: Sauté onion in oil until soft. Add remaining ingredients, cover and simmer for 20 minutes. Remove bay leaf and use as it is or press through a sieve for a smooth sauce.

Spaghetti Springtime

Serves: 2-4
Cooking time: 15 minutes

250 g (8 oz) spaghetti
1½ cups chopped, peeled tomatoes
1 green capsicum, seeded and chopped
½ cup chopped spring onions
¼ cup chopped black olives
salt and pepper
1 tablespoon lemon juice
⅓ cup olive oil
chopped parsley for garnish
grated Parmesan cheese for serving

Cook spaghetti in boiling, salted water until just tender, drain and keep hot.

Heat tomatoes in saucepan. Stir until hot. Add hot spaghetti, green capsicum, spring onions, olives, salt and freshly ground pepper to taste and lemon juice. Finally add olive oil and toss well.

Garnish with chopped parsley and serve immediately with Parmesan cheese.

Rice Pilaf

Serves: 4-6
Cooking time: 25 minutes

2 tablespoons oil
2 cups long grain rice
1 teaspoon salt
3 cups boiling stock or water and chicken stock cubes

Heat oil in a large saucepan. Add rice and sauté, stirring continuously, until it is well coated and rice turns opaque in appearance (approximately 5 to 7 minutes). Add salt and stock. Stir well and bring to the boil. Turn heat to very low and cook for 20 minutes.

All the liquid should be absorbed and rice grains separate. If any liquid remains, cook a little longer. Leave covered and allow to stand for 5 to 10 minutes before serving. Serve with kebabs and barbecued meats.

Tomato pilaf: Sauté 1 small chopped onion and ¼ cup chopped capsicum with rice, add ½ cup chopped, peeled tomatoes and proceed as above.

Pilaf with pine nuts: Sauté ¼ cup pine nuts with rice and proceed as above.

Rice Rissoles

Serves: 6
Cooking time: 40-60 minutes

1 onion, finely chopped
2 tablespoons butter
1 cup short grain rice
3 cups chicken stock
2 eggs, beaten
fine breadcrumbs
oil for frying
parsley sprigs for garnish

Sauté onion in butter until soft, add rice and stir until grains are coated with butter.

Add chicken stock, bring to the boil, stirring occasionally. Cover and cook over low heat for 30 minutes. Leave until cool enough to handle, then take large tablespoons of rice mixture and mould around a heaped teaspoon of filling which can be as given below or any other desired. The rissoles may be moulded into oval or round shapes. When all are made, dip into beaten egg and coat with breadcrumbs. Fry in deep hot oil until golden brown all over and heated through. Drain on paper towels and serve very hot, garnished with parsley. The rissoles may be kept hot in the oven for 10 minutes.

Ham and prawn filling: Finely dice ½ cup cooked ham and ½ cup cooked, shelled and deveined prawns. Chop a small onion finely, heat 1 tablespoon butter and gently fry onion until soft and golden. Mix with the ham and prawns, season to taste.

Savoury mince filling: In 1 tablespoon hot oil fry 1 finely chopped onion and 1 clove of crushed garlic. Add 250 g (8 oz) lean minced steak and stir until steak changes colour. Add salt and pepper to taste. If desired, add 2 chopped bacon rashers. Cover and cook over low heat for 20 minutes.

Mozzarella cheese filling: Cut 2 cm (¾ inch) cubes of Mozzarella cheese or any other cooking cheese and enclose in rice. When the rissoles are fried, the cheese melts slightly and when broken open it separates in long strands.

Macaroni Casserole

Serves: 4
Cooking time: 60 minutes
Oven temperature: 150-160° C (300-325° F)

250 g (8 oz) macaroni
3 tablespoons butter
1 onion, thinly sliced
1 garlic clove, crushed
1 x 220 g (7¾ oz) can mushrooms in butter sauce
1 x 425 g (15 oz) can peeled tomatoes, chopped
1 x 140 g (5 oz) can tomato paste
250 g (8 oz) ham, finely chopped
4 tablespoons dry white wine or sherry
1 teaspoon sugar
salt
freshly ground pepper
grated Parmesan cheese
finely chopped parsley

Cook macaroni in boiling, salted water until just tender. Drain and rinse. Melt butter in a flameproof casserole, saute onion and garlic until tender. Add macaroni and all remaining ingredients except Parmesan cheese and parsley and mix together thoroughly. Cover and cook in a slow oven for approximately 45 minutes or until hot.

Sprinkle with Parmesan cheese and parsley and serve with hot crusty French bread.

Cooking tip: Macaroni pieces often stick together during cooking. To prevent this pour macaroni into boiling, salted water, stirring constantly. Keep stirring until water returns to the boil, boil rapidly for 2 minutes, remove from heat, cover pan and leave for 30 minutes.

Spaghetti Bolognese

Serves: 4
Cooking time: 30 minutes

2 green capsicums
2 tablespoons olive oil
1 garlic clove, crushed
3 onions, chopped
500 g (1 lb) minced steak
1 tablespoon chopped parsley
1 x 425 g (15 oz) can peeled tomatoes
2 tablespoons tomato paste
¼ cup dry red wine
½ teaspoon sugar
salt
freshly ground pepper
375 g (12 oz) spaghetti
1 tablespoon butter
grated Parmesan cheese for serving

Remove seeds and white membrane from capsicums and chop. Heat oil in a pan, saute capsicum, garlic and onion until tender and onion is golden brown. Add minced steak and cook until meat changes colour, stirring frequently. Add chopped parsley, tomatoes, tomato paste, wine, sugar and salt and pepper to taste. Mix together thoroughly, cover and simmer gently for 20 minutes.

Meanwhile, cook spaghetti in boiling, salted water until just tender, drain and rinse with hot water.

Place spaghetti in dish, add butter and 2 tablespoons grated Parmesan cheese and toss well. Spoon hot sauce on top and serve with additional cheese.

Spaghetti Marinara

Serves: 4-6
Cooking time: 25 minutes

500 g (1 lb) spaghetti
250 g (8 oz) fish fillets (flounder, sole or John Dory)
500 g (1 lb) cooked prawns
2 garlic cloves, crushed
2 tablespoons oil
500 g (1 lb) tomatoes, skinned and chopped
salt and pepper
½ teaspoon sugar
½ cup dry white wine
1 teaspoon dried oregano
2 tablespoons melted butter
chopped parsley for garnish

Cook spaghetti in boiling, salted water until just tender. While spaghetti is cooking skin fish fillets and cut into bite-sized pieces. Shell and devein prawns. Gently fry garlic in oil in a frying pan, increase heat and add fish pieces. Cook until lightly tinted, remove from pan. Pour off any oil left in pan, add tomatoes, salt and pepper to taste and sugar. Cook rapidly for approximately 15 minutes, stir in wine, oregano, fish pieces and prawns. Simmer until fish and prawns are heated through.

Meanwhile drain spaghetti and toss with melted butter. Serve seafood sauce over spaghetti and sprinkle with chopped parsley before serving.

Paella Barcelona

Serves: 8-10
Cooking time: 50 minutes

1 chicken, about 1.5 kg (3 lb)
¾ cup Spanish olive oil
500 g (1 lb) chipolata sausages, pricked
2 onions, sliced
1 large green capsicum, seeded and sliced
2 garlic cloves, crushed
1 cup chopped, peeled tomatoes
2½ cups long grain rice
¼ teaspoon powdered saffron
8 cups boiling chicken stock
½ cup young green peas
250 g (8 oz) squid, cleaned and cut into rings
salt and pepper
8-10 canned artichoke hearts
½-1 cup cooked shelled prawns
½-1 cup cooked shelled mussels

Cut chicken into 8 or 10 pieces. Heat oil in paella or large frying pan, add chicken and sausages, fry until evenly browned. Remove from pan.

Sauté onion in remaining oil, add capsicum and garlic, cook a little longer, then add tomatoes. Cook for 5 to 10 minutes and return chicken and sausages to pan. Add rice and stir until golden brown. Mix saffron with boiling stock and add with peas and squid to pan. Season to taste with salt and pepper. Stir well and allow paella to cook without stirring again.

While paella is cooking, add artichoke hearts, prawns and mussels. Place them in the rice so that they heat through and look attractive. Cook paella over a moderate heat until all the liquid has been absorbed, about 25 minutes. Serve from pan.

Indian Ghee Rice

Serves: 4-6
Cooking time: 30-35 minutes

3 tablespoons ghee
1 onion, chopped
½ teaspoon powdered saffron
½ teaspoon ground turmeric
2 cups long grain rice, washed and drained
2 cloves
6 peppercorns
4 cardamom pods
8 cm (3 inch) cinnamon stick
2 teaspoons salt
4½ cups chicken stock
⅓ cup sultanas
1 cup cooked, hot green peas
2 tablespoons blanched almonds, fried in ghee or oil until
    golden
4 hard-boiled eggs, shelled
extra turmeric, salt and ghee

Heat ghee and gently fry onion until transparent. Add
saffron and turmeric and mix thoroughly. Add rice and
cook, stirring continuously, until well coated and golden in
colour. Add cloves, peppercorns, bruised cardamom pods,
cinnamon stick and salt. Add chicken stock and stir
thoroughly. Bring to the boil, cover and lower heat. Cook
gently until all the liquid has been absorbed, approximately
15 to 20 minutes.

Sprinkle sultanas on top of rice for last 10 minutes of
cooking time, do not stir. When rice is cooked, remove lid
and allow to stand for 5 minutes. Add peas and almonds, stir
lightly with a fork and serve immediately, garnished with
halved eggs.

To prepare eggs: Rub hard-boiled eggs with extra turmeric
and salt. Prick all over with a fine skewer and fry in ghee
until a golden crust forms.

Spaghetti with Quick Pesto Sauce

Serves: 4-6
Cooking time: 8-10 minutes

60 g (2 oz) butter, softened
3 tablespoons chopped fresh basil*
3 tablespoons chopped parsley*
250 g (8 oz) cream cheese softened at room temperature
⅓ cup grated Parmesan cheese
¼ cup olive oil
1 garlic clove, crushed
freshly ground pepper
½ cup boiling water
375 g (12 oz) thin spaghetti or vermicelli
grated Parmesan cheese for serving

In a bowl, cream together butter, basil, parsley, cream
cheese, Parmesan cheese, oil and garlic. Grind in a generous
amount of fresh black pepper. Stir in boiling water gradually
until smoothly combined.

Cook spaghetti in boiling, salted water until tender. Drain
and place on warm serving dish. Spoon some of the sauce
over the spaghetti, serve remainder separately with additional grated Parmesan cheese.
Note: The sauce is not meant to be piping hot. If it is
heated, the butter and cream cheese will melt and the
consistency of the sauce be lost. Ensure spaghetti is piping
hot when served. Sauce will keep in a screw top jar in
refrigerator.

* Dried herbs cannot be substituted.

VEGETABLES

How often a good meal is ruined by 'inadequate' vegetables! The French hold vegetables in such high esteem they frequently serve them as a separate course. The recipes following are drawn from many cuisines, and some can be served as the main course for a light luncheon or supper. Try Ratatouille with crusty bread, a side salad and a glass of crisp, white wine. For a more substantial dish, poach eggs in it.

Serve Hasselback Potatoes with your next roast, Potatoes Anna and Beans Amandine with your dinner party main course. What vegetables will you serve tonight?

Beans Amandine

Serves: 6
Cooking time: 10-15 minutes

500 g (1 lb) green beans
salt
sugar
60 g (2 oz) butter
¼ cup blanched, slivered almonds
freshly ground pepper

Top and tail beans, string only if necessary. Leave whole or slice French-style by splitting down centre. Cook in a small quantity of boiling, salted water with a pinch of sugar added. Do not cover. When tender, drain, place in a vegetable dish and keep hot.

Melt butter in a small pan, add almonds and sauté until golden brown. Pour butter and almonds over beans, season with pepper and serve immediately.

Variations: Serve almond butter on cooked cauliflower, broccoli or Brussels sprouts.

Asparagus and Ham Casserole

Serves: 4
Cooking time: 40 minutes
Oven temperature: 190-200° C (375-400° F)

1 cup sliced celery
2 tablespoons butter
1 x 440 g (16 oz) can asparagus soup
½ cup water
freshly ground pepper
1½ cups cooked rice
1 cup chopped ham
1 x 440 g (16 oz) can asparagus pieces, drained
¼ cup grated Parmesan cheese

In a saucepan, sauté celery in butter until tender. Add asparagus soup, water and pepper.

Grease a shallow ovenproof dish. Place rice in dish and cover with chopped ham and asparagus pieces. Gently pour soup mixture over dish contents and sprinkle cheese on top. Cook in a moderately hot oven for 20 to 30 minutes or until heated through. Serve with crusty French bread.

Zucchini Provencale

Serves: 6
Cooking time: 1 hour
Oven temperature: 180-190° C (350-375° F)

500 g (1 lb) zucchini
salt
1 onion, chopped
1 garlic clove, crushed
3 tablespoons butter
500 g (1 lb) tomatoes
2 tablespoons oil
1 tablespoon chopped parsley
¾ cup grated tasty cheese

Wash zucchini and cut into 5 cm (2 inch) slices or halve lengthways. Sprinkle with salt and leave for 30 minutes. Pat dry with paper towels.

Sauté onion and garlic in butter until onion is transparent, add zucchini and sauté for further 10 minutes. Peel tomatoes and slice thickly. Heat oil in a separate pan, add tomatoes and sauté for 5 minutes, turning once. Sprinkle with parsley.

Grease an ovenproof dish and place in a layer of tomatoes followed by a layer of zucchini. Sprinkle between layers with grated cheese, salt and pepper. Finish with a layer of tomatoes sprinkled with cheese. Bake in a moderate oven for 45 minutes. Serve hot as a separate course or as a vegetable accompaniment.

Brussels Sprouts Polonaise

Serves: 6
Cooking time: 18-20 minutes

750 g (1½ lb) Brussels sprouts
salt
sugar
90 g (3 oz) butter
⅓ cup soft white breadcrumbs (optional)
2 tablespoons lemon juice
2 hard-boiled eggs
freshly ground pepper

Wash Brussels sprouts well, remove coarse outer and damaged leaves and trim stems. Cook in boiling, salted water with a pinch of sugar added until tender, about 15 minutes. Cook uncovered for first 5 minutes, cover for remainder of cooking time. Drain well and keep hot in a vegetable dish.

Heat butter until foaming, add breadcrumbs, if used, and cook until golden brown. Add lemon juice and pour over sprouts. Finely chop whites of hard-boiled eggs, press yolks through a sieve. Sprinkle on top of sprouts with a good grind of black pepper. Serve immediately.

Variations: Cauliflower and asparagus may be used instead of Brussels sprouts.

Fried Vegetables Oriental

Serves: 6
Cooking time: 8-10 minutes

4 tablespoons peanut oil
small piece fresh root ginger, bruised
1 garlic clove, crushed
2 small onions, quartered
1 green capsicum, seeded and cut in strips
1 red capsicum, seeded and cut in strips
½ cup finely sliced celery
½ cup finely sliced carrot
1½ cups thinly sliced cauliflower or broccoli flowerets
1 cup sliced mushrooms
1 tablespoon sherry
1 tablespoon soy sauce
½ teaspoon sugar

Heat oil in a wok or large frying pan and fry ginger for 1 minute. Remove. Add garlic, onions (separated into 'leaves'), capsicum, celery and carrot. Stir-fry for 2 minutes, tossing vegetables as they cook. Add cauliflower or broccoli and mushrooms and cook, stirring and tossing constantly for a further 4 to 5 minutes, adding a little more water to wok if necessary. The water is used to create steam to help cook the vegetables. Season with a sprinkling of sherry, soy sauce and sugar, stir again. Serve immediately as a vegetable accompaniment to Asian-style dishes or grills.
Note: Chinese or savoy cabbage, or spinach leaves torn into pieces may be added. Vary vegetables to use those on hand. An excellent means of using up bits and pieces of vegetables.

Hot Herbed Tomatoes

Serves: 4-5
Cooking time: 10 minutes

8-10 ripe tomatoes
3 tablespoons butter
¼ cup finely chopped celery
1 garlic clove, crushed (optional)
salt
freshly ground black pepper
1 teaspoon sugar
2 tablespoons snipped chives
2 tablespoons finely chopped parsley
1 tablespoon chopped fresh oregano (or ¼ teaspoon dried oregano)

Choose even-sized, rather small tomatoes. Place in a bowl, cover with boiling water, leave 30 seconds and pour off water. Peel off skins.
Heat butter in a frying pan, add celery and garlic and sauté 5 minutes. Add tomatoes, sprinkle with salt, pepper and sugar and spoon butter over them. Cover and cook gently for 5 minutes. Sprinkle on herbs, baste again with butter and cook, uncovered for further 5 minutes, basting often. Spoon sauce once more over tomatoes before serving. Serve hot with roast poultry, beef, veal and grilled meats.

Stuffed Mushrooms

Serves: 6
Cooking time: 25 minutes
Oven temperature: 180-190° C (350-375° F)

6 large mushrooms
¼ cup melted butter
red capsicum strips for garnish
Stuffing
2 tablespoons butter
1 small onion, finely chopped
1 tablespoon chopped red capsicum
½ cup chopped ham
1 tablespoon chopped parsley
salt and pepper
1½ cups soft white breadcrumbs
½ cup Béchamel Sauce (page 16)

Wipe mushrooms with a damp cloth and remove stalks. Chop stalks finely and reserve for stuffing. Brush mushroom caps on each side with melted butter and place in baking dish. Cook in a moderate oven for 10 minutes. Remove mushrooms from oven and fill each mushroom with prepared stuffing. Return to oven, bake for a further 15 minutes or until mushrooms are tender. Serve hot, garnished with red capsicum strips.

Stuffing: Melt butter in a small saucepan, add onion and sauté gently until soft but not brown. Add chopped red capsicum, ham, parsley, salt and pepper, chopped mushroom stalks and breadcrumbs. Mix thoroughly and bind together with bechamel sauce.

Asparagus Rolls Supreme

Serves: 6
Cooking time: 10 minutes
Oven temperature: 200-230° C (400-450° F)

sliced bread
1 x 430 g (15 oz) can asparagus spears
butter
olives or parsley sprigs for garnish
Sauce
1 x 440 g (16 oz) can cream of chicken soup
1 tablespoon cornflour
1 cup milk
salt and pepper

Cut crusts from bread, place a spear of asparagus on each slice, roll up tightly and secure with wooden cocktail sticks. Brush rolls lightly with softened or melted butter, place on a baking tray and bake in a hot oven for 10 minutes or until lightly browned and crisp.

To make sauce: Heat soup in a small saucepan. Blend cornflour with milk, add to soup and stir constantly until boiling. Simmer for 1 minute. Add salt and pepper to taste.

To serve, place rolls on a heated dish and remove cocktail sticks. Pour sauce over rolls, garnish with chopped olives or parsley and serve hot.

Cooking tip: These rolls make excellent appetisers without the sauce. Prepare rolls, brush with butter and place in a plastic or foil container. Cover rolls closely with plastic film and seal container with lid. Store in freezer until required for heating and serving.

Braised Red Cabbage

Serves: 6-8
Cooking time: 45 minutes

1 medium-sized red cabbage
salt
freshly ground pepper
3 tablespoons butter
1 onion, sliced
2 tablespoons vinegar
½ cup dry red wine
2 green cooking apples
2 tablespoons brown sugar
pinch grated nutmeg
pinch ground cloves
2 tablespoons redcurrant jelly

Shred washed cabbage and discard hard core. Sprinkle with salt and pepper. Melt butter in a large saucepan and sauté onion until transparent. Add cabbage, vinegar and red wine. Cover and cook over a low heat for 10 minutes, stirring occasionally. Peel, core and slice apples, add to cabbage with sugar, nutmeg and cloves. Cover saucepan and simmer cabbage gently for 30 minutes or until tender.

Stir in redcurrant jelly and simmer for a further 5 minutes. Adjust seasoning, thicken liquid with a cornflour and water paste if desired. Serve with grilled beef or lamb, sausages or frankfurters.

Ginger Orange Pumpkin

Serves: 4-5
Cooking time: 45 minutes
Oven temperature: 200-220° C (400-425° F)

1 kg (2 lb) butternut or other smooth-skinned pumpkin
3 tablespoons butter
1 tablespoon honey
1 teaspoon ground ginger
juice of 1 large orange
shredded orange rind for garnish

Cut pumpkin in 5 mm (¼ inch) slices, remove skin and seeds. Melt butter in a saucepan, add honey, ginger and orange juice. Stir to combine and dip pumpkin slices in mixture. Arrange pumpkin, with slices overlapping, in a buttered ovenproof dish. Pour remaining orange mixture on top and cook in a hot oven for 45 minutes until tender and top is lightly browned. Baste occasionally during cooking with orange mixture.

While pumpkin is cooking, remove peel from orange skin with a vegetable peeler taking care not to remove pith. With a sharp knife cut into fine shreds. Cook in a little water until tender. Drain and rinse under cold water.

Garnish with orange shreds and serve with roast or grilled poultry, pork and veal.

Hasselback Potatoes

Serves: 4-6
Cooking time: 45-50 minutes
Oven temperature: 200-230° C (400-450° F)

8-12 medium-sized potatoes
50 g (2 oz) butter
1 tablespoon oil
salt and pepper
3 tablespoons grated Parmesan cheese (optional)

Choose even-sized, oval-shaped potatoes if possible. Peel and if too rounded on both sides, cut off a thin slice from one side so that potatoes can sit in dish without rolling. Cut each potato in thin slices from rounded side, cutting almost to but not through the base. Melt butter in an ovenproof dish until foaming, add oil and blend. Place potatoes cut side up in dish and spoon butter mixture over potatoes. Sprinkle with salt and freshly ground pepper and cook in a hot oven for 30 minutes, basting frequently with butter mixture. Sprinkle with cheese if desired, and cook for further 15 to 20 minutes until potatoes are golden brown. Serve immediately.

Eggplant Casserole

Serves: 4
Cooking time: 35-40 minutes
Oven temperature: 180-190° C (350-375° F)

3 eggplants
salt
2 tablespoons oil
2 tablespoons tomato paste or ½ cup smooth Tomato Sauce
  (page 17)
1 cup yoghurt
pepper

Slice the eggplants without peeling, sprinkle with salt and leave 30 minutes. Dry the slices and fry quickly in a frying pan in oil until coloured. Place them into a round cake tin or ovenproof casserole, as they come from the frying pan, layering them with tomato paste or sauce and yoghurt. Season layers with pepper. Cover the tin or casserole and bake in a moderate oven for 35 to 40 minutes. Turn out for serving.

Zucchini with Sour Cream

Serves: 6
Cooking time: 30-35 minutes
Oven temperature: 180-190° C (350-375° F)

1 kg (2 lb) zucchini
1 cup sour cream
2 tablespoons grated Parmesan cheese
paprika

Wash and trim zucchini. Slit in halves lengthways if small, otherwise, cut into 1 cm (½ inch) slices. Drop into boiling salted water and boil, uncovered, for 7 to 8 minutes until just tender. Drain well.

Place zucchini in a buttered ovenproof dish and spread sour cream on top. Sprinkle with grated Parmesan cheese. Bake in a moderate oven for 25 to 30 minutes until top is golden brown. Sprinkle with paprika and serve immediately. Serve with roast or grilled meats and poultry or as a vegetable accompaniment to braised and casseroled meat dishes.

Ratatouille

Serves: 12
Cooking time: 55 minutes

1 red capsicum
2 green capsicums
2 medium-sized eggplants
6 zucchini
½ cup olive oil
1 garlic clove, crushed
3 large onions, thinly sliced
3 large ripe tomatoes, peeled and chopped
¼ teaspoon dried basil
¼ teaspoon dried marjoram
1 tablespoon chopped parsley
freshly ground black pepper
crusty French bread for serving

Wash capsicums, remove seeds and white membrane and slice into rings. Wash eggplants and zucchini and cut into cm (½ inch) slices. Sprinkle slices with salt, leave for 3 minutes and pat dry with paper towels.

Heat oil in a heavy-based frying pan or flameproof casserole and sauté onion and garlic for 10 minutes. Add prepared capsicums, eggplants, zucchini and tomatoes, cover and simmer gently for 30 minutes.

Add herbs and salt and pepper to taste. Simmer gently uncovered for a further 15 minutes. The oil should be absorbed entirely by the vegetables. Serve cold with crusty French bread to mop up the juices, as an hors d'oeuvre or light luncheon dish; serve hot as a accompaniment to grilled beef or lamb.

Potatoes Anna

Serves: 6
Cooking time: 45-60 minutes
Oven temperature: 200-230° C (400-450° F)

750 g (1½ lb) potatoes
½ cup melted butter
salt
freshly ground black pepper

Select medium-sized, new potatoes if possible. Peel and slice thinly into a bowl of cold water. Soak for 10 minutes, drain and spread onto a clean tea towel. Dab dry with another cloth.

Brush a shallow round ovenproof dish or an 18 cm (7 inch) layer cake tin with some of the melted butter. Place a layer of potato slices in the base, overlapping the slices. Arrange in 2 or 3 graduating circles beginning at the outer edge. This is the most important layer as far as appearance is concerned, so choose even-sized slices for it. Sprinkle with salt and pepper and drizzle some butter on top. Repeat with remaining potato slices, seasoning and butter until dish is filled. Brush top slices well with butter. Bake in a hot oven for 45 to 60 minutes until cooked. Test with a fine skewer. Invert potato cake onto a heated serving dish, preferably ovenproof. Potatoes should be golden brown on base and sides; if not place under a hot grill for a minute or two to brown. Serve immediately as a vegetable accompaniment to main meals.

Curried Carrots

Serves: 4-6
Cooking time: 20-25 minutes

750 g (1½ lb) small carrots
1 large onion, sliced
2 tablespoons butter
1-2 teaspoons curry powder
2 tablespoons plain flour
½ cup milk
1 teaspoon tomato paste
salt

Scrape carrots and trim tops. Cook until tender in boiling salted water with a pinch of sugar added. Strain, measure liquid and make up to ¾ cup if necessary.

Sauté onion in butter until transparent, stir in curry powder and cook for 2 minutes. Blend in flour and cook a little longer. Add carrot liquid and milk, stirring constantly until sauce thickens and bubbles. Blend in tomato paste and add salt to taste. Add carrots to sauce and heat through gently. Alternatively, keep carrots hot and pour sauce over just before serving. Serve with corned meats and grills.

SALADS

A salad can be a meal in itself or served as an appetising accompaniment. Salad greens, such as lettuce, endive, spinach and silver beet, should be washed well under running water, placed in a salad basket or tea towel and the excess moisture removed with a vigorous swinging movement. Wrap loosely in a dry tea towel and place in the refrigerator. The cold atmosphere helps the leaves to absorb the remaining moisture and they come out crisp and dry. If not required immediately, place the crisped greens loosely in a plastic bag, seal with a tie and leave in the refrigerator.

Macaroni Salad
Serves: 4-6

3-4 cups cooked macaroni
¼ cup bottled French dressing
¼ cup chopped pickled onion
¼ cup diced tasty Cheddar cheese
½ cup chopped celery
½ cup chopped green capsicum
½ cup Mayonnaise (page 16)
salt
freshly ground pepper
crisp lettuce leaves or endive
sliced stuffed olives to garnish

Combine macaroni with French dressing, pickled onions, finely diced cheese, celery and capsicum. Toss and chill well. Add mayonnaise, toss to coat ingredients and adjust seasoning with salt and pepper.

Line a salad bowl with lettuce leaves and fill with the macaroni salad. Garnish with the stuffed olives.

Zucchini Salad
Serves: 4-6

500 g (1 lb) zucchini
½ cup bottled Italian dressing
2 tablespoons finely chopped parsley
2 tablespoons finely chopped green capsicum
2 spring onions, finely chopped
3 tablespoons finely chopped pickles (gherkins, onions, pimiento)
salt
freshly ground pepper
crisp lettuce leaves for serving

Wash zucchini, and slice thinly. Place in a frying basket and plunge into boiling, salted water. Boil rapidly for 3 minutes (timed after water returns to the boil). Stir zucchini gently while blanching. Lift out and drain well. Place in bowl. Add remaining ingredients except lettuce, seasoning to taste with salt and a good grind of black pepper. Cover and leave in refrigerator several hours or overnight. Serve in a bowl lined with crisp lettuce leaves.

Caesar Salad

Serves: 6-8

1 lettuce
1 endive
1 garlic clove
1 teaspoon salt
1 teaspoon dry mustard
1 tablespoon lemon juice
dash of Tabasco sauce
3 tablespoons olive oil
2 tablespoons grated Parmesan cheese
4 anchovy fillets, chopped into 3-4 pieces
1 egg, boiled for 1 minute
garlic croutons

Wash lettuce and endive. Place in salad basket or tea towel and swing to remove excess moisture. Wrap loosely in a dry tea towel and place in refrigerator to crisp.

Rub salad bowl with cut clove of garlic and add salt, mustard, lemon juice and Tabasco sauce. Stir with a wooden spoon until salt dissolves. Add olive oil and blend well.

Tear crisped salad greens into bite-sized pieces and add to salad bowl. Sprinkle with grated cheese and add chopped anchovy fillets. Break in the coddled egg and toss well until all ingredients are well coated.

Just before serving, sprinkle with garlic croutons and toss again.

Garlic croutons: Add 1-2 cloves of garlic to butter or oil in frying pan when frying croutons.

Waldorf Salad

Serves: 6

1 green apple
1 red apple
juice of ½ lemon
1 cup finely chopped celery
½ cup walnuts, broken
¼ cup Mayonnaise (page 16)
crisp lettuce cups
1 red apple for garnish
lemon juice

Chill apples, core and dice. Pour lemon juice over apples.

Combine apples with celery, walnuts and mayonnaise. Serve piled into lettuce cups. Slice red apple thinly, brush slices with lemon juice.

Garnish salad with red apple slices.

Chicken waldorf salad: Add 1 cup chopped, cooked chicken to above ingredients.

German Cauliflower Salad
Serves: 6-8

1 large cauliflower
1 small lettuce
6 bacon rashers, rind removed
2 tablespoons vinegar
3 tablespoons oil
salt
freshly ground pepper
chopped parsley

Cook cauliflower in boiling, salted water until just tender. Drain and chill. Separate into flowerets and discard any hard stems. Arrange flowerets on a bed of crisp lettuce leaves.

Fry bacon until golden brown and crisp, drain on absorbent paper and crumble. Beat vinegar with oil and add salt and pepper to taste.

Pour dressing over cauliflower. Sprinkle with crumbled bacon and chopped parsley.

Anchovied Vegetable Salad
Serves: 4-6

4 medium-sized tomatoes
125 g (4 oz) button mushrooms
1 small cucumber
1 large green capsicum
4-6 radishes
1 tablespoon finely chopped parsley
1 tablespoon snipped chives
Anchovy dressing
4-6 anchovy fillets
½ cup olive oil
1 garlic clove, crushed
2 tablespoons lemon juice
salt to taste
freshly ground black pepper
1 teaspoon chopped parsley
1 teaspoon capers, chopped

Remove cores from tomatoes, slice into wedges. Wipe mushrooms and slice thinly. Wash cucumber and score with skin on (peel if desired), slice thinly.

Remove seeds and membrane from capsicums and cut into short strips. Place salad ingredients in a bowl, sprinkle with parsley and chives and chill. Pour over half of the warm anchovy dressing, toss lightly. Serve in a salad bowl with remaining warm dressing served separately.

Anchovy dressing: Mash anchovy fillets, number used depends on size. Warm the olive oil and blend into anchovies. Add remaining ingredients and beat well with a fork to blend.

Swedish Herring Salad

Serves: 4-6

2 pickled herrings
6 boiled potatoes, peeled and diced
3 small gherkins, chopped
2 small pickled cucumbers, chopped
3 tablespoons chopped walnuts
2 green cooking apples, peeled, cored and chopped
3 beetroot, cooked, peeled and chopped
1 tablespoon caster sugar
1 tablespoon finely snipped chives
3 tablespoons Mayonnaise (page 16)
salt and pepper
French Dressing (page 70)
crisp lettuce leaves for serving

Rinse herrings in cold water. Drain and dry with paper towels and cut into small squares.

In a large bowl combine prepared ingredients adding 2 tablespoons of the mayonnaise and enough French dressing to moisten. Chill well.

Pile salad on a bed of crisp lettuce leaves and garnish with remaining mayonnaise and additional snipped chives, if desired.

Ham and Rice Salad

Serves: 10-12

500 g (1 lb) long grain rice
250 g (8 oz) lean ham
1 cup sliced French beans
1 cup diced carrots
chicken stock
1 cup thinly sliced celery
1 large cucumber, peeled and diced
1 tablespoon chopped chives
1 tablespoon chopped parsley
1 teaspoon chopped capers
½ cup French Dressing (page 70)
salt and pepper
parsley for garnish

Boil rice in salted water for 12 to 15 minutes or until just cooked. Rinse well in a colander and allow to dry thoroughly. Cut ham into fine strips. Cook beans and carrots in chicken stock until just tender, drain and cool. Place rice, ham and vegetables in a salad bowl, add the chives, parsley, capers and French dressing. Mix together thoroughly and season to taste with salt and freshly ground pepper. Chill thoroughly. Serve garnished with parsley.

Mushroom Salad

Serves: 6

500 g (1 lb) button mushrooms
2 tablespoons lemon juice
¼ cup olive oil
½ cup other salad oil of milder flavour
salt
freshly ground black pepper
1 tablespoon snipped chives
1 tablespoon finely chopped parsley
crisp lettuce leaves for serving

Choose firm, white button mushrooms. Wipe with a cloth and trim stems. Slice mushrooms thinly into a bowl. Beat lemon juice with the oils, about 1 teaspoon salt and a good grind of black pepper. Add half the chives and parsley and blend well. Pour over mushrooms, cover and chill for at least 2 hours. Toss now and then to distribute dressing. Pile into a salad bowl lined with lettuce and sprinkle with remaining chives and parsley.

Italian Bean Salad

Serves: 6-8

1 cup dried Lima beans
salt
3 medium-sized potatoes, cooked and sliced
1 cup chopped celery, blanched
freshly ground pepper
¼ cup Mayonnaise (page 16)
lettuce leaves
2 hard-boiled eggs, sliced
½ cup cocktail onions
3 tablespoons snipped chives
Salad dressing
1 teaspoon paprika
pinch salt
pinch sugar
¼ teaspoon dry mustard
2 tablespoons vinegar
4 tablespoons olive oil

Wash beans well, cover well with cold water and bring slowly to the boil. Simmer for 1½ hours. Add 2 teaspoons salt and cook further 30 minutes until tender. Drain.

Combine beans, potato and celery. Pour over salad dressing, toss lightly and chill for 2 hours in refrigerator. Add salt and pepper to taste and mix in mayonnaise.

Line a salad bowl with crisp lettuce leaves and fill with bean salad. Garnish with sliced hard-boiled eggs and sprinkle with cocktail onions and chives.

Salad dressing: Place all ingredients in a screw top jar, seal and shake well. Let it stand until required and shake just before using.

Bean and Egg Salad

Serves: 6

1 x 283 g (10 oz) packet frozen broad beans
1 x 298 g (10½ oz) can red kidney beans
⅓ cup bottled French dressing
4 hard-boiled eggs
salt and pepper
crisp lettuce leaves
mayonnaise for serving (optional)

Cook broad beans according to packet directions. Drain well. Drain kidney beans. Combine with broad beans in a bowl. Mix in French dressing, season if necessary, cover and chill. Shell eggs and cut into quarters. Combine 3 eggs with chilled beans, keep one quartered egg aside.

Line a salad bowl with lettuce, add bean and egg salad. Arrange reserved egg quarters on top. Serve with a bowl of mayonnaise if desired.

Boiling eggs: So that the yolks will be in the centre of the eggs when cooked, stir eggs gently during first 5 minutes of cooking. Hard-boiled eggs take about 12 to 15 minutes to cook. Cool under running cold water and shell as soon as possible to prevent a dark ring forming around the yolk.

Marinated Fish Salad

Serves: 5

1 kg (2 lb) fresh fish fillets (snapper, John Dory, Jewfish)
lime or lemon juice
1 teaspoon salt
1 medium-sized onion, finely chopped
1 cup coconut milk (see below)
1 red capsicum, seeded and thinly sliced
1 green capsicum, seeded and thinly sliced
halved coconut shells or lettuce leaf cups for serving
sliced lemon for garnish

Cut raw fish into 1 cm (½ inch) pieces (remove any skin or bones) and cover with lime juice. Add salt and stand in a cool place (refrigerate in hot weather) for at least 4 hours, stir occasionally.

Add onion, coconut milk and red and green capsicum, mix thoroughly. Chill until ready to serve.

Serve fish salad in coconut shells and garnish with sliced lemon.

Coconut milk: Place 1 cup coconut with 1¼ cups water in a saucepan. Bring slowly to the boil. Pour through a fine strainer (or cloth) pressing well to extract as much milk as possible.

Spinach Salad

Serves: 6-8

⅓ cup salad oil
2 tablespoons wine vinegar
1 tablespoon dry white wine
1 teaspoon soy sauce
½ teaspoon sugar
½ teaspoon dry mustard
½ teaspoon curry powder (optional)
garlic salt
salt
freshly ground pepper
500 g (1 lb) young spinach or silver beet leaves
250 g (8 oz) bacon rashers
2 hard-boiled eggs, finely chopped

In a screw top jar, combine oil, vinegar, wine, soy sauce, sugar, mustard and curry powder, if used. Seal and shake well. Add garlic salt, salt and pepper to taste, shake well and leave in refrigerator to chill.

Remove stalks from spinach or silver beet before weighing. Wash thoroughly, drain well and roll in a tea towel. Place in refrigerator and leave until crisp.

Remove rind from bacon, chop and fry until crisp. Drain on absorbent paper.

Gently tear spinach into small pieces and place in a large salad bowl. Add bacon and chopped egg, pour on dressing and toss gently to coat leaves. Serve immediately.

Brazilian Salad

Serves: 4

500 g (1 lb) cooked prawns
½ cup French dressing (see below)
3 oranges, peeled
500 g (1 lb) roast pork, sliced
1 fresh, ripe pineapple, peeled
1 cup cottage cheese
2 tablespoons flaked Brazil nuts, toasted
Mayonnaise (page 16) for serving

Shell and devein prawns, reserving some unshelled prawns for garnish. Marinate shelled prawns in French dressing for 30 minutes. Cut oranges into slices or segments, cut sliced pork into strips and toss together. Cut pineapple into 12 slices, remove inner core. Drain prawns with a slotted spoon, arrange on centre of platter with pork and oranges. Top pineapple slices with scoops of cottage cheese and sprinkle with flaked, toasted nuts. Arrange around prawns, pork and oranges. Garnish with reserved prawns and serve with mayonnaise. If desired salad may be arranged on a bed of crisp salad greens.

French dressing: The proportions for French dressing are 3 parts oil to 1 part vinegar with dry mustard, salt and freshly ground black pepper added to taste. Make up a quantity using ¾ cup good salad oil and ¼ cup vinegar (use wine, white, malt or tarragon vinegar), add seasonings and shake well in a screwtop jar. Use required amount, store remainder in a cool place. A pinch of sugar or chopped fresh herbs may be added if desired. If you like the flavour of garlic, add a halved clove to the dressing.

Tangy Chicken Salad

Serves: 4-6

750 g (1½ lb) chicken breasts
bouquet garni
½ teaspoon whole peppercorns
juice of ½ lemon
strip of lemon peel
salt
crisp lettuce leaves
1 large grapefruit
2 large oranges
3 tablespoons French Dressing (page 70)
radishes or cherry tomatoes
watercress for garnish
mayonnaise or sour cream for serving

Rinse chicken, place in a saucepan with bouquet garni, peppercorns, lemon juice and rind. Almost cover with water and bring to a slow simmer. Skim, add salt, cover and simmer gently 25 minutes until breasts are tender. Do not boil chicken as it will go stringy. Cool in liquid, lift out chicken and remove skin and bones. Reserve stock for other cooking uses.

Cut chicken breasts into generous strips and arrange on a bed of lettuce in a bowl. Peel grapefruit and oranges, remove pith, break into segments and peel off membrane. Halve grapefruit segments. Add to chicken and sprinkle with French dressing. Add colour to salad with whole radishes or cherry tomatoes and garnish with watercress. Serve mayonnaise or sour cream separately.

Salade Nicoise

1 x 420 g (15 oz) can tuna or salmon, drained
4 hard-boiled eggs
1 small green capsicum
1 cucumber
4 tomatoes
½ cup black olives
¼ cup onion rings
1 x 45 g (1¾ oz) can flat anchovy fillets
Herb dressing
3 tablespoons olive oil
1 tablespoon lemon juice
2 tablespoons each finely chopped parsley and chives
good pinch of thyme, crumbled
½ garlic clove
¼ teaspoon salt
pinch of sugar
freshly ground black pepper

Break tuna or salmon into chunks. Shell eggs and cut into quarters. Remove seeds and membrane from capsicums and cut into strips. Wash cucumber well, score and slice thinly, arrange in a bowl, sprinkle with salt and leave for 30 minutes, pressing with a weight to remove excess water. Peel tomatoes and cut into wedges. Arrange tuna, eggs, capsicum, drained cucumber and tomatoes in a salad bowl. Garnish with plump black olives, onion rings and drained anchovy fillets. Moisten with dressing, toss lightly and serve.

Herb dressing: Combine oil, lemon juice, parsley, chives and thyme. Crush garlic to a pulp with salt, add to oil mixture, season with sugar and pepper to taste. Shake or beat well before using.

Prawn Chef's Salad
Serves: 4-5

1 grapefruit
250 g (8 oz) shelled prawns or 1 x 220 g (7 oz) can tuna or
    salmon
2 tomatoes, cut into wedges
¼ cup stuffed olives
1 avocado pear
1 tablespoon lemon juice
1 small lettuce, crisped
250 g (8 oz) matured Cheddar cheese
Pickle dressing
1 cup sour cream
2 tablespoons piccalilli pickles
¼ teaspoon dry mustard
½ teaspoon salt
freshly ground pepper to taste

Remove flesh from grapefruit, divide into segments and
remove membrane and seeds. Halve segments. Devein
prawns cut in half lengthways if large. If using canned fish
instead, drain and flake roughly. Halve avocado pear,
remove seed and peel. Cut into wedges and sprinkle with
lemon juice. Tear lettuce into bite-sized pieces. Cut cheese
into sticks. Toss ingredients lightly together in a large salad
bowl. Add dressing and toss, or serve dressing separately.

Pickle dressing: Combine ingredients and chill for one
hour.

Potato Salad
Serves: 4-6

500-750 g (1-1½ lb) potatoes
½ cup finely chopped spring onions
½-¾ cup Mayonnaise (page 16)
1 tablespoon chopped parsley or mint (optional)

Boil potatoes in jackets. Peel, slice or dice and add spring
onions. When cold mix with enough mayonnaise to moisten.
Sprinkle with parsley or mint before serving.

Variations
1. Rub salad bowl with a cut garlic clove—omit spring
    onion.
2. Fold in 1 cup diced, processed Cheddar cheese.
3. Crumble 4 well-fried streaky bacon rashers over salad.
4. Fold in 1 cup chopped celery heart, cucumber cubes,
    grated carrot or 1 tablespoon celery seeds.
5. Add 1 cup flaked tuna, salmon, prawns or lobster.
6. Fold in 3 finely chopped hard-boiled eggs and ¼ cup
    chopped gherkins or 2 tablespoons finely chopped
    chives.
7. Use a French dressing, preferably when potatoes are still
    warm. Sprinkle with paprika.
8. Substitute mayonnaise with yoghurt flavoured with ½
    teaspoon garam masala.
9. Fold 1½ teaspoons curry powder into mayonnaise.
Note: Garam masala may be obtained from a quality
grocery store.

Avocado Salad Mould

Serves: 6

1 large or 2 small avocado pears
1 small onion, grated
1 teaspoon salt
freshly ground black pepper
dash of Tabasco sauce
1 tablespoon gelatine
½ cup cold water
¼ cup boiling water
¼ cup cream, whipped
¼ cup Mayonnaise (page 16)
lettuce leaves
1 small avocado pear, sliced, for garnish
French Dressing (page 70)

Choose well-ripened avocado pears, peel and stone. Blend with onion, salt, pepper and Tabasco sauce until smooth. Soften gelatine in ¼ cup cold water. Add boiling water, stir until dissolved. Stir in remaining cold water, pour into a large bowl and cool. When gelatine mixture is consistency of egg white, gradually fold in whipped cream, mayonnaise and avocado mixture. Pour into a mould, previously rinsed with cold water, chill until set. Invert and unmould onto a chilled plate lined with lettuce leaves.

Coat sliced avocado with French dressing and garnish mould.

Curried Rice Salad

Serves: 4-6

1 cup long grain rice
1 x 185 g (6 oz) packet frozen peas
500 g (1 lb) cooked prawns
1 cup chopped celery
1-2 teaspoons curry powder (see below)
pinch of dry mustard
1 tablespoon lemon juice
3 tablespoons olive oil
salt
freshly ground pepper

Cook rice in a large saucepan of boiling, salted water for 12 to 15 minutes. When tender, drain and rinse thoroughly. Drain again and cool. Cook peas in boiling, salted water until tender, drain. Shell and devein prawns, reserving 3 or 4 for garnish.

Combine all ingredients in a large mixing bowl, toss together lightly. Season to taste with salt and pepper. Chill and garnish with reserved prawns. Serve in a salad bowl.
Note: Some varieties of curry powder are hotter than others, so add according to taste.

MAIN MEAT DISHES
FAMILY FARE

Beef, lamb, pork and veal make satisfying and nourishing family meals. Most dishes in this section are cooked by moist heat, that is in liquid. Because they use less expensive cuts which take some time to cook to make them deliciously tender, you have the advantage of being able to cook them ahead. Refrigerate the dish for 2 to 3 days then reheat to serve. Flavour improves in storing. For meat pies, cook the filling ahead, store in refrigerator and enclose or top with pastry when required for final cooking. If storing in the freezer, leave the thickening until the dish is reheated. If this is not possible, you might find it necessary to thicken again on reheating as some starches break down during freezing.

Veal and Pork Casserole

Serves: 6
Cooking time: 2 hours
Oven temperature: 180-190° C (350-375° F)

500 g (1 lb) boned shoulder of veal
500 g (1 lb) lean belly pork
2 tablespoons caraway seeds
1 x 430 g (15 oz) can sauerkraut
1 x 454 g (1 lb) jar red cabbage pickle
1 teaspoon salt
1½ cups sour cream
1 teaspoon paprika for garnish
boiled potatoes for serving

Trim gristle and excess fat from meat, cut into 4 cm (1½ inch) pieces.

Heat oil in a flameproof casserole, brown meat evenly all over. Add caraway seeds and mix together. Add drained and well-rinsed sauerkraut, red cabbage with its liquid and salt. Cover and cook in a moderate oven for about 1½ hours or until meat is tender. Remove from oven, add sour cream and mix thoroughly, adjust seasoning if necessary. Place back in oven for 15 minutes.

Sprinkle with paprika and serve with boiled potatoes.

Oxtail Ragoût

Serves: 3-4
Cooking time: 3¾ hours
Oven temperature: 180-190° C (350-375° F)
   reducing to 150-160° C (300-325° F)

1 oxtail, cut into joints
seasoned flour
3 tablespoons bacon fat
2 large onions, chopped
1 bay leaf
pinch of dried thyme
1 × 425 g (15 oz) can tomatoes
2 beef stock cubes
1 cup red wine
salt and pepper
1 stalk celery, sliced
2 leeks, sliced
1 parsnip, sliced
1 carrot, sliced
125 g (4 oz) button mushrooms
2 tablespoons butter

Place oxtail in a large bowl, pour boiling water over and stand for 10 minutes, drain and wipe dry with absorbent paper. Coat oxtail with seasoned flour. Heat bacon fat in a frying pan, brown oxtail evenly on all sides and remove to casserole dish. Add onion to pan and sauté until transparent. Add to casserole with bayleaf, thyme, tomatoes, crumbled stock cubes, red wine, salt and freshly ground pepper to taste.

Cover casserole and cook in a moderate oven for 1 hour, lower oven temperature to slow and cook for a further 1½ hours. Add prepared celery, leeks, parsnip and carrot and cook for a further hour. Skim fat from surface. Sauté mushrooms in butter and add to casserole.

Georgian Lamb Casserole

Serves: 6
Cooking time: 2¼ hours
Oven temperature: 160-170° C (325-350° F)

750 g (1½ lb) boneless lamb
1 medium-sized eggplant
1 onion, chopped
1 garlic clove, crushed
2 tablespoons oil or butter
1½ cups chopped, peeled tomatoes
1 cup sliced green beans
2 cups beef stock
3 tablespoons chopped parsley
salt
freshly ground black pepper
750 g (1½ lb) medium-sized potatoes, peeled and quartered

Trim lamb and cut into large cubes. Slice eggplant and quarter each slice. Sprinkle eggplant with salt and leave for 30 minutes. In a frying pan, brown meat in oil or butter, a single layer at a time. Remove to casserole dish as it browns. Add onion and garlic to pan and cook gently until soft. Dry salted eggplant with paper towels and add to onion. Cook for 5 minutes. Add tomatoes, sliced beans, stock, 2 tablespoons parsley, salt and pepper to taste. Simmer for 5 minutes and pour over lamb in casserole. Stir and cover with a well-fitting lid. Cook in a moderately slow oven for 1 hour. Add potatoes to casserole and return to oven for further hour or until meat and potatoes are tender. Sprinkle with remaining chopped parsley and serve from casserole at the table.

Steak with Orange Dumplings

Serves: 5-6
Cooking time: 2 hours
Oven temperature: 180-190° C (350-375° F)

750 g (1½ lb) blade or skirt steak
1 tablespoon plain flour
salt
freshly ground pepper
1 teaspoon dry mustard
1 teaspoon brown sugar
2 tablespoons tomato sauce
1 teaspoon Worcestershire sauce
1 cup stock or water and beef stock cube
1 onion, finely chopped
1 tablespoon finely chopped parsley
Orange dumplings
1 cup self-raising flour
½ teaspoon salt
2 tablespoons butter
1 teaspoon grated orange rind
combined orange juice and water to mix (about ½ cup)

Cut meat into 4 cm (1½ inch) pieces. Combine flour, salt, pepper, mustard and sugar and coat meat. Place in an ovenproof casserole.

Combine remaining ingredients and pour over meat. Cover casserole and cook in a moderate oven for 1½ hours. Place dumplings on top of meat in casserole, cover and cook for a further 20 minutes.

Orange Dumplings: Sift flour and salt into a mixing bowl, rub in butter. Add orange rind and mix to a soft dough with combined orange juice and water. Using a wet tablespoon drop portions on top of bubbling casserole. Keep away from sides of casserole dish to allow heat to circulate evenly.

Pot Roast

Serves: 5-6
Cooking time: 2½ hours

2 large carrots
1 large parsnip
5-6 small onions
3 tablespoons dripping or butter
1 topside or bolar blade pot roast, about 1.5 kg (3 lb)
salt
freshly ground pepper
½ cup stock or water
beurre manié (see Glossary)
mustard or horseradish relish for serving

Peel vegetables and cut carrots and parsnip into 3 or 4 pieces, leave onions whole.

Heat dripping in a heavy-based saucepan and brown meat evenly on all sides. Remove meat from pan and brown vegetables in remaining fat.

Return meat to pan, season with salt and pepper and add stock or water. Cover pan with greased paper or aluminium foil and tightly fitting lid. Cook over a gentle heat for 2 to 2½ hours until meat is tender, turning meat occasionally. Remove meat and vegetables and keep warm. Thicken liquid with beurre manié.

Serve pot roast with gravy and mustard or horseradish relish.

Note: Chicken, rabbit, breast of veal or mutton may be cooked in the same way.

Family Meat Pie

Serves: 6
Cooking time: 2½ hours
Oven temperature: 190-200° C (375-400° F)

1 kg (2 lb) chuck or skirt steak
2 tablespoons oil
2 onions, chopped
½ cup chopped celery
½ cup chopped carrot
1½ cups beef stock
salt and pepper
¼ teaspoon ground nutmeg
3 tablespoons plain flour
1 × 284 g (10 oz) packet flaky pastry mix

Cut steak into cubes. Heat oil in a large saucepan, brown meat, remove. Sauté onion until transparent, add celery and carrot and cook a few minutes. Return meat, add stock, salt, pepper and nutmeg, cover and simmer gently for 2 hours, until cooked. Blend flour to a smooth paste with a little cold water, add to saucepan, stir until thickened. Adjust seasoning. Place in a 3 to 4 cup pie dish, placing a pie funnel in centre.

Make pastry according to directions on packet. Roll out on lightly floured board 4 cm (1½ inches) larger than top of dish. Cut a strip off 1 cm (½ inch) wide, place on edge of dish previously moistened with water. Moisten strip of pastry, place pastry top in position. Press edges together, trim and decorate. Glaze with beaten egg. Cut a vent in the centre for steam to escape. Bake in a moderately hot oven for 25 minutes or until cooked.

Variation: Add 2 lamb's kidneys or ½ ox kidney to steak. Wash well, trim, skin and chop into small pieces.

Steak and Kidney Pudding

Serves: 3-4
Cooking time: 3-3½ hours

Suet crust pastry
2 cups plain flour
1 teaspoon salt
2 teaspoons baking powder
125 g (4 oz) suet, shredded
cold water to mix
Steak and kidney filling
500 g (1 lb) chuck or blade steak
125 g (4 oz) beef or lamb kidney
1 tablespoon seasoned flour
1 onion, chopped
3 tablespoons beef stock
parsley for garnish

Sift flour, salt and baking powder into a bowl, stir in suet using a round-bladed knife, mix to a firm dough with cold water (about ½ cup). Shape into a ball, cover and rest for 5 to 10 minutes. Knead pastry lightly, cut off two-thirds, and roll into a round to line a 15 cm (6 inch) pudding basin.

Wipe meat, cut into cubes. Wash kidney, remove core and cut into small pieces. Toss meat and kidney in seasoned flour. Put meat and onion, mixed together, in pastry-lined pudding basin, add stock. Roll out remaining third of pastry, moisten edge of pastry in basin and place lid on top. Press edges well to seal. Cover with greased greaseproof paper and then aluminium foil. Tie paper and foil securely under rim of basin. Place in a steamer and steam for 3 to 3½ hours. When pudding is cooked, remove the paper, garnish with a sprig of parsley and serve.

Veal Birds

Serves: 4-6
Cooking time: 1½ hours
Oven temperature: 160-170°C (325-350°F)

6 thin slices veal from leg
3 tablespoons butter
1 onion, chopped
3 tablespoons plain flour
1½ cups chicken stock or water and chicken stock cube
salt and pepper
Stuffing
2 cups soft breadcrumbs
¼ cup finely chopped suet
1 tablespoon chopped parsley
1 teaspoon thyme or mixed herbs
½ teaspoon grated lemon rind
½ teaspoon salt
¼ teaspoon pepper
1 egg, beaten

Flatten steak between 2 sheets of plastic film. Prepare stuffing (see below) and divide into 6 portions. Spread on each slice of veal. Roll up and secure with cotton or cocktail sticks. Heat the butter in a frypan and brown the rolls. Place rolls in an ovenproof casserole. Sauté onion in butter until soft, stir in flour and cook for 1 minute. Add the stock and stir until thickened and bubbling. Season to taste with salt and pepper. Pour sauce over veal rolls, cover and cook in a moderately slow oven for 1¼ hours or until the meat is tender. Remove the cotton or cocktail sticks before serving.

Stuffing: Combine stuffing ingredients together and mix thoroughly.

Navarin of Lamb

Serves: 4-6
Cooking time: 2¾ hours
Oven temperature: 150-160° C (300-325° F)

1 kg (2 lb) boneless lamb
2 tablespoons butter or oil
1 medium-sized onion, chopped
1 garlic clove, crushed
2 tablespoons flour
1 cup stock
2 tablespoons tomato paste
½ teaspoon sugar
1½ teaspoons salt
¼ teaspoon pepper
bouquet garni
6-8 small whole onions
1 turnip, sliced
12 small whole potatoes
1 cup fresh shelled peas

Trim lamb and cut into cubes. Heat butter or oil in a heavy pan and brown meat on all sides. Transfer to a casserole. Add onion and garlic to pan and sauté over lower heat until onion is soft. Stir in flour and cook until lightly coloured. Add stock, stirring until it bubbles. Stir in tomato paste, sugar, salt and pepper and pour over lamb. Add bouquet garni.

Cover and cook in a slow oven for 1½ hours. Discard bouquet garni. Add onions, turnip, potatoes and peas to casserole, cover and cook for a further hour or until meat is tender. Sprinkle with chopped parsley if desired before serving from casserole. Accompany with fresh crusty bread.
Note: If using mutton, cook for 1¾ hours before adding main vegetables.

Ragoût of Beef

Serves: 4
Cooking time: 2 hours
Oven temperature: 180-190° C (350-375° F)

750 g (1½ lb) topside or blade steak
2 tablespoons dripping or oil
8 small onions
1 tablespoon plain flour
½ cup red wine
1 cup beef stock or water and beef stock cube
bouquet garni
1 garlic clove, crushed
salt and pepper
1 cup sliced celery
1 tablespoon butter or margarine
¼ cup walnut halves
extra ½ teaspoon salt
rind of 1 orange, finely shredded and blanched for garnish

Cut steak into cubes. Heat dripping in a flameproof casserole or frying pan, and fry meat until golden brown. Remove meat to a plate or ovenproof casserole, add whole onions and sauté until golden brown. Pour all but 1 tablespoon of fat from pan, add flour, blend together and cook for a few minutes. Stirring continuously add wine and stock, bring to the boil. Add bouquet garni, garlic and salt and pepper to taste. Return meat to flameproof casserole or pour sauce over meat in ovenproof casserole. Cover and cook in a moderate oven for 1½ to 2 hours or until meat is tender.

Meanwhile heat butter in a frying pan and sauté celery and walnuts with extra salt until lightly brown but still crisp. Add to casserole, adjust seasoning if necessary and garnish with orange rind.

Serve with boiled rice or buttered new potatoes.

Steak and Mushroom Pie

Serves: 6
Cooking time: 2½ hours
Oven temperature: 180-190° C (350-375° F)
*   increasing to 220-230° C (425-450° F)*

1 kg (2 lb) stewing steak
2 tablespoons dripping or oil
1 large onion, chopped
3 tablespoons flour
1½ cups beef stock
1 teaspoon Worcestershire sauce
pinch ground nutmeg
1 tablespoon chopped parsley
salt and pepper
250 g (8 oz) small mushrooms, sliced
2 tablespoons butter
1 x 340 g (12 oz) packet puff pastry

Cut beef into cubes. Brown in dripping and transfer to a deep pie dish. Add onion to pan and sauté until soft. Stir in flour and cook 2 minutes. Add stock, stirring constantly until sauce bubbles. Stir in Worcestershire sauce, nutmeg and parsley and season to taste. Pour over meat, cover and cook in a moderate oven for 1½ hours. Sauté mushrooms in butter, add to meat and cook for further 10 minutes. Cool.

Roll out pastry 4 cm (1½ inches) larger than top of dish. Cut off this extra width. Moisten rim of dish with water, place trimmed pastry around rim and moisten pastry. Place a pie funnel in centre of meat and position pastry top. Press edges well to seal. Trim and glaze with milk.

Cut a vent in the centre. Cut decorations from trimmings and place in position, glazing with milk. Cook in a hot oven for 15 minutes. Reduce heat to moderate and cook for further 20 to 25 minutes.

Stuffed Capsicums

Serves: 6
Cooking time: 1 hour
Oven temperature: 180-190° C (350-375° F)

6 large capsicums
2 tablespoons olive oil
1 large onion, finely chopped
1 garlic clove, crushed
1 kg (2 lb) minced steak
½ cup short grain rice
4 tablespoons tomato paste
1 bay leaf
1 bacon stock cube
2 cups hot water
salt
freshly ground pepper
2 tablespoons finely chopped parsley
½ teaspoon sugar

Cut tops off capsicums, remove seeds and membrane. Reserve tops.

Heat oil in a saucepan and sauté onion and garlic until golden. Add steak and cook until evenly brown. Add rice, 2 tablespoons of the tomato paste, bay leaf and stock cube dissolved in 1½ cups of the hot water. Season to taste with salt and pepper. Cover and simmer gently for 15 minutes. Remove bay leaf and add parsley.

Meanwhile, blanch capsicums in a large saucepan of boiling salted water. Drain well. Place the meat mixture into the capsicums and cover with reserved tops.

Place capsicums in a greased ovenproof casserole. Mix remaining tomato paste with remaining water and season with salt, pepper and sugar and pour around capsicums. Bake in a moderate oven for 40 minutes or until capsicums are tender. Baste occasionally while cooking.

Enchiladas

Serves: 6
Cooking time: 1¼ hours
Oven temperature: 180-190°C (350-375°F)

12 taco shells
2 tablespoons olive oil
1 large onion, chopped
1 garlic clove, crushed
1 × 425 g (15 oz) can tomatoes, chopped
salt to taste
1 teaspoon ground cumin
¼ teaspoon dried oregano
¼-½ teaspoon chilli powder
Savoury filling
500 g (1 lb) minced beef
2 tablespoons olive oil
1 garlic clove, crushed
1 large onion, chopped
1 cup chopped, peeled tomatoes
¾ cup red wine
1 green capsicum, seeded and chopped
salt and pepper

Fill taco shells with savoury filling (see below). Arrange in an ovenproof dish in one layer.

Heat oil and sauté onion and garlic until soft. Add tomatoes, salt, cumin, oregano and chilli powder to taste. Cover and simmer gently for 30 minutes until thick. Spoon over filled tacos. Cover and heat in a moderate oven for 20 minutes. Serve with boiled rice.

Savoury filling: Brown minced beef in oil, add garlic and onion and fry for 2 minutes. Add remaining filling ingredients. Cover and simmer for 30 minutes.
Note: Traditionally Enchiladas are made with tortillas, a type of corn pancake. Tortillas can be purchased at some specialty food stores. Taco shells are more readily obtainable.

Sauté of Kidneys Turbigo

Serves: 4
Cooking time: 20 minutes

8 sheep's kidneys
2 tablespoons oil
1 cup Espagnole Sauce (page 18)
salt and pepper
125 g (4 oz) button mushrooms
2 tablespoons butter
4 thin sausages or 8 chipolatas
chopped parsley for garnish
toast triangles for serving

Remove skin from kidneys, cut in half and remove fatty cores. Sauté in oil in a frying pan for 4 to 5 minutes. Do not overcook. Drain well and place in small saucepan with espagnole sauce. Leave on low heat to heat through gently.

Sauté mushrooms in butter. Fry sausages in oil left from kidneys, cut in half if long.

Place kidneys and sauce in a serving dish, arrange mushrooms and sausages on top, sprinkle with chopped parsley and place toast triangles around sides of dish. Serve immediately.

Lamb Cassoulet

Serves: 6
Cooking time: 5 hours
Oven temperature: 160-170° C (325-350° F)

1½ cups dried haricot or navy beans
750 g (1½ lb) boneless lamb
125 g (4 oz) streaky bacon pieces
1 tablespoon butter or oil
2 onions, chopped
2 garlic cloves, crushed
1½ cups chopped, peeled tomatoes
2 cups stock
bouquet garni
salt
freshly ground black pepper

Wash beans well, place in saucepan and cover well with cold water. Cook gently for 2 hours. Cut lamb into cubes. Place bacon in a heated pan and cook until fat renders and bacon browns. Remove bacon to a deep casserole dish, leaving fat in pan. Add butter or oil and brown meat. Remove to casserole when browned. Add onion and garlic to pan and sauté until onion is soft. Add tomatoes, stock, bouquet garni and salt and pepper to taste. Stir in cooked, drained beans (they should be slightly undercooked). Cover with a well-fitting lid and cook in a moderately slow oven for 2½ hours. Stir cassoulet every half hour during cooking. Remove bouquet garni and serve from casserole at table. Accompany with a tossed green salad.
Note: 250 g (8 oz) lamb may be replaced with garlic-flavoured sausage cut in thick slices.

Continental Rolled Steak

Serves: 4-6
Cooking time: 1 hour
Oven temperature: 180-190° C (350-375° F)

750 g (1½ lb) skirt steak, in a piece
2 bacon rashers, chopped
4 slices salami, chopped
½ cup cooked rice
2 hard-boiled eggs, chopped
1 tablespoon Mayonnaise (page 16)
1 teaspoon salt
¼ teaspoon pepper
½ teaspoon ground ginger
1 tablespoon sherry

Trim steak and beat with a meat cleaver or a rolling pin. Gently fry bacon and salami, combine with rice, chopped hard-boiled eggs, mayonnaise, salt, pepper and ginger and mix well. Spread rice mixture over steak, roll up carefully and secure with skewers. Place meat roll in a roasting dish, pour sherry over and cover with lid or with aluminium foil. Place in a moderate oven and bake for 1 hour. Remove from roasting dish and serve hot in slices with crisp green vegetables and new or sauté potatoes. Make a gravy from pan juices, if desired.

Curried Lamb

Serves: 6
Cooking time: 1½ hours

1 kg (2 lb) boneless lamb
2 tablespoons ghee
2 large onions, chopped
2 garlic cloves, crushed
1-2 tablespoons curry powder
small piece fresh root ginger
½ cup chopped capsicum
½ cup stock
1 cup coconut milk (see below)
salt to taste
1-2 tablespoons lemon juice

Trim lamb and cut into cubes. Heat ghee in a heavy-based saucepan and sauté onion and garlic until onion is soft. Stir in curry powder to taste and cook for 2 minutes. Add bruised ginger and capsicum and cook a little longer. Increase heat and add lamb. Cook, stirring often until meat is browned. Reduce heat and add stock, coconut milk and salt. Cover and simmer gently for 1½ hours or until lamb is tender and sauce has thickened. Remove ginger root. Stir in lemon juice to taste and serve over fluffy boiled rice with traditional curry accompaniments.

Coconut milk: Place 1 cup desiccated coconut with 1¼ cups water and a pinch of salt in a small saucepan and bring slowly to simmering point. Strain through a fine sieve into a basin, pressing coconut firmly with the back of a spoon to extract all liquid. Coconut may be returned to saucepan with a half cup of water and process repeated to extract more milk if necessary. Discard coconut.

Beef Strips in Sour Cream

Serves: 6
Cooking time: 1½ hours

1 kg (2 lb) blade steak
3 tablespoons butter
250 g (8 oz) small mushrooms, sliced
1 large onion, chopped
1 cup beef stock
1 tablespoon tomato paste
1½ teaspoons salt
freshly ground pepper
⅛ teaspoon ground nutmeg
2 tablespoons cornflour
½ cup sour cream

Trim beef and cut into thin strips. Melt half the butter in a saucepan and sauté sliced mushrooms for 5 minutes. Remove to a plate. Add remaining butter and sauté onion until soft. Remove to another plate, leaving butter in pan. Brown beef strips quickly over high heat, a few at a time. Remove to plate with onion as they brown. Return beef and onions to pan, add stock, tomato paste, salt, pepper and nutmeg. Stir to lift off browned meat juices, cover and simmer gently for 1 hour. Add cooked mushrooms and simmer for further 15 to 30 minutes until beef is just tender (do not overcook). Mix cornflour to a paste with cold water and thicken pan contents. Allow to boil gently for 1 minute. Stir in sour cream and heat through without bringing to the boil. Serve immediately with boiled rice or noodles and a tossed salad or green vegetable.

Cabbage Rolls

Serves: 4
Cooking time: 1½ hours
Oven temperature: 180-190° C (350-375° F)

1 large cabbage
500 g (1 lb) minced steak
½ cup short grain rice
1 onion, finely chopped
1 tablespoon chopped parsley
½ cup water
salt and pepper
2 tablespoons sour cream
Sauce
1 cup finely chopped onions
2 tablespoons olive oil
2 tablespoons tomato paste
1 tablespoon flour
1½ cups water
salt, pepper and sugar

Remove 12 outer leaves from cabbage, being careful not to break them. Keep the tight centre leaves for other purposes. Blanch leaves in boiling salted water for a few minutes, drain and cool.

In a bowl, mix the minced steak, rice, onion, parsley and water, season to taste. Place some of the filling on each cabbage leaf and folding the ends in, roll up neatly. Place seam side down in an ovenproof casserole dish. Make sauce (see below) and pour over rolls. Cover and cook in a moderate oven for 1½ hours. Add sour cream to casserole just before serving.

Sauce: Sauté onion in oil until transparent, add the tomato paste and flour. Stirring continuously, pour in the water and season to taste with salt, pepper and sugar.

Lamb Pie

Serves: 6
Cooking time: 1½ hours
Oven temperature: 220-230° C (425-450° F)
reducing to 180-190° C (350-375° F)

750 g (1½ lb) boneless lamb
2 tablespoons butter or oil
12 small onions
½ cup diced carrot
2 tablespoons flour
1 cup beef stock
½ teaspoon dried thyme
½ teaspoon dried marjoram
½ teaspoon sugar
salt and pepper to taste
1 cup shelled green peas
1× 284 g (10 oz) packet flaky pastry mix

Cut lamb into cubes. Brown in butter in a pan and remove to a plate. Add onions and carrot to pan and fry gently for 5 minutes. Stir in flour and cook for 2 minutes. Add stock and cook, stirring constantly, until liquid bubbles. Return lamb to pan and add herbs, sugar, salt and pepper. Cover and simmer gently for 30 minutes. Add green peas and cook for further 15 minutes or until lamb is just tender. Turn into a pie plate and leave to cool. Make pastry according to packet directions. Roll out 4 cm (1½ inches) larger than top of pie plate. Trim off this excess pastry and place it round moistened pie plate rim. Moisten with water and lift top into position. Press and crimp edge to seal. Brush with cold water and arrange decorations cut from pastry trimmings.

Glaze with beaten egg yolk, cut a vent in the centre and bake in a hot oven for 15 minutes. Reduce heat to moderate and cook for a further 20 minutes.

Apricot Lamb Roll

Serves: 6-8
Cooking time: 1 hour
Oven temperature: 180-190° C (350-375° F)

1 kg (2 lb) minced, lean lamb (from shoulder)
1 egg
salt
freshly ground pepper
Stuffing
¼ cup finely chopped onion
2 tablespoons butter
½ cup chopped, dried apricots
½ teaspoon dried marjoram
1 egg, lightly beaten
2 cups soft breadcrumbs
1 small can apricot halves for garnish

Mix lamb mince with egg, salt and pepper to taste until well blended. Turn onto a piece of waxed paper and press into a square 1 cm (½ inch) thick. Spread prepared stuffing over meat, leaving a 1 cm (½ inch) border of meat uncovered.

Roll up as for a Swiss Roll, beginning the rolling with the aid of the paper. Let the paper drop away as you roll. Press ends together to seal and lift roll into a greased baking dish, using two spatulas. Pat roll into shape in pan and brush with melted fat or oil. Cook in a moderate oven for 1 hour. Heat canned apricots, drain and garnish roll to serve.

Stuffing: Sauté onion in butter until transparent. Combine with remaining ingredients.

Spiced Apricot Short Ribs

Serves: 6
Cooking time: 2½-3 hours
Oven temperature: 220-230° C (425-450° F)
  reducing to 180-190° C (350-375° F)

1½-2 kg (3-4 lb) beef short ribs
1 small onion, grated
2 cups apricot nectar
½ cup tomato sauce
1 tablespoon Worcestershire sauce
1 tablespoon vinegar
½ teaspoon ground allspice
pinch ground cloves
1 tablespoon brown sugar
1½ teaspoons salt
pepper to taste

Place short ribs in a large roasting dish and brown in a hot oven for 30 minutes. Drain off fat. Mix together remaining ingredients and pour over browned ribs. Cover dish with foil and return to moderate oven. Cook for 2½ hours or until meat is very tender. Remove foil for last 10 minutes, adding a little water to pan if necessary.

Place short ribs in a warm serving dish. Tilt pan and skim off fat. Pour sauce over ribs and serve with vegetables. Rice is also a good accompaniment.

Beef and Mushroom Rolls

Serves: 4
Cooking time: 1¾ hours

750 g (1½ lb) topside steak, thinly sliced
2 tablespoons butter
1 small onion, finely chopped
½ cup sliced muchrooms
1 cup stock
salt and pepper
beurre manié (see Glossary)
Mushroom stuffing
2 tablespoons chopped spring onion
2 tablespoons butter
½ cup chopped mushrooms
2 teaspoons lemon juice
1½ cups soft breadcrumbs
1 tablespoon chopped parsley
salt and pepper to taste
1 egg, beaten

Flatten steaks and cut into 4 large or 8 small pieces. Spread with stuffing (see below), roll up and secure with cocktail sticks or white string. Heat butter in a pan and brown rolls. Remove. Add onion to pan and sauté until soft, add mushrooms and cook 5 minutes. Stir in stock and season to taste. Return rolls to pan, cover and simmer gently for about 1½ hours until tender. Place rolls on a heated platter and remove cocktail sticks or string. Thicken liquid with beurre manié. Pour over rolls and serve.

Mushroom stuffing: Sauté spring onion in butter until soft, add mushrooms and lemon juice and cook 2 minutes. Combine with remaining ingredients, binding with beaten egg.

Goulash and Noodles

Serves: 6
Cooking time: 2½ hours
Oven temperature: 150-160° C (300-325° F)

1 kg (2 lb) blade or chuck steak
3 tablespoons butter or oil
3 onions, chopped
1 green capsicum, seeded and chopped
1 garlic clove, crushed
1 cup chopped, peeled tomatoes
salt and pepper
1 tablespoon paprika
½ cup stock
375 g (12 oz) French beans, sliced
2 carrots, sliced
Poppy seed noodles
250 g (8 oz) noodles
1½ tablespoons poppy seeds
2 tablespoons butter

Cut meat into large cubes. Heat half the butter or oil in a frying pan and brown meat on all sides, remove to casserole dish. Add remaining butter to pan and sauté onion, capsicum and garlic until onion is transparent. Stir in tomatoes, salt and pepper to taste, paprika and stock. Bring to the boil and pour over meat in casserole. Cover and cook in a moderately slow oven for 1½ hours.

Add prepared beans and carrots. Cover and cook for a further 30 to 45 minutes or until meat and carrots are tender. Serve with poppy seed noodles.

Poppy seed noodles: Cook noodles in boiling, salted water for 12 to 15 minutes or until tender. Drain, add poppy seeds and butter, toss together gently and serve immediately with goulash.

QUICK MEAT DISHES

Meats for grilling or frying, minced meats, fancy meats (offal) and small goods are all convenient and quick to prepare for a satisfying meal. They can also be economical. Leftover roast and canned meats in Kromeskies and Instant Steak Casserole will have the family thinking you are a kitchen wizard. So when time is at a premium and there is a meal to prepare, you will find a recipe in this section to suit the occasion, and whatever is on hand.

Bean and Frank Pot

Serves: 4-6
Cooking time: 20-25 minutes
Oven temperature: 180-190° C (350-375° F)

8 thin frankfurters
2 tablespoons lard or dripping
1 large onion, chopped
1 small green capsicum
2 x 454 g (16 oz) cans baked beans in tomato sauce
salt
freshly ground pepper
grilled bacon for serving

Cut frankfurters into 5 cm (2 inch) lengths. Melt lard in a flameproof casserole or a heavy-based saucepan, and sauté onion until transparent. Remove seeds and white membrane from capsicum and chop. Add to onion in pan, cook a few minutes longer, then add baked beans, frankfurters and season to taste with salt and pepper. Mix well, cover and cook in a moderate oven or simmer on top of stove for approximately 15 minutes or until hot. Serve with grilled bacon.

Orange Cheeseburgers

Serves: 4-5
Cooking time: 10-12 minutes

500 g (1 lb) minced steak
1 medium onion, finely chopped
½ cup soft breadcrumbs
1 teaspoon grated orange rind
1 egg, lightly beaten
¼ teaspoon dried sage
salt and pepper
1 tablespoon butter
1 tablespoon oil
4-5 processed Cheddar cheese slices
halved hamburger buns or thickly sliced bread
crisp lettuce leaves
1 small orange
mint sprigs

Combine steak, onion, breadcrumbs, orange rind, egg, sage and season to taste with salt and pepper. Mix well. Shape into 4 or 5 even-sized patties and fry gently in combined butter and oil until cooked. Remove and drain on paper towels. Top each hamburger with a cheese slice and grill until cheese melts.

Toast buns or bread and spread with butter. Cover with crisp lettuce and a hamburger on each. Slice orange with peel, cut half way through 4 or 5 slices, twist and place on top of cheese.

Garnish with mint sprigs and serve.

Kromeskies

Serves: 4
Cooking time: 4-5 minutes

1½ tablespoons butter
2-3 spring onions, chopped
2 tablespoons plain flour
½ cup milk
1 teaspoon chopped parsley
1 teaspoon lemon juice
salt and pepper
¾ cup finely diced cooked meat (pork, veal, lamb)
2-3 bacon rashers, rind removed
oil for frying
Fritter batter
¾ cup plain flour
pinch salt
1 tablespoon oil
½ cup tepid water
1 egg white

Melt butter and sauté spring onions until soft. Stir in the flour and cook for 1 minute. Add milk, stir until boiling. Add parsley, lemon juice, salt and pepper. Cook for 2 minutes, stirring continuously then add the meat. Set aside to cool.

Dip bacon into boiling water, leave for 1 minute and cut into 8 cm (3 inch) strips. Put a tablespoon of the mixture on to a piece of bacon, roll into a cork shape. Dip into batter, deep fry in hot oil. Drain and serve at once accompanied with tomato sauce.

Fritter batter: Sift flour and salt into bowl. Pour oil into centre and gradually add the water, mixing to a smooth batter. Beat until bubbles rise. Whisk egg white until stiff and fold in just before using.

Frankfurters and Rice

Serves: 4
Cooking time: 1 hour
Oven temperature: 180-190° C (350-375° F)

3 tablespoons olive oil
1 large onion, sliced
1 green capsicum
2 cups chopped, peeled tomatoes
1 teaspoon sugar
salt
freshly ground pepper
pinch ground cloves
1 bay leaf
1 cup long grain rice
8 thick frankfurters, split lengthways

Heat oil in a saucepan and gently fry onion until transparent. Remove seeds and white membrane from capsicum, and chop. Add to onion with tomatoes and sugar, salt and pepper to taste, ground cloves and bay leaf. Simmer for approximately 10 minutes. Add the rice, stir thoroughly and cover saucepan with lid. Simmer for 20 minutes, or until rice is tender. During cooking add water gradually to keep the mixture moist. Split frankfurters in half lengthways and halve each piece. Arrange some of the quartered frankfurters around the side of a greased deep ovenproof dish. Layer remaining frankfurters alternately with the rice mixture in the centre. Cover with aluminium foil and cook in a moderate oven for 30 minutes until well heated.

Instant Steak Casserole

Serves: 4
Cooking time: 30 minutes
Oven temperature: 180-190° C (350-375° F)

1 x 454 g (16 oz) can braised steak
1 x 310 g (10 oz) packet frozen mixed vegetables, thawed
1 packet dehydrated French onion soup
1 tablespoon cornflour
1½ cups stock or water and beef stock cube
2 large potatoes, cooked and thinly sliced
2 tablespoons finely chopped parsley for garnish

Place steak in an ovenproof casserole and add vegetables. Blend soup, cornflour and stock together, pour over ingredients in casserole. Top with a layer of potatoes. Cook in a moderate oven for approximately 30 minutes or until hot and potatoes are lightly browned on top.

Sprinkle with finely chopped parsley before serving.

Kofta Curry

Serves: 6
Cooking time: 1 hour

750 g (1½ lb) minced beef
1 medium onion, grated
1 garlic clove, crushed
1 cm (½ inch) piece root ginger, grated
1 teaspoon ground allspice
1 teaspoon salt
¼ teaspoon pepper
2 tablespoons plain flour
1 egg
¼ cup oil
Curry sauce
3 tablespoons butter or ghee
2 large onions, finely chopped
1 garlic clove, crushed
2 tablespoons curry powder
1 cup beef stock
1 tablespoon tomato paste
2 tablespoons sour cream (optional)

Mix ingredients except oil until well blended. With moistened hands, roll into small balls about the size of a walnut. Heat oil in a frying pan and fry meat balls until browned. Do this in 2 or 3 lots. Lift out and drain on absorbent paper.

Make curry sauce (see below) and add meat balls. Cover and simmer gently for 45 minutes. Stir in the sour cream if used, heat a little without boiling and serve.

Curry sauce: Heat butter or ghee in a saucepan, add onion and garlic and fry gently until soft. Stir in curry powder and cook for 2 minutes. Add remaining ingredients except sour cream and cook until boiling. Cover and simmer for 10 minutes.

Sweet and Sour Pork

Serves: 4
Cooking time: 15-30 minutes

500 g (1 lb) lean pork leg or fillet
2 teaspoons soy sauce
1 tablespoon dry sherry
1 egg, beaten
4 tablespoons cornflour
peanut oil for frying
2 onions, quartered and separated into leaves
1 teaspoon finely chopped root ginger
1 carrot, sliced thinly
½ red and ½ green capsicum cut in squares
1 stalk celery, sliced diagonally
1 x 425 g (15 oz) can pineapple pieces
1 tablespoon sugar
3 tablespoons white vinegar
1 tablespoon cornflour
2 teaspoons soy sauce
3 tablespoons cold water

Cut pork into 2 cm (¾ inch) cubes and marinate in a mixture of soy sauce, sherry, egg and cornflour for 20 minutes.

Heat 2 tablespoons oil and stir-fry onion, ginger, carrot, capsicum and celery for 5 minutes. Add pineapple with liquid, sugar and vinegar and bring to the boil. Add cornflour blended with soy sauce and 3 tablespoons cold water. Cook, stirring, until mixture boils and thickens. Keep aside.

Heat oil in deep fryer to 180°C (350°F). Stir pork. Lift out pieces. Deep fry a few pieces at a time until cooked and golden. When all are cooked, bring oil temperature up to 190°C (375°F) return all the pieces of pork to the oil and cook for a few seconds to crisp them. Drain well, reheat sauce, and serve pork coated with hot sauce, accompanied by boiled rice.

Orange Glazed Lamb Chops

Serves: 4-6
Cooking time: 15-20 minutes

6-8 lamb grilling chops
shreds of orange rind
Orange glaze
1 teaspoon dry mustard
2 tablespoons brown sugar
1 cup orange juice
¼ cup cider vinegar
2 tablespoons honey
1 tablespoon soy sauce
freshly ground black pepper

If short loin chops are used, secure 'tails' with wooden cocktail picks. Peel orange rind thinly and cut into fine shreds. Boil rind in a little water for 5 minutes until tender, drain and keep aside.

Mix mustard with brown sugar to break up lumps. Add remaining glaze ingredients and stir until sugar is dissolved. Brush some glaze on each side of chops and leave at room temperature for 30 minutes. Cook chops under pre-heated grill, basting often with orange glaze (do not use all the glaze). When chops are cooked, arrange on serving dish and keep warm.

Heat remaining glaze in a saucepan and thicken with a cornflour and water paste. Add prepared orange shreds, let glaze boil for 1 minute and pour over chops. Serve immediately.

Devilled Meat Balls

Serves: 6-8
Cooking time: 20-30 minutes

750 g (1½ lb) finely minced beef
2 eggs
½ cup fine dried breadcrumbs
¼ cup milk
1 teaspoon salt
½ teaspoon dried mixed herbs
2 tablespoons oil
½ cup finely chopped onion
½-1 cup coarsely grated apple
¼-½ cup chutney
1½ cups hot water
2 beef stock cubes
1 tablespoon brown sugar
1 tablespoon soy sauce
1 tablespoon cornflour

Mix together minced beef, eggs, breadcrumbs, milk, salt and herbs. Shape into very small balls with damp hands, making 40 to 60 balls. Heat the oil in a large frypan and cook 20 to 30 balls at a time. Rotate the pan constantly to keep the balls from sticking or flattening during cooking. As soon as meat balls are brown (3 to 5 minutes) remove and drain on absorbent paper.

When all meat balls are browned, pour off all but about two tablespoons of fat from pan. Add onion to pan and sauté until tender. Add grated apple, chutney, hot water and beef stock cubes, brown sugar and soy sauce. Thicken gravy with the cornflour blended to a thin paste with cold water. Add meat balls and reheat in the sauce. Serve with buttered noodles.

Fricassee of Brains

Serves: 4
Cooking time: 20 minutes

4-6 sets lamb's brains
3 cloves
1 garlic clove, whole
sprig parsley
4 peppercorns
1 teaspoon salt
1 tablespoon vinegar
2 tablespoons butter
2 tablespoons flour
1 cup milk
125 g (4 oz) button mushrooms
extra 2 tablespoons butter
2 teaspoons lemon juice
salt and pepper

Soak brains in cold water for 1 hour, changing water several times. Remove any loose skin and place in a saucepan with cloves, garlic, parsley, peppercorns, salt and vinegar. Add enough water to just cover, bring to boil then simmer gently for 10 minutes. Remove brains, slice or cut into small pieces and place in a serving dish. Keep warm.

Melt butter in a saucepan and stir in flour. Cook for 2 minutes without colouring roux. Take off heat and stir in the milk. Return to heat and cook, stirring constantly, until sauce thickens and boils.

Meanwhile sauté mushrooms in extra butter with lemon juice. Add mushrooms and juices to the sauce. Adjust seasoning with salt and pepper, and heat through gently. Pour sauce over brains and serve with toast triangles.

Meat Loaf

Serves: 4-6
Cooking time: 1 hour
Oven temperature: 180-190°C (350-375°F)

750 g (1½ lb) minced beef
¾ cup dry breadcrumbs
1 onion, grated
½ cup grated carrot
2 tablespoons finely chopped green capsicum (optional)
¼ cup tomato purée
¼ cup milk
1 egg
2 tablespoons chopped parsley
½ teaspoon mixed herbs
1½ teaspoons salt
freshly ground black pepper

Place minced beef in a mixing bowl. In another bowl blend together the breadcrumbs, onion, carrot, capsicum, if used, tomato purée and milk. Stir in the beaten egg, herbs and seasoning. Combine the mixture with the minced beef and blend ingredients lightly together until well mixed. Spoon into a greased loaf tin and bake in a moderate oven for 1 hour. Drain off liquid, unmould onto a warm serving platter and serve.

Tomato-cheese loaf: Unmould meat loaf as above, lay slices of cheese and tomato on top, return to oven until cheese melts and browns lightly.

Potato frosted loaf: Frost with 2 cups mashed potatoes into which 30 g (1 oz) butter and 1 egg have been mixed. Bake for 15 minutes in hot oven, 200-230°C (400-450°F).

Mexican Beef Medley

Serves: 6
Cooking time: 25-30 minutes

2 cups spiral or shell noodles
1 large onion, chopped
1 garlic clove, crushed
1 cup chopped green and red capsicum
1 tablespoon oil or butter
750 g (1½ lb) minced beef
1 cup frozen or canned whole kernel corn
1 cup frozen or canned baby Lima beans
1 × 425 g (15 oz) can condensed tomato soup
1 teaspoon Mexican-style chilli powder
salt and pepper

Cook noodles in boiling salted water for 10 minutes. Drain and keep aside. In electric frypan or frying pan with lid to fit, sauté onion, garlic and capsicum in oil until onion is transparent. Remove to a plate. Shape minced beef into a flat cake, or use flat-packed mince straight from the freezer. Brown mince 'cake' in oil on each side, then break up into chunky pieces with a fork while still in the pan. Cook until red colour disappears. Return onion and capsicum to pan with corn kernels, Lima beans, tomato soup, chilli powder and salt and pepper to taste. Stir well, cover and simmer gently for 20 minutes. Add pre-cooked noodles and simmer for further 5 minutes or until noodles are tender. Serve immediately with a tossed salad and crusty bread.
Note: Noodles may be completely cooked separately and arranged in a border. Place meat mixture in centre.

OUTDOOR MEAT DISHES

There is something about serving meals outdoors which makes them taste so much better than when served in the confines of the dining room. Most of these recipes can be served indoors, but are very successful al fresco.

Scotch Eggs

Serves: 4-6
Cooking time: 5-7 minutes

500 g (1 lb) sausage mince
1 tablespoon bottled barbecue sauce
1 tablespoon flour
salt and pepper
6 hard-boiled eggs, shelled
1 egg, beaten with 1 tablespoon water
dry breadcrumbs
oil or fat for frying

Mix sausage mince with sauce and divide into 6 equal portions. Mix flour with a little salt and pepper and coat eggs. Shape a portion of sausage mince around each egg, enclosing it completely. Brush with beaten egg and coat with crumbs.

Heat oil or fat, but not to fuming point, as sausage coating has to cook through before crumb coating becomes too brown. Deep fry Scotch Eggs for 5 to 7 minutes, lift out and drain on absorbent paper. Serve whole or cut in half, with tomato sauce and vegetables. They may also be served cold with salad and make excellent picnic fare.

Bush Barbecue

Serves: 4-8

4 grilling steaks (T-bone, rump or cross-cut blade)
4-8 lamb chops (short loin or forequarter)
4-8 thick sausages
commercial barbecue sauce
salt
mustard
salad vegetables
Marinade
1 cup red wine
½ cup oil
1 small onion, sliced
1 garlic clove, crushed
1 crumbled bay leaf
2 sprigs each thyme and parsley
freshly ground black pepper

Place steaks and chops in a plastic container with a good seal. Combine marinade ingredients, pour over meats, seal and refrigerate for several hours. Turn container over occasionally to redistribute marinade.

Place sausages in cold water to cover, slowly bring to simmering point, leave off heat for 10 minutes, drain and store in a sealed container in refrigerator.

Pack containers of meats and salad ingredients in a portable insulated cooler with ice. Don't forget remaining ingredients (plus tongs, a brush, the billy can and tea).

To cook meats have fire at glowing coals stage, put meats on grid and baste steaks and chops with marinade, sausages with barbecue sauce. Cook until done to taste, turning with tongs. Season with salt and serve with salad vegetables, mustard, crusty bread rolls and billy tea.
Note: Put the fire out thoroughly before going home!

Shish Kebabs

Serves: 6
Cooking time: 15-20 minutes

1 kg (2 lb) lamb from leg or shoulder
2 green capsicums
2 red capsicums
3 small white onions
1 cup pineapple pieces
salt
Marinade
1 x 425 g (15 oz) can pineapple juice
¼ cup oil
1 tablespoon brown sugar
freshly ground pepper
1 teaspoon dried thyme
1 teaspoon dry mustard
½ cup chopped onion
¼ cup chopped parsley

Cut lamb into 4 cm (1½ inch) cubes and place in marinade. Cover and store in refrigerator for several hours or overnight. Stir meat occasionally. Remove seeds and white membrane from capsicums and cut into 4 cm (1½ inch) pieces. Peel onions and cut into quarters. On long skewers, thread pieces of lamb alternately with green and red capsicum, onion and pineapple. Barbecue over hot coals or cook under a hot grill, turning frequently and basting with the marinade. Season with salt when cooked.

Marinade: Combine all ingredients in a glass or china bowl and mix together thoroughly.

Chilli Con Carne

Serves: 4-6
Cooking time: 45 minutes

1 onion, chopped
2 garlic cloves, crushed
1 tablespoon oil
500 g (1 lb) minced steak
1 x 425 g (15 oz) can condensed tomato soup
1 teaspoon salt
1 tablespoon chilli powder
½ cup water
1 green pepper, seeded and chopped
2 cups cooked red kidney beans or 2 x 310 g (10 oz) cans
   kidney beans drained

Sauté onion and garlic in hot oil in a large, heavy-based frying pan. Add minced beef and cook until meat browns, stir continuously. Add soup, salt, chilli powder and water. Cover and simmer for 10 minutes, stir occasionally. Add green pepper and beans, simmer for a further 20 minutes and serve hot. Serve with boiled rice.

A good dish to serve at a barbecue. Heat in the pan, stirring occasionally. Serve with a rice salad.
Note: Use the chilli powder which is a mixture of spices specially for such dishes. Do not use the red-hot chilli powder used in curries.

93

Barbecued Hamburgers

Serves: 6
Cooking time: 12-16 minutes

750 g (1½ lb) finely minced steak
1 onion, finely chopped
1 teaspoon salt
freshly ground pepper
6 hamburger rolls
2 tomatoes
crisp lettuce leaves
Barbecue sauce
1 cup tomato ketchup
2 teaspoons Worcestershire sauce
½ teaspoon celery salt
few drops chilli sauce

Combine minced steak, onion and seasoning in a mixing bowl, mix together thoroughly. Shape into 6 hamburgers, about 1 cm (½ inch) thick.

Barbecue over hot coals for 6 to 8 minutes on each side or until cooked. Baste hamburgers with the barbecue sauce while cooking.

Split rolls, toast and butter. Place hamburgers in the prepared rolls, add sliced tomato and lettuce. Serve any remaining barbecue sauce with the hamburgers.

Barbecue sauce: Combine all ingredients and mix together thoroughly.

Hawaiian hamburgers: Lightly brown slices of canned pineapple on barbecue, place on top of hamburgers instead of tomatoes and lettuce. Serve with any remaining sauce.

Glazed Pork Spareribs

Serves: 4-5
Cooking time: 2 hours
Oven temperature: 200-230° C (400-450° F)
  reducing to 180-190° C (350-375° F)

8-10 pork spareribs
salt
freshly ground pepper
1½ cups Tomato Sauce, strained (page 17)
½ cup dry sherry
¼ cup honey
2 tablespoons wine vinegar
½ teaspoon Worcestershire sauce

Season spareribs with salt and pepper and place in a roasting dish in a hot oven for 45 minutes. Drain off excess fat.

Combine tomato sauce, sherry, honey, wine vinegar and Worcestershire sauce, pour over spareribs.

Reduce oven temperature to moderate, return spareribs to oven and roast for a further 1 hour or until tender. Baste during cooking, adding a little water to dish if sauce is scorching. Serve with rice, salad or vegetable accompaniments.

For serving outdoors reheat on barbecue in a flameproof dish or large frying pan, turning frequently.

Minted Lamb Kebabs

Serves: 4
Cooking time: 15-20 minutes

1 kg (2 lb) lean lamb
8 small tomatoes
12 small mushrooms
Marinade
2 tablespoons chopped fresh mint
½ cup vinegar
2 tablespoons brown sugar
pinch of dry mustard
½ teaspoon salt
3 tablespoons butter or oil
grated rind of 1 lemon
¼ cup white wine

Cut lamb into 4 cm (1½ inch) cubes. Place in a bowl, add marinade and mix well. Cover and stand for 1 or 2 hours. If marinating for longer, place in refrigerator. Lift meat from marinade and alternate meat, tomatoes and mushrooms onto skewers.

Barbecue over hot coals or cook under pre-heated grill for 20 minutes, or until cooked to taste. Turn and baste frequently with marinade while cooking.

Marinade: Place all ingredients except white wine in a saucepan. Bring to the boil, take off heat and allow to stand for 30 minutes. Add white wine.

Polynesian Pork Saté

Serves: 4
Cooking time: 25 minutes

750 g (1½ lb) lean pork
Marinade
1 onion, grated
1-2 garlic cloves, crushed
4 Brazil nuts, grated
¼ cup lemon juice
¼ cup soy sauce
½ teaspoon pepper
3 drops Tabasco or other hot pepper sauce
1 teaspoon ground coriander
2 tablespoons brown sugar
2 tablespoons salad oil

Trim excess fat from pork, leaving some on and cut into 3 cm (1¼ inch) cubes. Combine marinade ingredients in a glass or pottery bowl and add pork pieces, mix well. Allow to marinate for 2 hours or more. When ready to cook, thread pork on four metal or bamboo skewers and place under a hot grill. Cook for 25 minutes or until cooked through (reduce heat after first 3 minutes on each side). Brush pork with marinade and turn often during cooking. Serve on a bed of hot rice. Heat any remaining marinade and serve over satés.
Note: Satés may also be cooked over a barbecue for outdoor eating.

SPECIAL OCCASION MEAT DISHES

Whether entertaining or celebrating a special family occasion, you will find just the right recipe here to do you proud. Try a special roast or a moist-cooked dish such as Beef Bourguignonne for a crowd, Pepper Steak or Weiner Schnitzel for a more intimate dinner. There is a recipe for any occasion and every budget.

Peach Baked Ham

Cooking time: 2½ hours
Oven temperature: 160-170° C (325-350° F)

1 small leg cooked ham
½ cup brown sugar
2 teaspoons dry mustard
1 × 812 g (29 oz) can peach halves
glacé cherries

Remove skin from ham leaving an 8 cm (3 inch) strip around the bone end. Place in a large roasting dish and bake in a moderately slow oven for 1½ hours.

Mix brown sugar with mustard, drain peaches, reserving liquid. Spread brown sugar over fat surface and arrange peach halves, cut side down, over ham, securing them with toothpicks. Pour peach liquid in dish. Return to oven and bake for a further hour until ham is well glazed. Half way through, baste with liquid in dish, adding a little water if liquid shows signs of scorching.

When cooked, remove ham to serving platter, replace toothpicks with cocktail sticks and place a cherry in the centre of each peach half, over protruding cocktail sticks.

Serve hot for preference, but it is just as delicious served cold.

Pepper Steak

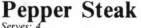

Serves: 4
Cooking time: 8-12 minutes

4 portions rump or fillet steak, thickly cut
2 tablespoons black peppercorns
1 tablespoon butter
salt
½ teaspoon Worcestershire sauce
squeeze of lemon juice
2 tablespoons brandy
2 tablespoons cream

Leave steaks at room temperature for 30 minutes. Crack peppercorns, using a mortar and pestle, or by placing in a plastic or paper bag and beating with a mallet. Coat steaks with cracked pepper, pressing it well into the steak with the heel of the hand (do not beat in).

Heat butter in a heavy frying pan and add steaks. Cook over high heat, 1 minute each side, to seal in the juices. Continue to cook over moderate heat until cooked to taste.

While steaks are in the pan sprinkle on sauce and lemon juice. Warm brandy, ignite and pour over steaks. When flames die down lift steaks onto platter and season with salt. Swirl cream into pan juices and pour over steaks.

Crusted Corned Beef

Serves: 6-8
Cooking time: 3¼ hours
Oven temperature: 180-190° C (350-375° F)

1 piece corned silverside, about 2 kg (4 lb)
2 tablespoons vinegar
4 tablespoons brown sugar
1 cup soft breadcrumbs
2 tablespoons chopped parsley
melted butter
Wine sauce
30 g (1 oz) butter
30 g (1 oz) flour
1 cup dry red wine
¼ cup redcurrant jelly
1 teaspoon powdered or ready-mixed mustard
salt and black pepper

Rinse meat, put into a saucepan and just cover with warm water. Add vinegar and 2 tablespoons of the brown sugar. Slowly bring to the boil, skim surface and simmer, covered, for 2½ hours or until tender. Transfer beef to a greased baking dish. Combine breadcrumbs, remaining brown sugar, parsley and enough melted butter to moisten. Press evenly over fat surface of beef and bake in moderate oven for 30-40 minutes until crust is golden brown. When cooked place on serving platter and serve with vegetables and Wine Sauce.

Wine Sauce: Melt the butter, add flour and stir for 2 minutes. Slowly stir in the wine and cook, stirring constantly until almost boiling. Add jelly, mustard, salt and pepper and simmer, stirring until jelly has melted. Pour into a sauce boat.

Pork Chops with Apple Pancakes

Serves: 4
Cooking time: 45 minutes

4 pork chops
flour
salt
cayenne pepper
butter or oil for frying
½ quantity pancake batter (page 41)
1 cup apple sauce

Coat chops in flour seasoned with salt and cayenne pepper. Heat butter in a frying pan and fry pork until cooked. Remove from pan and keep warm.

Make pancake batter using ½ quantity of ingredients listed, only ½ cup milk and add 1 tablespoon brandy. Cook as directed.

Spread a little apple sauce over the pancake and fold over into quarters. Remove from pan and keep warm. Repeat until all batter is used.

Return all chops and apple pancakes to pan and heat through. Serve piping hot with tossed salad or a crisp green vegetable.

Fondue Bourguignonne
Serves: 4-6

1 kg (2 lb) fillet steak
peanut oil
Accompaniments
Béarnaise Sauce (page 19)
Garlic Mayonnaise (Aioli, page 16)
Mushroom Sauce (page 18)
Tomato Sauce (page 17)
pickles (olives, gherkin, onions)
relishes (horseradish, mustard)
salad vegetables in French Dressing (page 28)
tossed green salad

Remove fat and sinews from fillet and cut into bite-sized cubes.

Pour enough oil into fondue pot so that it is almost half full. Heat oil until a cube of bread will brown in less than a minute. Adjust burner to maintain this temperature.

Supply each guest with a long-handled fondue fork, a dinner fork and a plate. Each guest spears a piece of meat on to a fondue fork and places it in the hot oil. When piece of meat is cooked as desired, transfer to a dinner fork to eat.

Select 2 or 3 sauces from those given and serve in small bowls so that cooked steak can be dipped into them. Arrange various pickles, relishes and salads in individual bowls or plates. Serve tossed salad in a large bowl and have plenty of crusty French bread on hand.

Crown Roast of Pork
Serves: 6
Cooking time: 1½ hours
Oven temperature: 160-170° C (325-350° F)

1 crown roast of pork (12 cutlets)
salt and pepper
1 tablespoon plain flour
1 cup chicken stock
Sage and onion stuffing (optional)
1 cup chopped onion
2 tablespoons butter
2 cups soft breadcrumbs
2 tablespoons chopped fresh sage
1 egg, beaten
salt and pepper

Have butcher prepare crown roast.

Rub surfaces with salt and pepper. Fill centre with stuffing, if used (see below) or place a jar or crumpled foil in centre to keep crown shape. Cover bare rib bones with aluminium foil to prevent burning. Place on a rack in a roasting dish and roast in a moderately slow oven for 1½ hours. Remove pork, place on a carving platter and keep warm.

Drain off all but 1 tablespoon fat from dish, stir in flour over medium heat until browned. Add stock and stir until gravy thickens and boils. Season to taste and strain into gravy boat.

Remove foil and place a cutlet frill on each bone. Carve by cutting between each cutlet. Serve with gravy, apple sauce, roast potatoes and pumpkin and a green vegetable.

Sage and onion stuffing: Sauté onion in butter until soft, add to breadcrumbs with sage. Bind with egg and season to taste.

Loin of Lamb Provencale

Serves: 6
Cooking time: 1¼ hours
Oven temperature: 180-190° C (350-375° F)

1 loin of lamb, boned, rolled and tied
salt and pepper
1 tablespoon flour
125 g (4 oz) button mushrooms, sliced
2 tablespoons butter
1 beef stock cube
⅓ cup cream
Marinade
2 cups red wine
1 garlic clove, crushed
½ teaspoon whole peppercorns
1 sprig of thyme

Place loin in a casserole dish. Mix marinade ingredients and pour over lamb loin in casserole dish. Marinate for several hours in refrigerator, turning lamb occasionally.

Remove loin from marinade and reduce marinade in a saucepan to half original quantity. Strain and keep aside.

Place lamb on a rack in roasting dish and rub fat surface with salt and pepper. Roast in a moderate oven for 1 hour. Remove to platter and keep warm.

Drain off all but 1 tablespoon fat from dish. Place dish over heat and stir in flour, cook 2 minutes. Add reduced marinade and stir constantly until bubbling. Sauté mushrooms in butter and add with crumbled stock cube. Stir to blend and cook sauce until bubbling again. Stir in cream, adjust seasoning and heat through without boiling again. Pour into sauce boat and serve with lamb carved in thick slices, and accompanying vegetables.

Carpetbag Steak

Serves: 4
Cooking time: 12-15 minutes

1 slice middle-cut rump steak about 4 cm (1½ inches) thick
2 bottles oysters (about 20 oysters)
lemon juice
salt
freshly ground black pepper
1 tablespoon butter
1 teaspoon cornflour

Leave steak at room temperature for 30 minutes. Make a deep pocket in the steak, cutting through meaty edge. Drain oysters reserving liquor and some oysters. Flavour oysters with lemon juice and salt and pepper. Fill pocket and close slit by sewing or with cocktail sticks. Rub steak with pepper and spread half of the butter on top. Place under pre-heated grill and cook for 6 minutes each side, spreading remaining butter on other side when steak is turned.

Reduce oyster liquor in a saucepan to ½ cup. Add reserved oysters, lemon juice, salt and pepper to taste. Mix cornflour with a little cold water and thicken sauce. Cook for 1 minute. Place steak on a heated platter, season with salt and pour over the sauce. To serve, cut steak into thick slices with knife held at an angle to cut across grain of meat.

Wiener Schnitzel

Serves: 4-5
Cooking time: 8-10 minutes

750 g (1½ lb) veal steaks
flour
salt and pepper
1 egg
dry breadcrumbs
2 tablespoons butter
2 tablespoons oil
1 hard-boiled egg
lemon slices and anchovy fillets to garnish

Pound steaks until thin, dip in flour seasoned with salt and pepper. Dip in beaten egg, then breadcrumbs. Press breadcrumbs on firmly. Refrigerate 30 minutes to set crumbs.

Combine butter and oil in frying pan, heat until butter is melted and begins to sizzle. Add one steak at a time, so that the butter mixture retains the heat necessary to brown the steaks. Cook quickly on both sides, about 2 to 3 minutes, reduce heat, cook gently until tender. Use tongs when turning schnitzels during cooking, a fork would pierce the crust and cause the juices to escape.

Remove steaks from pan and drain on paper towels. Arrange on warm platter. Garnish with chopped egg white, sieved egg yolk, lemon slices and anchovy fillets.

Veal Reboux

Serves: 6
Cooking time: 55-60 minutes
Oven temperature: 180-190° C (350-375° F)

2 nuts of veal, each about 500 g (1 lb)
2 veal kidneys
60 g (2 oz) butter
2 cups Espagnole Sauce (page 18)
1-2 cups soft breadcrumbs
1 bacon rasher, chopped
2 tablespoons maderia

Ask your butcher to cut out the nut or heart of 2 legs of veal. Trim nuts of veal into neat shapes. Roast veal in a moderate oven for 30 minutes. Remove from oven and slice thinly.

Sauté kidneys in butter until they stiffen. Slice thinly. Combine ½ cup espagnole sauce with sliced kidneys and spread between each slice of veal. Reform nut to original shape, securing with skewers. Coat with another ½ cup of sauce and sprinkle with breadcrumbs. Return veal to a moderate oven and cook for a further 25 minutes, or until cooked and crumbs are golden.

Place bacon in a heated saucepan and cook until lightly coloured. Add remaining 1 cup espagnole sauce and reduce to half quantity. Stir in madeira and heat gently without boiling.

Remove skewers from veal. Arrange meat in a heated serving dish, pour sauce around meat and garnish as desired.

Veal Parmigiana

Serves: 4-6
Cooking time: 55 minutes
Oven temperature: 160-170° C (325-350° F)

750 g (1½ lb) veal steaks, thinly cut
salt
freshly ground pepper
1 egg
2 tablespoons milk
1 cup dry breadcrumbs
2 tablespoons grated Parmesan cheese
oil for frying
60 g (2 oz) Mozzarella or Cheddar cheese, sliced
Tomato sauce
1 small onion, chopped
1 garlic clove, crushed
1 tablespoon oil
1 cup chopped, peeled tomatoes
2 tablespoons tomato paste
½ cup water
½ teaspoon dried oregano
1 tablespoon chopped parsley
salt and pepper to taste
1 teaspoon sugar

Flatten steaks. Season with salt and pepper. Beat egg with milk. Mix crumbs with Parmesan cheese. Dip meat into egg and coat with crumbs. Shallow-fry in hot oil until coating is golden brown. Transfer to shallow oven dish. Top with sauce and cheese slices. Bake in a moderately slow oven, covering with lid or foil for first 30 minutes. Remove cover and cook for further 15 minutes.

Tomato sauce: Sauté onion and garlic in oil for 10 minutes. Add remaining ingredients and simmer for 15 minutes.

Carbonnade of Beef

Serves: 6
Cooking time: 2 hours
Oven temperature: 160-170° C (325-350° F)

1 kg (2 lb) chuck, round or blade steak
2 tablespoons butter
2 large onions, sliced
2 garlic cloves, crushed
2 tablespoons flour
1 cup beer
¼ cup hot water
bouquet garni
1½ teaspoons salt
freshly ground black pepper
pinch nutmeg
3 teaspoons brown sugar
finely chopped parsley to garnish

Wipe and trim beef. Cut into cubes and brown in butter. Remove to a plate when browned. Reduce heat and sauté onion until soft, add garlic and cook a little longer. Stir in flour and cook 2 minutes. Return beef to pan and pour in beer and water. Stir constantly until mixture thickens and just begins to bubble. Add remaining ingredients, cover and simmer gently or place in casserole and cook in a moderately slow oven for 1½-2 hours, until beef is tender. Remove bouquet garni, adjust seasoning and sprinkle with chopped parsley before serving. Serve with whole boiled potatoes or buttered noodles and tossed green salad or green vegetables.

Stuffed Pork Fillet

Serves: 4-6
Cooking time: 1 hour

12 dried apricots
2 medium-sized pork fillets, each about 500 g (1 lb)
1 cooking apple
2 tablespoons butter
salt
freshly ground pepper
¾ cup water

Soak apricots in water overnight. Trim excess fat from the pork fillets and split carefully down the centre without cutting the fillet in half. Drain the apricots. Peel and slice the apple. Arrange the apricots and apple slices inside the fillet. Draw the edges together and tie securely with string. Melt the butter in a frypan and brown the meat on all sides. Season with salt and pepper. Add the water, cover and simmer for 1 hour or until the meat is tender. Remove the string before serving the meat. Slice the fillets and serve with a gravy made by thickening the meat juices in the frypan.

Loin of Pork with Prunes

Serves: 6-8
Cooking time: 2-2½ hours
Oven temperature: 180-190° C (350-375° F)

2 kg (4 lb) pork loin, boned and rind removed
salt and pepper
20 prunes, stoned
¼ cup prune juice
1½ cups stock or water
2 tablespoons plain flour
1 tablespoon redcurrant jelly

Rub pork all over with salt and pepper. Place prunes along the inside of the loin. Roll up and tie securely with white string. Place in a roasting dish and cook in a moderate oven for 2 to 2½ hours until meat is tender. When cooked, remove string, slice and keep warm.

Pour off excess fat from roasting dish. Add prune juice and stock and heat. Mix flour to a smooth paste with a little cold water and blend in. Simmer, stirring constantly, until thick and smooth. Season to taste with salt and pepper. Add redcurrant jelly, mix thoroughly and pour over meat. Serve immediately.

Note: Prune juice is manufactured in small tins by baby food manufacturers.

Cooking tip: Score the pork rind into 1 cm (½ inch) strips without cutting through the underlying fat. Rub rind with salt and place on rack in roasting dish, fat side down. Cook in a hot oven for 15 minutes until bubbly and crisp. Divide into strips and serve with pork loin.

Blanquette of Veal

Serves: 6
Cooking time: 1½ hours

1 kg (2 lb) stewing veal
3 tablespoons butter
1 onion, studded with 3 cloves
2 carrots, sliced
1½ cups stock
salt
white pepper to taste
bouquet garni
2 tablespoons flour
12 small onions, par-boiled
125 g (4 oz) button mushrooms
1 extra tablespoon butter
2 teaspoons lemon juice
2 egg yolks
3 tablespoons cream
pinch nutmeg

Cut veal into cubes. Soak in cold water for 1 hour and dry well. Fry quickly in 1 tablespoon butter without browning. Add onion with cloves, carrots, stock, salt, pepper and bouquet garni. Cover, bring to boil, skim, then simmer, covered, for 45 minutes. Remove veal pieces and carrots. Strain liquid and reserve; cleanse saucepan then melt remaining butter and mix in flour. Pour in veal stock, stirring until mixture thickens. Add veal pieces, carrots and whole onions. Sauté mushrooms in butter and lemon juice and add. Cover and simmer, stirring occasionally, for 20 to 30 minutes or until meat is tender. Remove from heat. Mix egg yolks, cream and nutmeg and stir into veal mixture. Reheat blanquette gently but do not bring to boil again.

Roast Scotch Fillet

Serves: 6-8
Cooking time: 1¼-1½ hours
Oven temperature: 190-200° C (375-400° F)

1 piece Scotch fillet about 1.5-2 kg (3-4 lb)
freshly ground black pepper
soft butter
Mushroom Sauce or Béarnaise Sauce for serving
  (pages 18, 19)

Wipe beef with a damp cloth. Place on a rack in a baking dish, rub surface with pepper and spread with butter. Place in a moderately hot oven and roast for about 45 minutes per kg (20 minutes per lb) — meat thermometer reading 70°C (160°F) for medium done beef. Baste during cooking.

When cooked, lift meat onto a warm carving dish and allow to stand in a warm place for 15 minutes before carving. Carve slices downwards through the joint in thick slices and serve with gravy made from pan drippings or with Mushroom Sauce or Béarnaise Sauce.

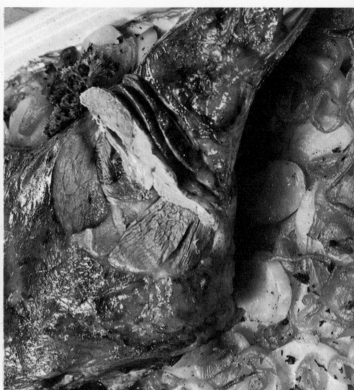

Sauerbraten

Serves: 6-8
Cooking time: 3-3½ hours

1 beef pot roast, about 2 kg (4 lb)
1½ cups dry red wine
½ cup red wine vinegar
2 large onions, sliced
2 large carrots, sliced
1 leafy celery stalk, chopped
½ lemon, sliced
2 bay leaves
4 parsley stalks
1 teaspoon black peppercorns
4 whole allspice
4 cloves
3 tablespoons butter
salt to taste
2 tablespoons plain flour
1 tablespoon brown sugar

Place meat in a deep bowl. In a saucepan combine wine, wine vinegar, vegetables, herbs and spices. Bring to the boil and pour over meat. Cover and place in refrigerator for 3 days, turn meat each day.

Remove meat from marinade, wipe dry. Heat half the butter in a deep pan and brown meat on all sides. Heat marinade and pour over meat. Add salt to taste. Cover tightly and simmer for 2½ to 3 hours or until meat is tender. Take meat out of pan and keep warm. Skim fat from liquid in pan and reduce over high heat until about 1½ cups liquid remains. Strain into a jug.

Melt remaining butter in pan, blend in flour and sugar until smooth, cook until lightly browned. Add reserved liquid and stirring continuously, bring to the boil. Simmer for 2 minutes. Return meat to pan, cover and leave on low heat for 10 minutes.

Slice meat and serve with sauce and buttered noodles.

Lamb Boulangère

Serves: 6-8
Cooking time: 2-2½ hours
Oven temperature: 200-230° C (400-450° F)
  reducing to 180-190° C (350-375° F)

1 leg lamb, about 2 kg (4 lb)
salt and pepper
1-2 garlic cloves
1 tablespoon butter
1 tablespoon oil
4 medium-sized onions, sliced
4 large potatoes
1 cup stock
chopped parsley for garnish

Season leg with salt and freshly ground black pepper. Cut garlic into slivers, make small slits in skin and insert slivers. Place in a large roasting dish and cook in a hot oven for 1 hour.

Meanwhile heat oil and butter in a frying pan and sauté onions until transparent and beginning to colour. Peel potatoes and slice thinly.

Remove lamb from dish and drain off fat. Arrange potato slices in base of dish, top with onions and season with salt and pepper. Pour on stock and place lamb on top. Return to moderate oven for further 1-1½ hours until lamb is cooked to taste. Turn leg to brown evenly during cooking.

Rest lamb in a warm place for 15 to 20 minutes, carve in thick slices and serve on bed of potatoes and onions sprinkled with parsley.

Beef Bourguignonne

Serves: 6-8
Cooking time: 3 hours
Oven temperature: 160-170° C (325-350° F)

1.5 kg (3 lb) topside, round or blade steak
freshly ground pepper
2 large onions, chopped
2 garlic cloves, crushed
bouquet garni
1 cup dry red wine
2 tablespoons olive oil
2 tablespoons dripping or bacon fat
125 g (4 oz) salted belly pork, diced
3 tablespoons seasoned flour
½ cup beef stock or water
2 tablespoons butter
12 small white onions
250 g (8 oz) button mushrooms
chopped parsley

Cut meat into large cubes, place in a bowl with pepper, 1 onion, 1 garlic clove, bouquet garni, red wine and olive oil. Cover and marinate for 3 to 6 hours.

Heat dripping or bacon fat in a frying pan, fry pork until golden brown, remove to casserole dish.

Lift meat from marinade and drain thoroughly. Toss in seasoned flour and brown in remaining fat. Remove to casserole and add remaining chopped onion and garlic clove to pan, sauté until onion is soft. Stir in any remaining flour, cook 1 minute, blend in strained marinade and stir until thickened and bubbling. Add stock and bouquet garni from marinade and pour over casserole contents. Cover and cook in a moderately slow oven for 2 hours. Skim fat from surface.

Heat 1 tablespoon butter in pan, add whole onions and sauté until lightly coloured. Remove, add remaining butter and sauté mushrooms. Add onions and mushrooms to casserole and cook for a further 30 to 45 minutes until tender. Remove bouquet garni and adjust seasonings. Sprinkle with chopped parsley and serve.

Beef Wellington

Serves: 6
Cooking time: 45 minutes
Oven temperature: 200-230° C (400-450° F)

1 beef fillet, about 1.5 kg (3 lb)
2 spring onions, finely chopped
3 tablespoons butter
125 g (4 oz) button mushrooms, sliced
¼ cup brandy
salt
freshly ground black pepper
3 tablespoons pâté
1 x 340 g (12 oz) packet puff pastry
1 egg yolk

Trim fat and silver skin from fillet. Sauté spring onions in half the butter in a pan, add mushrooms and cook until liquid evaporates. Put aside. Add remaining butter to pan and brown fillet well on all sides. Flame with brandy and allow to cool completely. Season with salt and pepper. Keep pan aside for making sauce.

Roll out pastry thinly. Place cold fillet on longer side. Spread with pâté then with mushroom mixture. Wrap fillet in pastry, trim off excess, moisten and press joins to seal. Cut decorations from trimmings and place on top. Beat egg yolk with a little water and glaze. Lift on to baking tray and bake in a hot oven for 30 minutes. Fillet should be medium rare. Serve with Madeira Sauce.

Madeira sauce: Blend 1 teaspoon flour into frying pan juices, add ½ cup beef stock and 2 tablespoons madeira. Stir over heat until smooth and thickened. Simmer for 1 minute, adjust seasoning.

POULTRY & GAME

Roast chicken on Sundays and turkey at Christmas. Not any longer! With modern expertise in its production and marketing, poultry, be it chicken, turkey, duck or goose, can be served more frequently. Chicken can also be purchased in pieces—breasts, drumsticks, thighs etc., or special casserole packs. Even turkey is available in halves.

If you have a hunter in the family, then game may not be difficult to come by. Unfortunately the only game readily available commercially is rabbit and the occasional hare, and even these are becoming difficult to obtain. There are recipes for game in this chapter if you are fortunate enough to bag some, one way or another.

Chicken Livers Bordelaise

Serves: 4-6
Cooking time: 10 minutes

500 g (1 lb) chicken livers
seasoned flour for coating
3 tablespoons bacon drippings or butter
1 onion, finely chopped
125 g (4 oz) mushrooms, chopped
½ cup dry white wine
6 bacon rashers
1 tablespoon chopped parsley
boiled rice for serving

Coat chicken livers lightly with seasoned flour.

Heat dripping or butter and sauté onion until transparent. Add chicken livers and brown lightly. Lower heat, stir in mushrooms, cook 2 minutes and add wine. Cover and simmer gently for 5 to 7 minutes.

Meanwhile remove rind from bacon rashers and cook bacon until crisp. Crumble and sprinkle over chicken livers with parsley. Serve immediately with boiled rice as an entrée or luncheon dish.

Chicken Paprika

Serves: 5-6
Cooking time: 45-55 minutes
Oven temperature: 160-170° C (325-350° F)

1 chicken, about 1.5 kg (3 lb)
3 tablespoons oil
2 onions, chopped
½ cup green and red capsicum strips
2 tablespoons flour
1½ cups stock or water
1 tablespoon paprika
1 tablespoon tomato paste
salt and pepper
½ teaspoon sugar
¼ cup sour cream

Cut chicken into serving pieces and wipe dry. Heat oil in a frying pan and brown chicken pieces. Remove to a casserole dish. Add onion to pan and sauté until transparent. Add capsicum strips, cook 2 minutes, stir in flour, and cook a little longer. Add stock or water, stirring constantly until sauce bubbles and thickens. Blend in paprika, tomato paste, salt and pepper to taste and sugar. Pour over chicken, cover and cook in a moderately slow oven for 45 minutes or until chicken is tender. Carefully blend in sour cream and serve with buttered noodles and a tossed salad or a green vegetable.

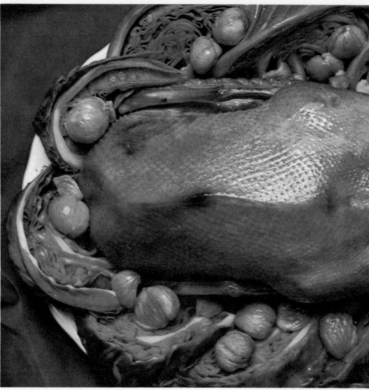

Duck with Sour Cherries

Serves: 4
Cooking time: 1¼-1½ hours
Oven temperature: 200-230° C (400-450° F)
  reducing to 180-190° C (350-375° F)

2 ducks, each about 1.5 kg (3 lb)
½ teaspoon celery salt
salt
freshly ground pepper
½ cup water
3 tablespoons butter
1 small onion, sliced
1 tablespoon flour
½ cup chicken stock
¼ cup port
about 1 cup liquid from cherries
1 x 480 g (17 oz) jar Morello cherries

Wipe ducks inside and out with a damp cloth. Sprinkle cavity with celery salt, salt and freshly ground pepper to taste. Place ducks in a roasting dish, breast side up and add water to prevent scorching. Spread the breast and legs with butter and cover loosely with a piece of aluminium foil. Roast ducks in a hot oven for 15 minutes. Reduce heat to moderate and continue to cook ducks until tender. Baste frequently with drippings during cooking.

Remove the ducks to a heated platter and keep warm. Pour off fat from roasting dish leaving 1 tablespoon fat with brown sediment, and add onion. Cook over gently heat until onion is soft, stir in flour, cook 1 minute, and add chicken stock. Stir continuously until sauce thickens and bubbles. Add port and cherry liquid. Bring sauce to the boil and cook, stirring continuously, until it is slightly thick. Add Morello cherries and heat through. Halve the ducks and pour half the sauce over them. Serve remaining sauce separately in a sauceboat.

Roast Goose

Serves: 10-12
Cooking time: 2½-3 hours
Oven temperature: 180-190° C (350-375° F)

1 goose, about 3.5 kg (8 lb)
1½ cups stock made from giblets
2 tablespoons arrowroot or cornflour
Chestnut stuffing (optional)
250 g (8 oz) chestnuts
½ cup finely chopped celery
3 tablespoons butter
liver of bird, chopped (optional)
2 cups soft white breadcrumbs
½ teaspoon ground allspice
salt and pepper to taste
¼ cup cream
2 tablespoons sherry

Wipe body cavity of goose with paper towels. Fill with stuffing if used (see below) and truss. Place goose in a roasting dish and cook in a moderate oven for 2½ to 3 hours. Baste towards end of cooking. When cooked remove to serving platter and keep warm. Deglaze dish with stock, skim off fat and add arrowroot blended to a smooth paste with a little cold water. Bring to the boil and strain into a sauceboat. Carve the goose and serve with braised red cabbage, additional chestnuts braised in butter and gravy.

Chestnut stuffing: Shell and peel chestnuts. Break into pieces. Sauté celery in butter for 10 minutes. Add chopped liver if used and stir over heat until just cooked. Thoroughly combine all ingredients.

Cooking tip: To shell and peel chestnuts: Make a slit on each side with a sharp knife. Drop into boiling water, boil for 10 minutes. Drain, cover with cold water, shell and peel as quickly as possible.

Chicken Grand-Mère

Serves: 4-6
Cooking time: 1 hour
Oven temperature: 160-170° C (325-350° F)

1 chicken, about 1.5-2 kg (3-4 lb)
1 bacon rasher, diced
125 g (4 oz) butter
10 small white onions
250 g (8 oz) potatoes, peeled and diced
Sausage stuffing
2 tablespoons butter
2 tablespoons chopped onion
125 g (4 oz) sausage meat
1 chicken liver, chopped
4 tablespoons soft breadcrumbs
1 teaspoon chopped parsley
¼ teaspoon each dried rosemary and thyme
salt

Fill chicken with sausage stuffing (see below). Truss the bird and place in a large ovenproof, earthenware casserole. Add bacon, butter and onions. Cover the casserole and cook the chicken in a moderately slow oven for 30 minutes. Add potatoes and cook, covered, for 20 minutes longer, or until chicken is tender. Serve hot from the casserole.

Sausage stuffing: Melt butter and sauté onion until soft. Stir in sausage meat, chicken liver, breadcrumbs, herbs and salt to taste. Cook mixture for 3 minutes, stirring constantly.

Coq au Vin

Serves: 4
Cooking time: 1¼ hours
Oven temperature: 160-170° C (325-350° F)

1.5 kg (3 lb) chicken pieces
1 tablespoon oil
2 tablespoons butter
4 rashers bacon, rind removed
8 small onions
125 g (4 oz) button mushrooms
2 garlic cloves, crushed
2 tablespoons brandy
1½ cups red wine
bouquet garni
salt
freshly ground pepper
beurre manié (see Glossary)

Dry chicken pieces with paper towels. Heat oil and butter in a frying pan, brown chicken and remove to a casserole dish. Chop bacon, add to pan with onions and sauté until golden. Add mushrooms and garlic and cook 5 minutes longer. Return chicken to pan. Pour over brandy and ignite. Allow to flame for 1 minute, shaking pan, extinguish with wine. Transfer contents to casserole, add bouquet garni and salt and pepper to taste.

Cover casserole and cook in a moderately slow oven for 1 hour or until chicken is tender. Remove bouquet garni and thicken casserole slightly with beurre manié, adjust seasoning if necessary. Garnish with chopped parsley and fried croûtes of bread before serving.

Rabbit with Prunes and Pine Nuts

Serves: 4-6
Cooking time: 1¼ hours

2 rabbits, each about 750 g (1½ lb)
¼ cup olive oil
2 onions, chopped
1 cup chopped, peeled tomatoes
1 bay leaf
2 garlic cloves
¼ cup blanched, toasted almonds
2 sprigs of parsley
½ cup water
salt
⅓ cup pine nuts
20 prunes

Wash and dry rabbits, cut into serving pieces. Heat oil in a flameproof casserole or large heavy saucepan. Brown rabbit pieces, lift out and keep aside. Sauté onions in pan until golden, add tomatoes and bay leaf, cook for 5 minutes. Return rabbit to pan and simmer, covered, for 30 minutes.

Crush garlic, almonds and parsley with a mortar and pestle, mix in water, or blend together in an electric blender. Add ground mixture to rabbit, salt to taste and continue cooking for 30 minutes or until tender. Simmer pine nuts and prunes in water in separate saucepans. The pine nuts will require 10 to 15 minutes. Cooking time of prunes varies according to size. Drain and add pine nuts and prunes to rabbit just before serving.

Note: If added earlier, the pine nuts will not remain white and the prunes will over-sweeten the sauce.

Chicken Pie

Serves: 6
Cooking time: 55-60 minutes
Oven temperature: 200-230° C (400-450° F)

6-8 small, whole onions
1 cup chicken stock
2 carrots, sliced
1 cup frozen peas
1 cup milk
1 onion, finely chopped
3 tablespoons butter
4 tablespoons plain flour
1 chicken stock tablet
3 cups diced, cooked chicken
salt and pepper
pinch ground nutmeg
¼ cup cream
1 × 284 g (10 oz) packet flaky pastry mix

Simmer whole onions in chicken stock for 10 minutes, add carrots and peas and cook until just tender. Drain, measure stock and make up to 1 cup with water. Combine with milk.

Sauté chopped onion in butter until soft, stir in flour and cook gently for 1 minute. Add combined liquid and stir constantly until thickened and bubbling. Crumble in stock tablet and stir until blended. Add diced chicken and cooked vegetables, season to taste with salt, pepper and nutmeg and blend in cream. Pour into an 8 or 9 cup deep pie dish.

Make pastry according to packet directions, roll out to an oval 4 cm (1½ inches) larger than top of dish. Trim off this excess and place around moistened rim of dish. Moisten pastry and place top in position. Press edges to seal and trim. Make decorations from trimmings and place on pie. Glaze top with milk and cut a hole in the centre. Bake in a hot oven for 25 to 30 minutes until cooked.

Chicken à la King

Serves: 4-6
Cooking time: 2½-3½ hours

1 stewing chicken, about 1.5 kg (3 lb)
1 onion, chopped
1 carrot, chopped
1 stalk celery, chopped
bouquet garni
rind and juice of 1 lemon
3 spring onions, chopped
60 g (2 oz) butter
1 cup sliced mushrooms
1 green capsicum, finely chopped
½ cup flour
2 cups milk
1 teaspoon nutmeg
salt and pepper
2 egg yolks
1 cup cream

Place chicken in a large saucepan with sufficient water to just cover. Add onion, carrot, celery and bouquet garni. Cover and simmer gently for 2 to 3 hours, until chicken is tender. When cooked, remove chicken from pan, cool, then prepare 4 cups of diced chicken meat. Strain stock and return to pan.

Add lemon rind and spring onions to stock and reduce liquid to 1 cup. Remove lemon rind. Melt butter in a saucepan and sauté mushrooms and capsicum until soft. Stir in flour and cook gently for 2 to 3 minutes. Add lemon juice, milk and stock, bring to the boil, stirring continuously. Add nutmeg, salt and pepper to taste and chicken and cook a further 5 minutes. Blend egg yolks with cream, stir in gradually and heat through without boiling. Serve hot with boiled rice.

Chicken with Cashews

Serves: 4
Cooking time: 12-15 minutes

500 g (1 lb) chicken breasts
1 tablespoon soy sauce
2 teaspoons cornflour
1 egg white, slightly beaten
1 green capsicum
3-4 spring onions
oil for frying
1 cup raw cashew nuts
small piece root ginger, bruised
1 tablespoon sweet sherry
pinch sugar

Remove skin and bone chicken breasts. Cut flesh into 1 cm (½ inch) dice. Place in a bowl, add 2 teaspoons of the soy sauce, cornflour and egg white. Mix well and leave aside for 10 minutes.

Remove seeds and white membrane from capsicum and cut into squares. Slice spring onions diagonally in 3 cm (1¼ inch) lengths.

Heat oil in a wok or large frying pan. Add cashew nuts and stir over heat until browned and crisp. Lift out and keep aside. Add garlic and bruised ginger to oil, cook a few seconds and remove ginger. Add capsicums and spring onions and stir-fry for 2 to 3 minutes. Remove.

Add chicken pieces and stir-fry for 5 to 7 minutes until cooked, return cashew nuts, peppers and spring onions to wok. Mix together sherry, remaining soy sauce and sugar and stir over heat for 1 minute until well coated. Serve with boiled rice.

Roast Wild Duck

Serves: 4-6
Cooking time: 1 hour
Oven temperature: 190-200° C (375-400° F)

2 wild ducks
salt and pepper
1 apple
1 orange
1 onion, chopped
4 bacon rashers, halved
1 tablespoon plain flour
½ cup combined orange and lemon juice
¼ cup chicken stock
2 tablespoons port

Clean ducks well and singe end feathers over a flame. Rub cavities with salt and pepper. Leave peel on orange and apple and chop roughly; combine with onion and place into cavities. Truss ducks and rub surfaces lightly with salt and pepper. Place bacon over the breast of each bird and place on a rack in a roasting dish. Cook in a moderately hot oven for 45 minutes. Remove bacon and cook until skin is crisp and brown, turn and brown other side. Lift ducks onto serving platter and keep warm. Skim most of the fat from pan drippings, stir in flour and heat on top of stove. Cook for a few minutes and stir in juice and stock. Bring to the boil, stirring constantly. Blend in port, adjust seasoning and strain into sauce boat.
  Carve ducks and serve with the sauce.

Curried Chicken

Serves: 4
Cooking time: 1¼ hours

1 chicken, about 1.5 kg (3 lb)
2 tablespoons butter or ghee
2 large onions, chopped
1 garlic clove, crushed
1 tablespoon curry powder
1 teaspoon curry paste
1 cup chicken stock or water and chicken stock cube
1 cup coconut milk (see below)
1 tablespoon lemon juice
salt and pepper

Cut chicken into serving pieces and dry well with paper towels. Melt butter in a heavy saucepan and fry chicken pieces until golden brown, remove and keep aside. Add onion and garlic to pan and sauté gently in remaining fat until onion is transparent. Add curry powder and paste and continue to cook for 3 to 4 minutes. Stir in stock, coconut milk and lemon juice, cover and simmer very gently for 15 minutes. Turn chicken in pan and season to taste with salt and pepper. Cover and simmer gently for 45 minutes or until chicken is tender. Sauce should be thick at end of cooking. If not, remove chicken pieces and reduce sauce over high heat until thickened. Serve curry with boiled rice, pappadums and traditional curry accompaniments.

Coconut milk: Put 1¼ cups water and 1 cup dessiccated coconut in a saucepan, bring slowly to the boil. Strain through a fine sieve, pressing coconut well with back of a spoon to extract all liquid.

Chicken Maryland

Serves: 6
Cooking time: 40-45 minutes
Oven temperature: 180-190° C (350-375° F)

6 chicken maryland pieces (drumsticks and thighs)
lemon juice
seasoned flour
2 eggs
2 tablespoons water
fine dry breadcrumbs
oil for frying
6 slices canned pineapple
3 bananas
3 bacon rashers, for garnish

Leave drumsticks and thighs joined together as purchased, or separate at joint for easier handling. Wipe dry and rub with lemon juice. Leave aside for 10 minutes. Roll pieces in seasoned flour. Beat eggs with water. Brush chicken with beaten egg and coat well with dry breadcrumbs, pressing them on well. Refrigerate if desired for 20 minutes to firm crumbs.

Heat oil in a large frying pan and shallow fry chicken until browned on all sides but not cooked through. Place in a baking dish and bake in a moderate oven for 25 to 30 minutes to complete cooking. Roll halved bacon rashers and fasten with cocktail sticks. Place around chicken during last 10 minutes of cooking. When chicken is almost done, cook fruit. Dry pineapple, peel bananas and halve lengthways. Dip fruits in remaining egg and coat with breadcrumbs. Shallow fry in hot oil until golden brown. Drain on paper towels. Serve chicken with pineapple and bananas and garnish with bacon rolls.

Spiced Chicken Breasts

Serves: 6
Cooking time: 30-35 minutes

6 large halved chicken breasts
1½ teaspoons salt
1 garlic clove, crushed
2 teaspoons grated root ginger
1 teaspoon turmeric
1 teaspoon ground coriander
pinch of chilli powder (optional)
oil for frying
Rice Pilaf (page 52)
2 tablespoons currants
1 teaspoon grated orange rind
1 tablespoon pine nuts, fried in a little oil

Wipe chicken and remove loose bones. Mix together salt, garlic, ginger and spices and rub into chicken. Cover and stand in refrigerator for several hours. Fry chicken breasts in hot oil until golden brown on each side and cooked through. Place in a covered dish and keep hot.

Make pilaf, adding currants and orange rind with the stock. When cooked spread in a warm serving dish and sprinkle with pine nuts. Arrange chicken breasts on top and serve immediately.

Braised Chicken and Potatoes

Serves: 4
Cooking time: 45 minutes

1 chicken, about 1.5 kg (3 lb)
3 bacon rashers, chopped
2 tablespoons butter
1 tablespoon oil
1 onion, finely chopped
½ cup dry white wine
½ cup chicken stock
bouquet garni
salt and pepper
beurre manié (see Glossary)
8-12 small potatoes, peeled and thoroughly dried
¼ cup oil
chopped parsley to garnish

Wipe chicken and cut into serving portions. In a heavy-based saucepan lightly brown bacon in butter, lift out with a slotted spoon. Add 1 tablespoon oil and brown chicken pieces on all sides. Remove to a plate. Add onion and sauté gently until soft. Add wine and stock and heat, stirring well to lift browned sediment. Return chicken and bacon to pan, add bouquet garni and season to taste. Cover and simmer gently for 45 minutes or until tender.

Meanwhile, heat oil in a saucepan large enough to take potatoes in one layer. Add potatoes, cover and cook gently in the oil for 25 to 30 minutes, turning to brown evenly.

When chicken is cooked, lift out and place on serving dish. Skim fat from liquid and thicken with beurre manié to taste. Arrange potatoes with chicken and pour sauce on top. Serve sprinkled with chopped parsley.

Roast Turkey

Serves: 8-12
Cooking time: 3 hours
Oven temperature: 180-190° C (350-375° F)

1 turkey, about 3.5 kg (8 lb)
salt
Chestnut stuffing (page 107)
Sausage stuffing (page 108)
½ lemon
freshly ground pepper
butter
2 tablespoons plain flour
2 cups stock made from giblets

Dry turkey and rub inside well with salt. Fill the body and neck cavity loosely with prepared stuffings. Use chestnut stuffing for body cavity and sausage stuffing for neck cavity (omit liver). Fold skin over neck opening.

Fold wing tips under body and pass a poultry skewer through wing tips, neck skin and back to secure. Truss to secure the legs close to the body. Rub surfaces with cut lemon, salt and pepper. Place turkey, breast side up, on a rack in a large roasting pan and spread thickly with softened butter. Cover loosely with aluminium foil and roast in a moderate oven for 3 hours until tender. Remove foil for last 30 minutes of cooking to brown. Insert a fork in the meatiest part of the leg—if cooked, the juices should not be pink. Transfer turkey to a heated platter and keep warm. Drain off all but 2 tablespoons fat from the roasting pan. Stir in flour and cook over a low heat for 1 minute. Gradually add stock, stir in the sediment and bring to the boil, stirring continuously. Simmer for 2 or 3 minutes. Adjust seasoning and serve with the turkey.

Duck in Red Wine

Serves: 6
Cooking time: 1¼ hours

1 duck, about 2 kg (4 lb)
3 tablespoons butter
125 g (4 oz) bacon pieces, chopped
salt
freshly ground pepper
1 tablespoon plain flour
1 cup dry red wine
2 teaspoons sugar
bouquet garni
250 g (8 oz) small white onions, peeled
250 g (8 oz) button mushrooms, sliced
2 tablespoons cognac

Truss duck. Heat half the butter in a heavy-based saucepan and lightly brown chopped bacon. Add duck and brown on all sides. Sprinkle with salt, pepper and flour. Heat wine and pour over. Add half the sugar and bouquet garni and bring to a gentle boil. Lower heat, cover tightly and simmer gently for 30 minutes.

Melt remaining butter with remaining sugar in a frying pan. Add onions and sauté until lightly browned. Add to duck and cook for further 30 minutes. Add sliced mushrooms and cook 10 minutes longer. Adjust seasonings if necessary. When duck is cooked warm cognac, pour over duck and flame.

Place duck on a serving platter with onions and mushrooms, strain pan juices and serve in a gravy boat.

French Colonial Style Chicken

Serves: 6
Cooking time: 25 minutes

3 chickens, each about 750 g (1½ lb)
Marinade
2 tablespoons sesame oil
¼ cup maize or peanut oil
¼ cup wine vinegar
1 teaspoon finely chopped fresh tarragon
1 teaspoon salt
few drops Tabasco sauce
1 garlic clove, crushed
¼ cup lemon juice
1 tablespoon Worcestershire sauce
1 teaspoon brown sugar
1 teaspoon paprika
freshly ground black pepper

Cut chickens in halves. Combine remaining ingredients in a glass or china dish and place chicken in marinade for 3 to 4 hours. Stand in refrigerator, turn chicken occasionally. Drain. Place under a hot grill, skin side down, and cook for 25 minutes or until chicken is tender and brown. Turn often during cooking and baste frequently with marinade.

Alternatively, chicken may be barbecued over glowing coals—have grid set high above fire bed so that chicken will cook slowly without burning. Lower grid towards end of cooking, if necessary.

Hare Hunter Style

Serves: 4-6
Cooking time: 2¼ hours

1 hare
2 tablespoons brandy
2 tablespoons olive oil
salt and pepper
1 onion, thinly sliced
dry red wine
250 g (8 oz) thickly sliced bacon, diced
90 g (3 oz) butter
20 small white onions
2 tablespoons (1 oz) plain flour
bouquet garni
250 g (8 oz) button mushrooms, cooked in butter
croutons

Cut hare into serving pieces and place in bowl with brandy, oil, a little salt and pepper and the onion. Cover with dry red wine. Refrigerate for several hours.

Fry bacon in butter in a large flameproof casserole. Drain the bacon when browned and keep aside. Sauté the onions in the butter and bacon fat until lightly browned. Remove and keep aside. Drain the hare, add to the fat and brown well. Remove. Sprinkle flour into casserole, blend and cook roux until lightly browned. Stir in sufficient strained wine marinade to make a thin sauce. Return hare to casserole, add bouquet garni, cover and simmer over gentle heat for 1 hour. Add bacon, onions and mushrooms and simmer a further hour, or until hare is tender.

Skim fat from sauce and if necessary thicken with beurre manié (see Glossary). Adjust seasoning. Serve garnished with croutons.
Note: Rabbit may be used in place of hare.

Barbecued Chicken

Serves: 4
Cooking time: 25-35 minutes

1.5 kg (3 lb) chicken pieces
Marinade
1 cup sherry or apple cider
½ cup salad oil
1 onion, finely chopped
1 tablespoon French mustard
1 tablespoon mixed dried herbs or 4 sprigs fresh thyme
1 teaspoon salt
freshly ground pepper
1 tablespoon Worcestershire sauce
1 teaspoon soy sauce

Place chicken pieces in a shallow china or glass dish. Mix marinade ingredients thoroughly together and pour over chicken. Cover and stand for several hours in refrigerator. Turn chicken occasionally. Drain chicken and reserve marinade.

Barbecue chicken over medium hot coals for approximately 25 to 35 minutes or until tender. Allow more cooking time on the bone side than the flesh side. Baste frequently with the marinade while cooking.

Turkey Tetrazzina

Serves: 6
Cooking time: 35-40 minutes

1 quantity Bechamel Sauce (page 16)
90 g (3 oz) butter
2 small onions, sliced
1 carrot, cut in 5 mm (¼ inch) slices
250 g (8 oz) button mushrooms, sliced
2 tablespoons flour
1 cup strong chicken stock
salt and pepper to taste
½ cup cream
3 cups diced, cooked turkey
250 g (8 oz) ribbon noodles, cooked and tossed in butter
grated Parmesan cheese

Make béchamel sauce and press a piece of buttered paper over the surface until required, to prevent a skin forming.

Melt butter in a saucepan and gently sauté onion and carrot for 15 minutes, stirring often. Add mushrooms and sauté until liquid evaporates. Sprinkle in flour and stir over heat for 2 minutes. Blend in chicken stock, stir constantly until sauce bubbles. Add salt and pepper, reduce heat to very low and simmer for 5 minutes or until carrots are tender. Blend in béchamel sauce, stir until smooth and stir in cream and turkey. Heat gently until hot, but not boiling.

Arrange hot buttered noodles in an ovenproof dish, top with turkey mixture and sprinkle with cheese. Brown lightly under a hot grill and serve immediately.

Blushing Duckling

Serves: 4
Cooking time: 1 hour
Oven temperature: 190-200° C (375-400° F)

1 duckling, about 1.5 kg (3 lb)
3 tablespoons butter
1 sprig fresh thyme
1 bay leaf
2 parsley stalks
salt and pepper
2 onions, thinly sliced
½ cup dry red wine
1 cup chicken stock
1 large orange
1 large red capsicum
2 teaspoons arrowroot
paprika
1 orange and red capsicum rings for garnish

Prepare duck, place 1 tablespoon butter and the herbs inside the bird and truss. Rub over with salt, pepper and butter. Gently fry onion in the remaining butter. Place duck and onions in ovenproof dish. Heat wine to just below boiling point, flame it and pour over the duck with the stock. Braise gently uncovered, in a moderately hot oven for about 1 hour, basting every 15 minutes.

While duck is cooking, blanch the orange for 5 minutes, slice finely and cut slices in half. Blanch and shred the capsicum. Add orange slices and shredded capsicum to duck for final 30 minutes of cooking. Take out duck, carve and keep hot. Strain and season the gravy to taste then thicken slightly with the arrowroot blended with a little cold water. Add paprika to taste and pour the gravy over the duck. Garnish with orange slices and red capsicum and sprinkle with chopped parsley.

Roast Chicken with Rice Stuffing

Serves: 4-5
Cooking time: 1½ hours
Oven temperature: 180-190° C (350-375° F)

1 chicken, about 1.5 kg (3 lb)
salt
freshly ground pepper
pinch of paprika
2 tablespoons butter
Rice stuffing
½ cup long grain rice
2 tablespoons butter
1 onion, chopped
3 bacon rashers, chopped
½ teaspoon dried mixed herbs
1 teaspoon finely chopped parsley
1 egg, beaten
salt and pepper

Wash and dry chicken and sprinkle cavity with salt and pepper. Fill with the stuffing (see below) and skewer the opening. Truss the bird and rub skin with salt and paprika, then with butter. Place in a roasting dish and roast in a moderate oven for 1½ hours until it is golden brown and crisp. Pierce meaty part of leg; chicken is cooked when juices run clear.

Rice stuffing: Cook the rice in boiling salted water, rinse and drain well. Melt butter in a saucepan, add onion and bacon and cook until lightly browned, cool. Combine all ingredients, mix well and season to taste.

Chicken Kebabs Teriyaki

Serves: 4
Cooking time: 10 minutes

750 g (1½ lb) chicken breasts
1 x 250 g (8½ oz) can water chestnuts
Teriyaki marinade
¾ cup pineapple juice
3 tablespoons soy sauce
3 tablespoons lemon juice
2 tablespoons oil
1 garlic clove, crushed
2 teaspoons grated root ginger
1 tablespoon honey

Remove skin and bones from chicken breasts and cut flesh into 3 cm (1¼ inch) pieces. Drain water chestnuts. Thread chicken and water chestnuts alternately onto washed bamboo skewers. Arrange in a single layer in a shallow glass or china dish. Mix marinade ingredients thoroughly together and pour over filled skewers. Cover and marinate for 30 minutes in refrigerator, turning occasionally. If using metal skewers marinate chicken and water chestnuts in a bowl and thread onto skewers before cooking.

Cook over glowing coals or under a pre-heated grill for 10 minutes, turning and basting frequently with marinade. Serve immediately with salad accompaniments and boiled rice.

PUDDINGS & DESSERTS

Winter appetites take some satisfying, so there is nothing like a hot pudding to finish a good meal. Choose a substantial pudding to follow a light main course, a light dessert to follow a rich main course. In the following selection of recipes there are proper puddings, delightful desserts, tempting tarts, pies and cheesecakes to suit any and every occasion.

HOT PUDDINGS

Crusted Pineapple Slices

Serves: 5-6
Cooking time: 6-7 minutes

1 large pineapple
½ cup chopped raisins
¼ cup chopped walnuts
2 egg whites
2 teaspoons lemon juice
¾ cup caster sugar
½ teaspoon grated lemon rind
flaked or desiccated coconut

Remove skin from pineapple, cut into slices and remove core. Fill the cavity of each slice with a mixture of raisins and walnuts. Combine the lightly beaten egg whites, lemon juice, sugar and lemon rind in a heatproof basin. Beat briskly over boiling water for 5 minutes, then remove from heat, and fold in the coconut. Cool slightly and pile onto each pineapple slice. Brown tops lightly under a medium-hot grill and serve at once.

Variation: Substitute 5 or 6 canned peach halves or 10 or 12 canned apricot halves for the pineapple.

Vanilla Soufflé

Serves: 4
Cooking time: 30 minutes
Oven temperature: 180-190° C (350-375° F)

1 teaspoon butter for soufflé dish
2 tablespoons caster sugar
2 tablespoons butter
3 tablespoons flour
1 cup milk
¼ cup sugar
1 teaspoon vanilla essence
3 egg yolks
4 egg whites

Butter a 5-cup soufflé dish and tie a collar of greased greaseproof paper around the outside. Lightly dust the inside with half the caster sugar. Melt butter in a large saucepan, stir in flour and cook gently for 1 minute without colouring. Add milk and stir continuously until mixture boils and thickens. Stir in sugar and vanilla essence and cool slightly. Beat in egg yolks. Whisk egg whites until stiff and fold into the vanilla mixture. Pour into the prepared soufflé dish and bake in a moderate oven for 30 minutes, until well risen and golden brown. Carefully remove the collar and lightly dust the surface with remaining caster sugar. Serve immediately with whipped cream.

Chocolate soufflé: Melt 90 g (3 oz) cooking chocolate in a small pan over hot water and add to thickened mixture with sugar and vanilla. Add 1 tablespoon rum if desired.

Quick Cherry Strudel

Serves: 6
Cooking time: 35-40 minutes
Oven temperature: 230-250° C (450-475° F)
 reducing to 190-200° C (375-400° F)

1 x 420 g (15 oz) can cherries
¾ cup very finely chopped walnuts
¼ cup sugar
grated rind of 1 lemon
1 teaspoon ground cinnamon
3 tablespoons melted butter
¾ cup soft white breadcrumbs
250 g (8 oz) commercial puff pastry
extra melted butter
icing sugar

Stone and halve cherries, put into a sieve and drain thoroughly. Mix together walnuts, sugar, lemon rind and cinnamon. Pour melted butter over crumbs, stir to combine.

Put pastry on a well-floured clean tea towel, roll out to a thin oblong about 35 x 50 cm (14 x 20 inches), having the longer side of pastry nearest to you. Brush over with extra melted butter, spread the crumbs over, leaving a 5 cm (2 inch) margin of pastry all round. Arrange cherries parallel with longer edge of pastry and near the centre. Fold in sides of pastry, brush folds with melted butter. Roll up and put on a large, greased baking tray. Brush all over with melted butter. Bake in a very hot oven for 10 minutes, reduce to moderately hot and bake another 25 to 30 minutes, or until golden brown, brushing with melted butter every 10 minutes. Dust with sifted icing sugar and serve warm.

Apricot Apple Cobbler

Serves: 5-6
Cooking time: 30-35 minutes
Oven temperature: 180-190° C (350-375° F)

1 cup dried apricots
2 cooking apples, peeled and chopped
½ cup sugar
Cobbler topping
90 g (3 oz) butter
½ cup caster sugar
½ teaspoon vanilla essence
2 eggs
1¼ cups self-raising flour
¼ cup milk

Rinse apricots, cover with hot water and leave to soak for 1 hour. Peel and slice apples, add to apricots with the sugar and cook until soft.

Place fruit in the base of a greased ovenproof dish, keep hot in oven.

Cobbler topping: Cream together the butter, sugar and vanilla essence, add eggs and beat well. Fold in the sifted flour and milk alternately and spread lightly over the hot fruit. Bake in a moderate oven for 30 to 35 minutes. Serve with custard or cream.

Variation: Use any stewed fruit, either one kind or a combination.

Cooking tip: Do not have too much liquid in the stewed fruit when topping goes on top, nor should fruit be over-sweetened as it could scorch. Fruit must be hot when topping is spread on top.

Fruit Fritters

Serves: 4-6

Fritter batter
1 cup plain flour
¼ teaspoon salt
2 eggs
1 cup milk

Select and prepare fruit from following:
bananas, peeled and sprinkled with lemon juice
apples, peeled, cored and cut into 1 cm (½ inch) rings
canned pineapple slices or chunks, well drained
icing or caster sugar
whipped cream or ice cream

Prepare batter (see below). Prepare chosen fruit and drop gently into batter. With a skewer, transfer coated fruit to a pan of deep, hot oil and deep fry until golden brown and fruit is hot and cooked. Drain well and serve piping hot sprinkled with icing or caster sugar and topped with whipped cream or ice cream.

Fritter batter: Sift the flour and the salt into a mixing bowl. Make a well in the centre and drop in the eggs, add half the milk gradually and mix to a smooth batter, using a wooden spoon, and working in the flour from the sides. When all the flour is worked in, beat the batter until smooth with the back of the wooden spoon. When the surface of the batter is covered with bubbles, stir in the remaining liquid to give the consistency of thin cream. If possible leave the batter to stand in a cool place for 1 hour before using.

Zabaglione

Serves: 4

6 egg yolks
½ cup sugar
¼ cup dry marsala wine or dry sherry
¼ cup brandy

Beat egg yolks with sugar in the top of a double boiler until foaming and pale in colour. Place over simmering water and slowly add marsala and brandy, beating continuously until the mixture thickens and becomes foamy. Do not overcook. Remove from heat, pour into glasses and serve immediately with sponge fingers or cream wafers. Zabaglione may also be served as a sauce with hot fruit pudding.

Strawberry sabayon: Wash and hull 1 punnet strawberries, halve or quarter if large and add to Zabaglione just before serving. (Sabayon in French is a corruption of the Italian Zabaglione.)

Cooking tip: It is important to beat Zabaglione over simmering, not boiling water. If water is too hot, the mixture will curdle.

Baked Apples

Serves: 6
Cooking time: 45 minutes
Oven temperature: 180-190° C (350-375° F)

6 cooking apples
½ cup brown sugar
¼ cup chopped walnuts
¼ cup chopped raisins
1 teaspoon ground cinnamon
2 tablespoons butter
whipped cream for serving

Wash and core apples. Score skin around the middle. Combine sugar, walnuts, raisins and cinnamon in a mixing bowl, mix together thoroughly. Place each apple on a square of aluminium foil, stuff with the mixture and dot with butter.

Wrap securely, sealing with double folds and bake in a moderate oven for 45 minutes or until tender. Place each apple in its foil wrapper on dessert plates. Open out foil and serve with whipped cream.

Note: Apples may be cooked on the barbecue as a dessert for a barbecue meal. Use doubled aluminium foil for each package, cook for 30 to 45 minutes on barbecue grid over glowing coals, turning once.

Steamed Jam Pudding

Serves: 6-8
Cooking time: 2 hours

125 g (4 oz) butter
½ cup caster sugar
½ teaspoon vanilla essence
2 eggs
1½ cups self-raising flour
pinch of salt
¼ cup milk
2 tablespoons raspberry jam

Cream butter, sugar and vanilla essence until light and fluffy. Add eggs, one at a time, beating well after each addition. Sift flour with salt and fold in alternately with milk.

Grease a 6 or 7 cup pudding basin and spread jam in the base. Spoon in pudding batter, cover basin with a square of buttered aluminium foil and place lid on top. If using a china basin, cover with two layers of buttered greaseproof paper, top with a layer of foil and tie on securely under rim of basin with string.

Place a round wire cake rack or invert a saucer in the base of a large saucepan of boiling water. Place pudding on this and make sure water comes half way up sides of basin. If not, add boiling water. Cover pan and steam for 2 hours. During cooking, add boiling water to pan when necessary. Invert onto serving dish and serve hot or warm with custard or cream.

Chocolate Fondue
Serves: 4

250 g (8 oz) dark chocolate
½ cup cream
¼ teaspoon each ground cinnamon, nutmeg and cloves
fresh fruit: peaches, apricots, strawberries, cherries, paw paw,
  banana
cake: sponge fingers, butter cake
marshmallows

Grate chocolate, place in a heatproof, earthenware fondue pot. Add cream and spices, blend well. Heat gently, stirring until smooth and blended. This can be done on the stove then transferred to table burner at serving time. Keep heat low.

Arrange your selection of fruits on a platter, cubed or sliced into bite-sized portions. Cut sponge fingers and butter cake (should not be too fresh) into squares or cubes and arrange in a napkin-lined basket. Place marshmallows in a bowl.

Desired food is speared onto fondue forks, dipped into chocolate mixture, then transferred to dessert fork.

Variation: Omit spices and add 1 tablespoon grated orange rind.

Apricot Shortcake
Serves: 6-8
Cooking time: 35-40 minutes
Oven temperature: 190-200° C (375-400° F)
* increasing to 200-230° C (400-450° F)*

3 cups self-raising flour
pinch of salt
½ cup caster sugar
125 g (4 oz) butter
1 egg, separated
⅔ cup milk
2 tablespoons blanched, slivered almonds
1 x 825 g (30 oz) can apricot halves
1½ cups cream, whipped and sweetened

Sift flour and salt into a bowl. Mix in all but 1 tablespoon sugar. Rub in butter until crumbly. Beat egg yolk with milk and stir into flour mixture with a round-bladed knife. Grease and flour two 20 cm (8 inch) layer cake tins and spread mixture evenly in each. Bake in a moderately hot oven for 30 minutes or until cooked. Turn onto a wire rack. Place one shortcake right side up on a baking tray and increase oven temperature to hot.

Beat egg white until stiff and beat in reserved sugar. Pile onto centre of shortcake on tray and sprinkle with slivered almonds. Return to oven for 5 to 7 minutes until meringue is lightly browned and set.

Drain apricots, reserve 8 or 10 for top, mash remainder and combine with two-thirds of the whipped cream. Place plain shortcake upside down on platter. Cover with whipped cream and apricot mixture. Place top in position, pipe remaining whipped cream around edge and arrange apricots on top. Serve warm.

Christmas Pudding

Serves: 12-15
Cooking time: 5-7 hours

250 g (8 oz) butter or margarine
1⅓ cups brown sugar
4 eggs
1 tablespoon treacle
grated rind of 1 lemon and 1 orange
1½ cups raisins, chopped
1½ cups sultanas
1 cup currants
1 cup dates, chopped
½ cup mixed peel, chopped
½ cup chopped, blanched almonds
1½ cups plain flour
1 teaspoon bicarbonate of soda
1 teaspoon nutmeg
1 teaspoon cinnamon
¼ teaspoon salt
3 tablespoons brandy
2 cups soft breadcrumbs

Cream butter and brown sugar until light and fluffy. Add eggs one at a time and beat well. Stir in treacle and grated lemon and orange rind. Mix fruit, peel and almonds together and blend half into creamed mixture with half the sifted dry ingredients. Add remaining fruit mixture, brandy and breadcrumbs and fold in remaining dry ingredients. Put mixture into a greased pudding basin or pudding steamer. Cover with two thicknesses of greased greaseproof paper and secure lid or tie paper on with string. Steam for 5 hours, then for 2 hours more on day when pudding is served. Flame with 2 tablespoons warmed brandy when serving.
Note: This quantity will fit a 3 litre (5 pint) basin or two smaller basins, in which case steam for 4 hours then 1 hour on day pudding is to be served.

Hard sauce: Cream ½ cup butter with ¾ cup sifted icing sugar until light and fluffy. Beat in 1 tablespoon ground almonds and 1 tablespoon brandy. Chill until required.

Bread and Butter Custard

Serves: 4
Cooking time: 40 minutes
Oven temperature: 180-190° C (350-375° F)

4 slices white bread, buttered
¼ cup sultanas
3 eggs
2 tablespoons sugar
pinch of salt
2 cups milk

Remove crusts from buttered bread and cut into fingers. Arrange bread fingers, buttered side down, in layers, sprinkling sultanas between layers, in an ovenproof dish.

Beat eggs, sugar and salt together. Blend in milk and stir until sugar is dissolved. Strain over top of bread.

Stand in a baking dish of hot water. Bake in a moderate oven for 40 minutes or until custard is set (test by inserting a knife in the centre). The top should be golden brown. Serve hot.
Note: Bread and Butter Custard may be served cold with cream.

Quick Creamed Rice

Serves: 6-8
Cooking time: 40 minutes

1 cup water
½ cup short grain rice
4 cups milk
pinch salt
1 tablespoon custard powder
2 tablespoons cold milk
3 tablespoons sugar
ground nutmeg

Place water in a lightly greased saucepan and bring to the boil. Add rice, stir until boiling, then simmer until water is absorbed. Add milk and a pinch of salt, stir well and leave over moderate heat until beginning to boil. Reduce heat so that milk simmers gently. Simmer for 25 to 30 minutes, stirring occasionally, until rice is very tender and mixture is creamy. Blend custard powder with cold milk, stir in half a cup of the hot mixture and pour back into the saucepan contents, stirring constantly. Add sugar and cook until bubbling gently. Pour into serving dish and dust with ground nutmeg. Serve hot or warm with stewed fruit.

Note: If you like rice custard with a browned 'skin' on top, leave to cool in dish until a skin forms and place under a hot grill until top is golden brown. Sprinkle with nutmeg after browning.

Apricot and Orange Pancakes

Serves: 4
Cooking time: 30-35 minutes
Oven temperature: 160-170° C (325-350° F)

1 quantity pancake batter (page 41)
2 tablespoons melted butter
2 large oranges
caster sugar
Filling
1½ cups dried apricots
4 tablespoons Seville orange marmalade
3-4 teaspoons rum or Curacao
caster sugar

Make pancakes and place them on a napkin-lined plate. Prepare filling (see below) and spread on each pancake. Roll up and place in a buttered ovenproof dish. Brush pancakes with melted butter and heat in a moderately slow oven for 10 minutes or until hot.

Meanwhile take two or three strips of peel from one orange with a potato peeler or sharp knife. Cut these strips into tiny shreds. Place shreds in a small pan, cover with cold water and bring to the boil. Strain and rinse under cold water, drain. Keep aside. Peel the oranges, removing all pith, and slice thinly. Arrange around heated pancakes and sprinkle with orange peel shreds and caster sugar.

Filling: Wash apricots thoroughly. Cover with cold water and cook gently until soft. Drain off cooking water and sieve fruit. Stir in marmalade and rum or Curacao and sweeten with a little sugar if too tart.

Baked Apple Dumplings

Serves: 4
Cooking time: 45 minutes
Oven temperature: 200-230° C (400-450° F)

Short crust pastry
2 cups plain flour
pinch salt
60 g (2 oz) butter
60 g (2 oz) lard
1 teaspoon lemon juice
about ¼ cup cold water
To finish dumplings
2 large apples
1 tablespoon butter
⅓ cup brown sugar
1 cup water

Short crust pastry: Sift flour and salt into a bowl. Blend fats together then rub into flour lightly with fingertips. Using a round-bladed knife, mix to a soft dough with lemon juice and water. Knead lightly, roll into a ball, wrap and chill for 15 to 30 minutes. Roll out thinly to a 40 cm (16 inch) square. Cut into 4 small squares.

Peel and core the apples. Cut each in half and place a half, cut side down in the middle of each pastry square. Dampen edges of pastry with a little cold water and bring the four corners together. Pinch the edges together tightly fluting or folding them to look attractive. Grease a large shallow baking dish and stand the four dumplings in it. Bake, uncovered, in a hot oven for 15 minutes. Heat together the butter, brown sugar and water and pour over dumplings. Baste after apples have cooked 15 minutes longer. If sauce evaporates too quickly add a little boiling water towards end of cooking time. Cook for 45 minutes in all. Spoon sauce over apples for serving.
Note: If sauce thickens too much it becomes toffee-like as it cools.

Sultana Lemon Delicious

Serves: 4-5
Cooking time: 40 minutes
Oven temperature: 180-190° C (350-375° F)

¾ cup caster sugar
¼ cup plain flour
finely grated rind of 1 large lemon
¼ cup lemon juice
60 g (2 oz) butter, melted
3 eggs, separated
1½ cups milk
3 tablespoons sultanas

Put ½ cup of the sugar, the flour, lemon rind and juice, melted butter and egg yolks into a mixing bowl. Beat until mixed. Heat milk just enough to remove chill. Add milk to lemon mixture, beat together. Whisk egg whites stiffly with remaining sugar, fold about 1 cup of mixture lightly into egg whites, then fold in remainder lightly. Sprinkle sultanas in base of ungreased ovenproof dish and pour mixture carefully on top. Stand in another dish of cold water. Bake in a moderate oven until cooked and set, about 40 minutes. Serve while still warm, or if preferred, cold.

COLD DESSERTS

Frozen Plum Pudding
Serves: 8-10

1½ cups mixed dried fruit
¼ cup chopped glacé cherries
½ cup chopped almonds or walnuts
2 tablespoons brandy
2 cups milk
2 tablespoons cornflour
½ cup sugar
2 eggs, beaten
1 egg yolk, beaten
1 cup cream, whipped
½ teaspoon vanilla essence
glacé fruits to decorate

Mix fruits and nuts and sprinkle with brandy. Cover and leave for several hours in refrigerator.

Blend milk, cornflour, sugar and beaten eggs in a heavy-based saucepan. Cook over medium heat, stirring constantly until thickened and beginning to bubble. Use a wire balloon whisk if custard goes lumpy. Turn into a mixing bowl and cover surface with a piece of plastic film to prevent skin forming. When cold fold in whipped cream and vanilla essence. Pour into a freezer container, cover and freeze until a solid rim 4 cm (1½ inches) wide, forms around edge. Spoon into a chilled bowl and beat with electric mixer until smooth. Fold in chilled fruit and pour into a mould. Cover and place in freezer. Unmould to serve and decorate with glacé fruits.

Raspberry Fool
Serves: 12

1.5 kg (3 lb) raspberries
1¼ cups water
1 cup sugar
1 cup cream
whipped cream to decorate
Custard
1 cup milk
2 tablespoons cornflour
2 tablespoons sugar
1 egg
1 egg yolk
½ teaspoon vanilla essence

Clean raspberries and remove stems, wash and put into a large saucepan with water and sugar. Stew raspberries until soft, cool then rub through a sieve or purée in an electric blender. Whip cream and mix with custard (see below) and raspberry purée. Serve in a glass bowl or in individual glasses. Decorate with swirls of whipped cream.

Custard: Combine milk, cornflour and sugar in a heavy-based saucepan. Beat whole egg and egg yolk thoroughly and stir into milk mixture. Place over moderately low heat and stir continuously with a wooden spoon or balloon whisk until thickened and just beginning to bubble. Remove from heat, stir in vanilla essence and turn into a bowl. Cover surface with a piece of plastic film to prevent skin forming and leave until cool.
Note: Frozen raspberries or fresh boysenberries may be used instead of fresh raspberries.

Summer Pudding
Serves: 4

500 g (1 lb) raspberries (or a mixture of raspberries,
   redcurrants, mulberries or blackberries)
½–¾ cup sugar
2 tablespoons water
1 tablespoon lemon juice (optional)
½ loaf stale white bread

Remove stalks from fruit. Place in a saucepan, sprinkle on ½
cup sugar, add water and lemon juice, if used. Heat, stirring
gently until sugar is dissolved, taste and add more sugar, if
necessary. Do not overcook fruit.

Slice bread thinly and trim off crusts. Line a china bowl
with slices of bread. Fill the lined bowl with stewed fruit,
placing two layers of bread in between the fruit, cover top
with another layer of bread. Press a plate or saucer over
pudding and 'place a heavy weight on top. Place in
refrigerator overnight and turn out of bowl before serving.

This pudding is delicious served with cream, ice cream or
hot custard.

Honeyed Grapes
Serves: 4

500 g (1 lb) seedless white grapes
2 tablespoons honey
1 teaspoon lemon juice
2 tablespoons brandy
whipped fresh cream or sour cream for serving

Remove grapes from stems, wash well and drain.

Combine honey, lemon juice and brandy and pour over
grapes. Stir gently, being careful not to break fruit. Cover
and stand in refrigerator overnight.

Serve chilled, topped with a spoonful of whipped cream or
sour cream.

Mandarin Layer Jelly

Serves: 4-6

1 x 310 g (11 oz) can mandarin segments
water
1 packet orange jelly crystals
250 g (8 oz) packaged cream cheese, softened at room
   temperature
1 teaspoon gelatine
2 tablespoons hot water
whipped cream

Drain mandarins, reserving syrup. Make syrup up to 1¾ cups with water, heat and dissolve jelly crystals in the liquid. Pour half the jelly mixture into a 3 to 4 cup mould and place in the freezer to set.

Beat the softened cream cheese until smooth. Chop most of the mandarins, reserving a few for decoration. Add chopped mandarins to the cream cheese. Dissolve gelatine in the hot water and cool, then add to the cream cheese, beating thoroughly.

Pour half the cream cheese mixture onto the set jelly and set as before. Repeat the two layers again with remaining jelly and cream cheese mixture, placing mould in refrigerator for final setting. When ready to serve, dip quickly in hot water and invert on a serving plate. Decorate with whipped cream and remaining mandarin segments.

Pineapple Mint Sherbet

Serves: 5-6

1 x 425 g (15 oz) can crushed pineapple
2 tablespoons bruised mint leaves
2 teaspoons gelatine
1 tablespoon boiling water
2 tablespoons lemon juice
½ cup cold milk
2 egg whites
2 tablespoons caster sugar
sugared mint sprigs or crème de menthe for serving

Drain pineapple and reserve ½ cup fruit pulp. Place pineapple liquid in a saucepan, heat until boiling and pour over mint leaves. Stand for 5 minutes, then strain liquid. Discard mint and cool liquid. Dissolve gelatine in boiling water. Put remaining pineapple pulp, pineapple liquid and lemon juice in an electric blender and mix to a purée. Add dissolved gelatine and milk and mix until blended. Place into refrigerator tray, freeze until set. Whisk egg whites stiffly, add sugar gradually, beat until dissolved. Place frozen mixture into a mixing bowl, beat well, then fold in the whisked egg whites. Empty into refrigerator tray, freeze until quite set. Serve topped with the reserved pineapple pulp and a sugared mint sprig or a drizzle of creme de menthe.

Vanilla Ice Cream

Yield: 1½ litres (2½ pints)

1 teaspoon gelatine
3 tablespoons cold water
4 tablespoons sugar
1 tablespoon butter
2 cups milk
1 cup full cream powdered milk
1 teaspoon vanilla essence
1 teaspoon vinegar

Place gelatine and water in a saucepan and allow to stand for 5 minutes. Add sugar and bring slowly to the boil to dissolve sugar and gelatine. Remove from heat, add butter and stir until butter has melted. Turn into a bowl and allow to cool. Beat until very thick.

Beat together milk and powdered milk and add the gelatine mixture. Flavour with vanilla essence, add vinegar and pour into a suitable container. Freeze at maximum temperature until mixture is firm. Break up with a spoon and place in a chilled mixing bowl. Beat until smooth. Return to container, cover and freeze until firm.

Chocolate ice cream: Melt 60 g (2 oz) dark chocolate over hot water, blend in a little milk, cool and add to mixture with vanilla essence.

Coffee ice cream: Add 3 teaspoons coffee essence instead of vanilla essence.

Chocolate Mousse

Serves: 6

125 g (4 oz) dark cooking chocolate
4 eggs, separated
⅓ cup sugar
1 tablespoon brandy or rum
½ teaspoon vanilla essence
1 cup cream, whipped
grated chocolate or chocolate curls

Cut chocolate into small pieces and melt in a bowl set in hot water. Beat egg yolks with sugar in a heatproof bowl over simmering water. Blend in melted chocolate, brandy or rum, and vanilla essence and remove from heat. Cool.

Whisk egg whites until stiff and fold into the chocolate mixture with 2 tablespoons of the whipped cream. Pour chocolate mousse into small mousse pots, or small individual glass sweet dishes and place in refrigerator until set, about 2 hours. Pipe a large rosette of cream onto each mousse and decorate with grated chocolate or chocolate curls.

Creamy Lemon Soufflé

Serves: 6-8

1½ tablespoons gelatine
¾ cup hot water
375 g (12 oz) packaged cream cheese, softened at room
    temperature
¾ cup caster sugar
⅓ cup milk
⅓ cup lemon juice
1½ cups cream, whipped
4 egg whites
whipped cream to decorate
glacé cherries

Prepare a 4-cup soufflé dish with a collar of greased greaseproof paper or foil. Dissolve gelatine in hot water. Set aside to cool. Beat softened cream cheese until smooth, gradually add sugar, milk, lemon juice and dissolved gelatine. Chill mixture until slightly thickened, beat again until frothy. Fold in whipped cream. Beat egg whites until stiff, and fold lightly into mixture. Pour into prepared dish and chill until set, about 2 hours.

Remove collar and decorate with swirls of whipped cream and glacé cherries.

Pavlova

Serves: 6-8
Cooking time: 2 hours
Oven temperature: 100-110° C (200-225° F)

3 egg whites
¾ cup caster sugar
½ teaspoon cornflour
½ teaspoon vinegar
½ teaspoon vanilla essence
Filling
1 cup cream
2-3 teaspoons icing sugar
½ teaspoon vanilla essence
1 punnet strawberries, hulled and cleaned
4 Chinese gooseberries (Kiwi fruit), peeled and sliced
pulp of 6 passionfruit

Whisk the egg whites until they are quite stiff. Add the sugar a spoonful at a time, beating well to dissolve each quantity. Add the cornflour with the last amount of sugar, then fold in the vinegar and vanilla essence. Draw an 18 cm (7 inch) circle on greaseproof paper placed on a greased baking tray. Sprinkle lightly with cornflour. Spread meringue mixture to cover the circle and shape into a cake, dome or pie shell shape as preferred. Place in a cool oven for 1½ to 2 hours until crisp and dry. Open the oven door slightly and cool before removing, then peel away the paper. Serve pavlova with whipped cream piled on top and fruit arranged over cream.

Filling: Whip the cream and sweeten slightly with icing sugar and vanilla. Prepare fruit.

Variations: Ice cream topped with passionfruit pulp. Fresh fruit salad, sliced tinned fruit or any sliced fresh fruit in season, topped with whipped cream. Lemon butter or curd topped with whipped cream.

Raspberry Mallow Ice
Serves: 4-6

250 g (8 oz) packaged cream cheese, softened at room
   temperature
1 x 250 g (8 oz) packet marshmallows
⅔ cup milk
⅔ cup thickened cream
2 tablespoons raspberry jam
125 g (4 oz) dark chocolate

Beat softened cream cheese until smooth. In a saucepan, melt
the marshmallows in the milk over a low heat. Cool. Fold
cream into cream cheese mixture and pour into an icecream
tray. Add the jam to the marshmallow mixture and pour into
the tray over the cream cheese mixture. With a skewer
marble the mixture and freeze.

Just before serving melt chocolate in a saucepan over hot
water. Scoop icecream into individual serving dishes and
drizzle melted chocolate over the top of each one.

Serve with crisp wafer biscuits, if desired.

Loganberry Soufflé
Serves: 6

1 x 425 g (15 oz) can loganberries
3 eggs
4 tablespoons caster sugar
1 tablespoon gelatine
1 cup cream
½-¾ cup chopped nuts
whipped cream to decorate

Tie a collar of doubled greaseproof paper or aluminium foil
round the outside of a china soufflé dish, to stand 8 cm (3
inches) above dish.

Drain liquid from loganberries into a measuring cup.
Separate eggs and whisk egg yolks, sugar and 2/3 cup
loganberry liquid in a heatproof bowl over boiling water
until thick and light. Dissolve gelatine in remaining
loganberry liquid and stir quickly into whisked mixture.
Both mixtures should be lukewarm to combine smoothly and
to prevent the soufflé separating.

Whip cream and fold into mixture with loganberries.
Whisk egg whites until stiff and gently fold into mixture,
using a tablespoon or a plastic spatula. Pour into prepared
soufflé dish and place in refrigerator to set. When set, remove
paper carefully, unrolling from the soufflé and easing it off
with a clean knife dipped in cold water. Press chopped nuts
on side of soufflé. Decorate top with swirls of whipped
cream.

Variation: Use canned raspberries, blackberries or boysenberries instead of the loganberries.

Solid Syllabub
Serves: 4-6

rind of 1 lemon, thinly sliced
4 tablespoons lemon juice
½ cup white wine or sherry
2 tablespoons brandy
⅓ cup caster sugar
1 cup cream, lightly whipped
grated nutmeg

Place the lemon rind, lemon juice, wine and brandy in a bowl, cover and leave a few hours or overnight. Strain into a large bowl and add the sugar. Stir until sugar is completely dissolved. Slowly pour in lightly whipped cream, stirring vigorously all the time. Whisk the mixture until it forms soft peaks.

Pile into a glass bowl or individual sweet glasses and sprinkle with nutmeg. Serve with sponge fingers.

Note: Solid syllabub will keep for 2 days in a cool place (not the refrigerator).

Summer Fruit Bowl
Serves: 6-8

1 rockmelon
4 peaches
juice of 1 lemon
4 tablespoons caster sugar
1 small pineapple
8 apricots
4 bananas
4 tablespoons Cointreau
6 passionfruit
whipped cream or ice cream for serving

Peel rockmelon, cut into cubes. Skin peaches and slice. Combine rockmelon and peaches and steep in lemon juice and 2 tablespoons sugar for 10 minutes. Peel and core pineapple, cut into chunks. Skin and quarter apricots. Peel bananas and slice diagonally. Combine prepared fruits, toss gently together with remaining sugar and Cointreau.

Serve in a bowl with passionfruit pulp spooned over. Serve with whipped cream or ice cream.

Festive Frozen Cake
Serves: 8

1 x 20 cm (8 inch) chocolate sponge
250 g (8 oz) unsalted butter
¾ cup caster sugar
6 eggs, separated
250 g (8 oz) dark chocolate
3 teaspoons gelatine
½ cup hot strong coffee
4 tablespoons chocolate or coffee liqueur
½ cup cream
¼ cup hazelnuts, chopped
extra 60 g (2 oz) dark chocolate

Split chocolate sponge through the centre. Cream butter and sugar together and gradually add beaten egg yolks until mixture is light and fluffy. Cut chocolate into small pieces and melt in the top of a double boiler or in a heatproof bowl over gently boiling water. Cool and stir into butter mixture. Dissolve gelatine in hot coffee, cool and add to filling. Lastly, whisk egg whites until stiff and fold into mixture. Place half chocolate sponge in spring-form tin and sprinkle with 2 tablespoons of the liqueur. Spread the prepared cream filling over and cover with other half of sponge, sprinkle with remaining liqueur. Cover cake with aluminium foil and place in the freezing compartment of the refrigerator for approximately 30 minutes. If desired the cake may be prepared to this stage 2 or 3 days in advance. When ready to serve, remove cake from freezer and take out of spring-form tin. Whip cream and swirl over top of cake. Decorate with hazelnuts and grated chocolate.
Note: If desired, chocolate may be melted and spread into neat, flat rounds on a greased baking tray. Leave until set, lift off with a spatula and arrange on the cream.

Coffee Gâteau
Serves: 6

18 sponge fingers
sherry or brandy
125 g (4 oz) butter
½ cup caster sugar
2 eggs
2 tablespoons very strong black coffee
1 cup cream
grated chocolate and walnuts for decoration

Line a pudding basin or charlotte russe mould with sponge fingers and sprinkle well with sherry or brandy.

Cream the butter and sugar until light and fluffy. Add lightly beaten eggs very slowly, beating continuously. Then add the black coffee very slowly while beating continuously. (If coffee is added too quickly the mixture will curdle). Pour into sponge lined basin and cover with more sponge fingers. Cover with greased aluminium foil. Place a plate on top to lightly weigh it down. Chill for several hours before serving.

To serve, turn coffee gâteau out onto a serving plate, cover with whipped cream and decorate with grated chocolate and walnuts.

Rich Short Crust Pastry

Cooking time: 25-30 minutes for cooked pastry case
Oven temperature: 190-200° C (375-400° F)

2 cups plain flour
pinch salt
125 g (4 oz) butter
1 tablespoon caster sugar
1 egg yolk
2 teaspoons lemon juice
2 tablespoons cold water

Sift flour and salt into a mixing bowl. Add butter and rub lightly into flour with the fingertips. When mixture resembles fine breadcrumbs, stir in sugar and make a well in the centre. Add egg yolk, lemon juice and enough cold water to mix to a slightly crumbly stiff dough. Knead lightly, cover with clear plastic and chill for at least an hour before using.

To make a cooked pastry case: Roll out pastry on a lightly floured board and line a 20 or 23 cm (8 or 9 inch) flan ring or pie plate. Trim edges and prick base with a fork. Line inside with a circle of greased greaseproof paper and fill with dried beans or peas.

Bake in the middle shelf of a moderately hot oven for 15 to 20 minutes. Remove paper and beans. Return to oven for a further 10 minutes or until golden brown.

Chocolate Rum Pie

Serves: 5-6

1 x 410 g (14 oz) can evaporated milk
1 tablespoon gelatine
¾ cup milk
¾ cup sugar
pinch salt
2 eggs, separated
125 g (4 oz) cooking chocolate
2 tablespoons rum
1 teaspoon vanilla essence
1 × 23 cm (9 inch) cooked pastry case (page 134)
1 cup cream
2 tablespoons caster sugar

Pour evaporated milk into ice cube tray, place in freezer and chill until mushy around edges. Soften the gelatine in ¼ cup of milk. Combine sugar, salt, egg yolks and the softened gelatine in top of a double boiler and mix well. Stir over boiling water until the mixture thickens slightly, remove from the heat. Melt half the chocolate and blend in, beat until smooth. Chill until slightly thickened. Whip chilled evaporated milk until thick. Fold whipped milk, rum and vanilla essence into chocolate mixture, pour into cooked pastry case and chill thoroughly.

Whip cream. Beat egg whites until frothy, add caster sugar gradually, continue to beat until soft peaks form. Fold into the whipped cream and spread over the pie. Shave remaining chocolate into curls and sprinkle over top of the whipped cream mixture in a lattice pattern or as desired.

No Bake Strawberry Flan
Serves: 6-8

Crumb crust
2 cups sweet biscuit crumbs
90 g (3 oz) butter, melted
Filling
250 g (8 oz) packaged cream cheese, softened at room
   temperature
3 tablespoons caster sugar
$\frac{2}{3}$ cup thickened cream
2 tablespoons gelatine
4 tablespoons hot water
1 x 425 g (15 oz) can strawberries, drained
whipped cream
pink food colouring
12 fresh whole strawberries

Crumb crust: Combine biscuit crumbs with melted butter. Press onto bottom and sides of greased 23 cm (9 inch) pie plate. Chill.

Filling: Beat softened cream cheese until smooth, then beat in sugar, and fold in cream. Dissolve gelatine in hot water, cool, and add to cream cheese mixture. Fold in drained strawberries. Pour into prepared pie plate and chill until set (1½ to 2 hours). Colour whipped cream delicately with pink food colouring. Decorate top of flan with swirls of whipped cream and whole strawberries.

Citrus Cheesecake
Serves: 6-8

Crumb crust
2 cups sweet biscuit crumbs
90 g (3 oz) butter, melted
2 teaspoons hot water
Filling
1 tablespoon gelatine
¼ cup hot water
500 g (1 lb) packaged cream cheese, softened at room
   temperature
½ cup caster sugar
1 teaspoon vanilla essence
grated rind and juice of 1 lemon
1 x 310 g (11 oz) can mandarin segments
2 egg whites

Crumb crust: Combine biscuit crumbs, melted butter and hot water. Press into a 23 cm (9 inch) spring-form tin.

Filling: Dissolve gelatine in hot water. Beat softened cream cheese until smooth, gradually add sugar, gelatine, vanilla essence and lemon rind. Make lemon juice up to ½ cup liquid with mandarin syrup. Add liquid to cream cheese mixture. Blend well. In a large bowl beat egg whites until just stiff and fold in cream cheese mixture, then drained mandarin segments. Pour into prepared crumb crust. Chill until firm. Decorate with additional mandarin segments and whipped cream if desired.

135

Honey Tart

Cooking time: 50-60 minutes
Oven temperature: 190-200° C (375-400° F)
  reducing to 150-160° C (300-325° F)

2 tablespoons sugar
1 cup plain flour
60 g (2 oz) butter
cold water to mix
Filling
1½ cups ricotta
3 tablespoons honey
3 eggs
1 teaspoon ground cinnamon

Combine sugar and flour and add butter and cut into flour with a knife, then rub ingredients together lightly with fingertips. Add just enough cold water to make a firm dough. Cover and rest pastry for 1 hour. Roll pastry out on a lightly floured board and line a 20 cm (8 inch) pie plate or flan ring.

Prepare filling (see below) and pour into pastry case. Sprinkle top with remaining cinnamon.

Bake tart in a moderately hot oven for 10 to 15 minutes. Reduce temperature to moderately slow and cook for further 40 to 45 minutes until set. Serve cold.

Filling: Press ricotta cheese through a sieve into a bowl, add honey and beat thoroughly on mixer. Add eggs and half the cinnamon, beating well.

Caramel Banana Tart

Serves: 6
Cooking time: 25-30 minutes
Oven temperature: 190-200° C (375-400° F)

Biscuit pastry
90 g (3 oz) butter
2 tablespoons caster sugar
1 egg
1½ cups plain flour
½ teaspoon baking powder
Filling
5 tablespoons plain flour
1 cup brown sugar
2 egg yolks, beaten
2 cups milk
2 tablespoons butter
½ teaspoon vanilla essence
3 bananas
lemon juice
whipped cream for serving

Biscuit pastry: Beat butter and sugar until light, add egg and beat well. Sift flour and baking powder and mix into butter mixture to form a firm dough. Turn onto a floured board and knead lightly. Roll into a circle and line a greased 23 cm (9 inch) pie plate. Crimp edge and prick base and sides with a fork. Bake in a moderately hot oven for 15 to 20 minutes until cooked and lightly browned. Cool.

Filling: Mix flour and sugar in a saucepan, gradually blend in egg yolks and milk. Add butter and cook over moderate heat, stirring constantly, until thickened and bubbling. Remove from heat, stir in vanilla essence and cool a little. Pour half into pie crust, cover with 2 sliced bananas, top with remaining caramel mixture. Leave until cool. Slice remaining banana and sprinkle with lemon juice. Decorate tart with swirls of whipped cream and banana slices.

Honey Fruit Pie

Serves: 6-8
Cooking time: 50-60 minutes
Oven temperature: 200-230° C (400-450° F)
* reducing to 180-190° C (350-375° F)*

2 cups mixed dried fruit
¼ cup honey
grated rind of 1 orange
½ cup orange juice
½ cup water
1 tablespoon arrowroot
1 tablespoon brandy
1 quantity rich short crust pastry (page 134)
beaten egg white to glaze
caster sugar for sprinkling
whipped cream for serving

Place dried fruits, honey, orange rind and juice and half the water in a saucepan and bring slowly to the boil. Simmer gently for 10 minutes. Blend arrowroot with remaining cold water and stir into fruit mixture. Stir constantly until thickened and bubbling. Stir in brandy, remove from heat and leave until cool.

Divide pastry into two portions, one slightly larger than the other. Roll out larger portion and line a greased 20 cm (8 inch) pie plate. Roll out remainder for top.

Fill lined pie plate with cooled fruit mixture, moisten pastry edge with water and place top in position. Press edges to seal, then crimp. Glaze with beaten egg white, sprinkle with caster sugar and prick top with a skewer. Bake in hot oven for 15 minutes, reduce to moderate and cook for further 25 to 30 minutes until pastry is golden. Serve warm or cold with whipped cream.

Strawberry Flan

Serves: 4-6
Cooking time: 25-30 minutes
Oven temperature: 180-190° C (350-375° F)

1 cooked pastry case (page 134)
Filling
¾ cup cream
1 tablespoon caster sugar
1 tablespoon kirsch
1 punnet strawberries
Glaze
3 tablespoons redcurrant jelly
1 teaspoon arrowroot
1 teaspoon lemon juice
2 teaspoons kirsch

Make and cook pastry case as directed, using a 20 cm (8 inch) flan ring. Cool on a wire rack.

Whip cream and flavour with sugar and kirsch. Cover the bottom of the flan with the whipped cream and arrange the strawberries attractively on top. Heat redcurrant jelly, add the arrowroot blended to a smooth paste with a little cold water and boil gently for 2 minutes, stirring all the time. Add the lemon juice and kirsch and glaze the fruit while the mixture is hot.

Baked Cheesecake

Cooking time: 45 minutes
Oven temperature: 180-190° C (350-375° F)

Biscuit crust
250 g (8 oz) plain sweet biscuits
90 g (3 oz) melted butter
1 tablespoon ground almonds (optional)
Filling
250 g (8 oz) cottage cheese
500 g (1 lb) cream cheese, softened at room temperature
¾ cup sugar
3 tablespoons cream
3 eggs
1 teaspoon vanilla essence
¼ teaspoon grated lemon rind
whipped cream and freshly grated nutmeg for serving

Biscuit crust: Crush biscuits and combine with melted butter and ground almonds if used. Spread over base and sides of a greased 20 cm (8 inch) spring-form tin. Press firmly and chill.

Filling: Press cottage cheese through a sieve into a bowl. Add cream cheese, sugar and cream and beat together thoroughly. Add eggs one at a time, then vanilla essence and lemon rind, beating well. Pour mixture into prepared biscuit case and cook in a moderate oven for 45 minutes. Turn off oven heat and leave cheesecake in oven to cool.

Chill for at least 2 hours. Top with whipped cream and nutmeg before serving.

Rhubarb Flan

Cooking time: 35-40 minutes
Oven temperature: 190-200° C (375-400° F)

1 quantity biscuit pastry (page 136)
1 egg white, beaten
2 cups stewed rhubarb with syrup
1 cup stewed apple
½ teaspoon ground ginger
sugar to taste
3 tablespoons arrowroot
3 tablespoons cold water
few drops red food colouring (optional)
icing sugar for sprinkling

Make pastry according to directions in Caramel Banana Tart recipe, roll out and line a 20 cm (8 inch) flan ring or pie plate. Roll out trimmings and cut into strips. Brush base and sides of pastry case with beaten egg white and leave to dry.

Combine rhubarb, apple and ginger in a saucepan, add sugar to taste and heat. Blend arrowroot with cold water and stir into rhubarb mixture, stirring constantly until bubbling. Add red food colouring if desired and cool. Spread into pastry case and arrange strips of pastry in a lattice pattern on top. Press ends of strips into side of case. Brush strips with egg white. Bake in a moderately hot oven for 35 to 40 minutes until golden brown. Dust pastry with icing sugar and serve warm or cold with custard or whipped cream.

Lemon Meringue Pie

Serves: 6
Cooking time: 40-45 minutes
Oven temperature: 150-160° C (300-325° F)

4 tablespoons cornflour
1¼ cups water
2 tablespoons butter
grated rind and juice of 1 large lemon
1 cup caster sugar
2 eggs, separated
1 × 20 cm (8 inch) cooked pastry case (page 134)

Combine cornflour, water, butter, lemon rind and juice and ½ cup caster sugar in a saucepan. Whisk over a moderate heat until boiling, whisk a further 2 to 3 minutes. Cool slightly. Beat in egg yolks and pour into pastry case.

Whisk egg whites until stiff. Add ¼ cup caster sugar and whisk until stiff again. Gently fold in the remaining sugar. Pile meringue over lemon mixture making sure it comes right down to the pastry all round. Bake in a slow oven for about 30 minutes until meringue is golden.

Latticed Apple Pie

Serves: 6
Cooking time: 50-55 minutes
Oven temperature: 200-230° C (400-450° F)
  reducing to 180-190° C (350-375° F)

1 quantity rich short crust pastry (page 134)
4 cooking apples
⅛ teaspoon ground cloves
½ teaspoon cinnamon
½ cup caster sugar
1 tablespoon flour
1 tablespoon melted butter
milk or egg to glaze
caster sugar for sprinkling

Roll pastry thinly and line a 20 cm (8 inch) pie plate. Roll out trimmings and cut into 1 cm (½ inch) strips.

Peel and core apples and slice thinly. Mix with spices, sugar and flour and place in uncooked pastry case. Drizzle butter over top of apples. Place pastry strips over top in a lattice, twisting strips if desired. Press ends of strips into inner edge of crust. Glaze with milk or egg and bake in a hot oven for 15 minutes, reduce to moderate and cook for further 35 to 40 minutes until cooked. Cover pie with a piece of foil if top browns too quickly.

When cooked, sprinkle with caster sugar and serve warm or cold with whipped cream or ice cream.

CAKES & BISCUITS

There is a cake here for every need—little cakes to please little ones, big cakes for cake lovers; biscuits for the barrel and treats to serve with after-dinner coffee; simple butter cakes and rich, hearty fruit cakes.

Though recipes stipulate butter, margarine may be substituted, and a combination of butter and margarine gives a very satisfactory result. Remember, if using the metric 250 ml cup measure, use 60 g (2 oz) eggs; if using the 8 fluid ounce cup measure, use 55 g (1¾ oz) eggs.

CAKES & TORTES

Rippled Coffee Liqueur Cake

Cooking time: 1-1¼ hours
Oven temperature: 180-190° C (350-375° F)

90 g (3 oz) packaged cream cheese, softened
1 cup caster sugar
2 tablespoons coffee flavoured liqueur
2 teaspoons instant coffee powder
125 g (4 oz) butter
½ teaspoon vanilla essence
2 eggs
2 cups self-raising flour
¼ cup milk
whipped cream flavoured with coffee liqueur for serving

Beat softened cream cheese with ¼ cup of the sugar until light, blend in coffee liqueur and instant coffee and beat until smooth. Keep aside.

Cream butter, sugar and vanilla until light and fluffy. Add eggs one at a time, beating well. Fold in sifted flour alternately with the milk.

Grease a 20 cm (8 inch) deep round cake tin and line base with greased greaseproof paper. Pour batter into tin, add cream cheese-coffee liqueur mixture on top and swirl through batter with a knife. Bake cake in a moderate oven for 1 to 1¼ hours until cooked when tested. Turn onto a wire rack to cool. Serve with whipped cream flavoured with coffee liqueur if desired.

Jaffa Cake

Cooking time: 45-50 minutes
Oven temperature: 180-190° C (350-375° F)

125 g (4 oz) butter
¾ cup caster sugar
grated rind of 1 orange
2 eggs
1½ cups self-raising flour
⅓ cup orange juice
2 tablespoons grated chocolate
2 tablespoons chopped, blanched almonds to decorate
Chocolate glacé icing
¾ cup icing sugar
1 tablespoon cocoa
1 teaspoon butter
1 tablespoon boiling water

Beat butter, sugar and orange rind until light and fluffy. Add eggs one at a time, beating well after each addition. Sift flour and fold in alternately with orange juice. Blend in grated chocolate. Turn into a greased and floured baba mould or ring cake tin and bake in a moderate oven for 45 to 50 minutes or until cake shrinks from sides of tin. Turn out onto a wire rack and cool. Pour icing on top and let it dribble down sides. Sprinkle with chopped almonds.

Chocolate glacé icing: Sift icing sugar and cocoa into a heatproof bowl, add butter and pour boiling water onto butter. Blend until combined, place over boiling water and stir for 1 minute until icing melts. Do not overheat as icing will go dull when it sets on cake.

Chocolate Swiss Roll

Serves: 6-8
Cooking time: 12-15 minutes
Oven temperature: 180-190° C (350-375° F)

125 g (4 oz) self-raising flour
2 tablespoons cocoa
3 eggs
125 g (4 oz) caster sugar
2 tablespoons hot water
additional caster sugar
sifted icing sugar
chocolate curls
Filling
250 g (8 oz) packaged cream cheese, softened at room
    temperature
½ cup cream
½ cup sifted icing sugar
1 teaspoon vanilla essence

Sift flour and cocoa together. Separate eggs, beat egg whites until stiff and gradually add the caster sugar, beating until mixture is thick and sugar completely dissolved. Beat in egg yolks and add hot water. Fold in sifted flour and cocoa. Pour mixture into a buttered Swiss Roll tin lined with greased greaseproof paper. Bake in a moderate oven 12 to 15 minutes.

Turn immediately on to a clean tea towel which has been well sprinkled with caster sugar. Quickly peel off paper and trim edges with a sharp knife. Roll in towel and cool on a wire rack for 1 hour at least.

Unroll cake, spread with filling and re-roll carefully. Dust cake with icing sugar and decorate with chocolate curls.

Filling: Beat softened cream cheese until smooth, add cream, icing sugar and vanilla essence.

Quick Mix Chocolate Cake

Cooking time: 50-55 minutes
Oven temperature: 180-190° C (350-375° F)

2 eggs
¾ cup caster sugar
½ teaspoon vanilla essence
1 cup self-raising flour
2 tablespoons cocoa
3 tablespoons melted butter
2 tablespoons milk
Butter frosting
60 g (2 oz) butter
1 cup icing sugar
2 tablespoons full cream powdered milk
1 teaspoon lemon juice
water

Beat eggs well, add sugar and beat for 5 minutes. Stir in vanilla essence. Sift flour with cocoa and fold into beaten eggs with melted butter and milk. Blend well and turn into a greased and floured 23 x 12 cm (9 x 5 inch) loaf tin. Bake in a moderate oven for 50 to 55 minutes or until cooked when tested. Turn out onto a wire rack and cool. Spread top with butter frosting, swirling it on with the back of a spoon.

Butter frosting: Cream butter until light. Sift icing sugar with powdered milk and beat into butter with lemon juice, adding enough cold water to give a spreading consistency.
Note: As an added touch, crush 1 tablespoon raw sugar with a rolling pin and sprinkle on top of frosting.

141

Butter Cake

Cooking time: 1 hour
Oven temperature: 180-190° C (350-375° F)

250 g (8 oz) butter
1 cup caster sugar
1 teaspoon vanilla essence
4 eggs, beaten
3 cups self-raising flour
¾ cup milk

Line and butter a deep 20 cm (8 inch) cake tin and set oven temperature at moderate. Cream butter, sugar and vanilla essence until light, white and fluffy. Add beaten eggs gradually, beating well after each addition. Sift the flour and fold in gently alternately with the milk. Place mixture into the prepared cake tin, smooth top and bake in a moderate oven for 1 hour or until cooked. The cake should shrink from the sides of the tin when cooked. Cool on a wire rack. Decorate as desired.

Orange cake: Add the grated rind and juice of 1 orange with sufficient milk to make up to ¾ cup liquid. Omit vanilla essence.

Lemon cake: Replace vanilla essence with grated rind of 1 lemon.

Cherry cake: Add 125 g (4 oz) chopped glacé cherries when folding in the flour.

Cherry Yoghurt Cake

Cooking time: 1 hour
Oven temperature: 180-190° C (350-375° F)

125 g (4 oz) butter
1 cup caster sugar
3 eggs, separated
1¾ cups self-raising flour
¼ teaspoon bicarbonate of soda
pinch of salt
¾ cup cherry flavoured yoghurt
icing sugar for sprinkling
glacé cherries to decorate

Beat butter and sugar until light and fluffy. Add egg yolks and beat well. Sift dry ingredients and fold in alternately with yoghurt. Beat egg whites until stiff and fold into batter using a metal spoon to avoid overmixing. Turn into a greased and floured baba mould or 20 cm (8 inch) deep cake tin and bake in a moderate oven for 1 hour until cake shrinks from sides of tin. Turn out onto a wire rack and cool. Sprinkle with sifted icing sugar and decorate with glacé cherries.
Note: Use any flavoured yoghurt instead of the cherry yoghurt to vary the flavour. If plain yoghurt is preferred, add the grated rind of 1 lemon when creaming the butter and sugar.

Coffee Layer Cake

Cooking time: 25-30 minutes
Oven temperature: 180-190° C (350-375° F)

125 g (4 oz) butter
½ cup caster sugar
2 eggs, separated
1 tablespoon instant coffee powder
1½ cups self-raising flour
¼ cup milk
Coffee frosting
60 g (2 oz) butter
2½ cups icing sugar
3 teaspoons instant coffee powder
milk to mix

Grease two 18 cm (7 inch) layer cake tins and line bases with greased greaseproof paper. Set oven temperature at moderate. Cream butter and sugar until light and fluffy. Add egg yolks beating well. Blend in instant coffee powder, beat until smooth. Sift flour, add alternately to creamed mixture with the milk. Beat egg whites until stiff and fold gently into batter. Spread into prepared tins. Bake in a moderate oven for 25 to 30 minutes. Allow to stand 5 minutes before turning onto a wire rack to cool.

Coffee frosting: Beat butter until creamy. Sift icing sugar with coffee powder and beat in gradually until light and fluffy, adding a little milk to give a spreading consistency. Swirl onto cake with a small spatula.

Rich Boiled Fruit Cake

Cooking time: 3½-4 hours
Oven temperature: 150-160° C (300-325° F)

8 cups mixed dried fruit
2 tablespoons golden syrup
3 tablespoons rum, sherry or brandy
¾ cup water
250 g (8 oz) butter
1⅓ cups brown sugar
5 eggs
2½ cups plain flour
½ cup self-raising flour
¼ teaspoon salt
2 teaspoons mixed spice
¼ teaspoon ground cinnamon
¼ teaspoon ground nutmeg

Place the mixed fruit, golden syrup, rum, sherry or brandy and the water in a saucepan. Bring to the boil, stirring occasionally and simmer for 2 minutes. Pour into a bowl, cover and allow to stand overnight. Set oven temperature at slow. Cream butter and brown sugar together until fluffy. Add eggs one at a time, beating well after each addition. Sift dry ingredients together, then sift half over the boiled fruit mixture. Mix lightly and stir into the creamed mixture. Fold remainder of sifted dry ingredients into mixture. Place in a 23 cm (9 inch) round cake tin, previously lined with three layers of brown paper and 1 layer of greaseproof paper. Bake in a slow oven for 3½ to 4 hours. Remove cake from tin, leaving paper on and leave on a wire rack until cool.

Mocha Torte

Cooking time: 30-35 minutes
Oven temperature: 180-190° C (350-375° F)

1 quantity Chocolate Layer Cake batter (page 146)
¼ cup strong black coffee
1 cup chopped toasted almonds
Coffee cream filling
250 g (8 oz) packaged cream cheese
½ cup cream
½ cup sifted icing sugar
1 teaspoon coffee-flavoured liqueur
Coffee glacé icing
2 cups icing sugar
3 teaspoons instant coffee powder
1 tablespoon butter
3 tablespoons hot water

Make cake batter and pour into 2 greased and floured 23 cm (9 inch) layer cake tins. Bake in a moderate oven for 30 to 35 minutes until cooked. Cool on a wire rack. Split each cake in two and place one layer on a plate. Sprinkle with a little of the coffee and spread with a quarter of the filling. Repeat with two more layers. Place top layer in position and leave plain. Keep remaining filling for decoration. Pour glacé icing over top and sides of cake, smoothing it with a knife dipped in hot water. Press chopped almonds around sides and pipe remaining filling on top.

Coffee cream filling: Beat softened cream cheese until smooth, add cream, icing sugar and coffee liqueur and beat until light.

Coffee glacé icing: Sift icing sugar and instant coffee into a heatproof bowl, add butter and pour hot water onto butter. Stir until icing has a soft dropping consistency and place over hot water for 1 minute, stirring constantly, until melted.

Passionfruit Sponge

Cooking time: 25 minutes
Oven temperature: 180-190° C (350-375° F)

4 eggs
¾ cup caster sugar
⅔ cup cornflour
¼ cup plain flour
1 teaspoon baking powder
Filling and icing
1 cup cream
2 tablespoons caster sugar
1 teaspoon melted butter
1 cup icing sugar
2 passionfruit

Set oven temperature at moderate. Grease two 20 cm (8 inch) sandwich tins and flour the bases lightly. Separate the eggs and whisk the egg whites until stiff. Add sugar gradually, beating continuously. Add the egg yolks one at a time and beat again. Sift together the cornflour, flour and baking powder three times and gently fold into the mixture with a metal spoon. Divide the mixture evenly between the two tins. Cook in a moderate oven for 20 to 25 minutes. Stand in tins for 2 or 3 minutes, loosen sides from tins with a knife, and turn onto a wire rack. Place another rack lightly on top and invert so that cakes cool right side up.

To fill and ice: Whip cream until soft peaks form, fold in caster sugar. Place one of the sponges on a serving plate. Spread thickly with whipped cream. Place the second sponge on top. Make the icing by adding the melted butter to the sifted icing sugar. Add the juice and pips of the passionfruit until the mixture is of a spreading consistency. Spread over top of sponge.

Marble Cake

Cooking time: 1 hour
Oven temperature: 180-190° C (350-375° F)

125 g (4 oz) butter
1 cup caster sugar
½ teaspoon vanilla essence
2 eggs
1¾ cups self-raising flour
pinch of salt
½ cup milk
3 teaspoons cocoa
few drops red food colouring
Butter Frosting (page 141)

Beat butter, sugar and vanilla essence until light and fluffy. Add one egg at a time, beating well after each addition. Sift flour with salt and fold in alternately with milk. Divide batter into three portions. Leave one plain. Add cocoa mixed to a paste with a little cold milk to second portion. Colour third portion pink with a little red food colouring. Grease an 18 cm (7 inch) square cake tin and line with greased greaseproof paper. Place batters into tin in alternate spoonfuls and swirl lightly with a skewer. Bake in a moderate oven for 1 hour until cooked when tested. Turn onto a wire rack and cool. Make Butter Frosting according to directions in Quick Mix Chocolate Cake recipe and swirl onto cooled cake.

Brandied Yule Cake

Cooking time: 2-2½ hours
Oven temperature: 150-160° C (300-325° F)

1½ cups shelled Brazil nuts
1 cup pecan or walnut halves
½ cup blanched almonds
1½ cups stoned dates
½ cup seeded raisins
½ cup coarsely chopped glacé fruits (apricots, pineapple, figs)
¾ cup red and green glacé cherries
1 cup plain flour
¼ teaspoon salt
½ teaspoon baking powder
½ cup caster sugar
3 eggs
1 tablespoon brandy

All nuts and fruits should be left whole, except for the larger glacé fruits which should be cut into chunky pieces. Grease a 25 x 15 cm (10 x 6 inch) loaf tin and line base and sides with greaseproof paper. Brush paper lining well with melted butter.

Place nuts and fruit in a mixing bowl. Sift dry ingredients on top of fruit, add sugar and stir. Beat eggs and stir into fruit and nut mixture with brandy until blended. Spoon into lined tin. Bake in a slow oven for 2 to 2½ hours until golden brown. Invert onto rack, peel off paper and leave until cool. Soak a piece of sterilised, dry muslin or cheesecloth in brandy and wrap cake in this. Place in a plastic bag and store in a sealed container for 3 weeks. Soak cloth in brandy once a week. Slice thinly to serve.
Note: Cake may be glazed with warmed honey before serving.

Orange Gâteau

Cooking time: 35-40 minutes
Oven temperature: 180-190° C (350-375° F)

185 g (6 oz) butter
¾ cup caster sugar
grated rind of 1 orange
3 eggs
2 cups self-raising flour
½ cup orange juice
1 cup cream, whipped and sweetened
1 cup flaked almonds, toasted
1 small orange, thinly sliced
Orange filling
grated rind and juice of 1 orange
water
1½ tablespoons cornflour
3 tablespoons sugar
1 tablespoon butter

Cream butter, sugar and orange rind until light and fluffy. Add eggs one at a time, beating well. Sift flour and fold in alternately with orange juice. Divide mixture equally into 2 greased and floured 20 cm (8 inch) layer cake tins. Bake in a moderate oven for 35 to 40 minutes until cooked. Turn out onto a wire rack to cool. Join layers with orange filling (see below). Spread three-quarters of the whipped cream on top and sides. Decorate sides with flaked almonds. Pipe swirls of remaining cream on top, and decorate with halved or quartered orange slices just before serving.

Orange filling: Measure orange juice and make up to ½ cup with water. Blend with remaining ingredients in a saucepan, stir over heat until thickened and bubbling. Cool and fill cake.

Chocolate Layer Cake

Cooking time: 30-35 minutes
Oven temperature: 180-190° C (350-375° F)

2 tablespoons cocoa
2 tablespoons hot water
185 g (6 oz) butter
1 cup brown sugar
1 teaspoon vanilla essence
3 eggs
2 cups self-raising flour
whipped, sweetened cream to fill
blanched almonds to decorate
Chocolate icing
1 cup icing sugar
1½ tablespoons cocoa
1 teaspoon butter
½ teaspoon vanilla essence
1 tablespoon boiling water

Blend cocoa with hot water and leave to cool. Cream butter, sugar and vanilla essence until fluffy. Add eggs one at a time, beating well after each addition. Fold in sifted flour alternately with cocoa mixture. Spread into 2 greased and floured 20 cm (8 inch) layer cake tins. Bake in a moderate oven for 30 to 35 minutes. Cool on a wire rack. Join layers together with whipped, sweetened cream. Spread chocolate icing on top, swirling it with the point of a knife. Decorate with blanched almonds.

Chocolate icing: Sift icing sugar and cocoa into a bowl, add butter and pour boiling water onto butter. Add vanilla essence and stir until combined, adding a little more water if necessary to give a spreading consistency.

Gala Fruit Ring

Cooking time: 1 hour
Oven temperature: 180-190° C (350-375° F)

125 g (4 oz) butter
¾ cup caster sugar
grated rind of 1 lemon
2 eggs
1½ cups self-raising flour
pinch salt
¼ cup milk
½ cup mixed dried fruit
Topping
1 slice glacé pineapple, chopped
2 tablespoons glacé cherries, halved
2 tablespoons slivered almonds
2 tablespoons raisins, halved

Beat butter, sugar and lemon rind until light and fluffy. Add eggs one at a time, beating well after each addition. Sift dry ingredients and fold into mixture alternately with milk. Blend in mixed fruit and turn into a greased and floured 20 cm (8 inch) ring cake tin. Combine topping ingredients and sprinkle lightly over batter. Bake in a moderate oven for 1 hour or until cooked. Turn onto a paper covered wire rack and invert onto another rack to cool.
Note: Fruit topping may be glazed with a little heated honey before serving.

Linzertorte

Serves: 6-8
Cooking time: 40 minutes
Oven temperature: 190-200° C (375-400° F)

1 cup plain flour
¼ cup caster sugar
½ teaspoon baking powder
½ teaspoon ground cinnamon
pinch of ground cloves
1 cup ground almonds
grated rind of 1 lemon
125 g (4 oz) butter
milk
1½ cups jam, raspberry, currant or strawberry
egg for glazing
fresh raspberries to decorate (optional)
whipped cream

Sift flour, sugar, baking powder and spices into a mixing bowl. Mix in almonds and lemon rind. Rub in butter with fingertips. Add milk if required to make a dry dough. Knead only until combined. Wrap in plastic film and chill in refrigerator for 30 minutes. Roll out two-thirds of the pastry and press onto base of 20 cm (8 inch) greased spring-form tin. Spread jam on top. Roll out remaining pastry, cut into 1 cm (½ inch) strips and arrange crosswise on top, using the last strip as an edging around the side of the cake. Press down lightly. Chill again. Brush pastry only with beaten egg and bake in a moderately hot oven for 35 to 40 minutes. Allow to cool in tin. Decorate with fresh raspberries if available and serve with whipped cream.

Light Fruit Cake

Cooking time: 3-3½ hours
Oven temperature: 150-160° C (300-325° F)

250 g (8 oz) butter
½ scant cup caster sugar
½ cup brown sugar
grated rind of ½ lemon
5 eggs, beaten
2½ cups plain flour, sifted
2 teaspoons baking powder
¾ cup currants
2 cups sultanas
1 cup chopped, dried apricots
1 tablespoon sherry or brandy
2 tablespoons slivered almonds

Line a 20 cm (8 inch) cake tin with 1 layer of brown and 1 layer of greaseproof paper. Beat the butter with the sugars and the lemon rind until very creamy. Add the well beaten eggs gradually, beating after each addition. Stir in the sifted flour and baking powder alternately with the prepared fruits and the sherry or brandy, mix well. Spoon carefully into the prepared tin to avoid air-holes. Sprinkle top with almonds. Bake in a slow oven for 3 to 3½ hours. Cool for 15 minutes before turning out of the tin.
Note: For a more economical light fruit cake use 3 eggs and ½ cup milk.

Cooking tip: To avoid air holes in fruit cakes, lift just-filled cake tin up to waist level and let it drop straight onto the bench.

Christmas Cake

Cooking time: 3½-4 hours
Oven temperature: 150-160° C (300-325° F)

2 cups raisins, chopped
1½ cups sultanas
1 cup currants
⅔ cup chopped glacé cherries
½ cup chopped mixed peel
½ cup rum or brandy
2½ cups plain flour
2 teaspoons baking powder
2 teaspoons mixed spice
½ teaspoon ground nutmeg
½ teaspoon bicarbonate of soda
250 g (8 oz) butter
1 cup brown sugar
2 tablespoons marmalade or plum jam
4 eggs
½ cup chopped blanched almonds

Place fruit in a bowl, sprinkle with rum or brandy, cover and leave for 1 or 2 days. Blend dry ingredients and sift twice. Cream butter and sugar until light, beat in marmalade or jam. Add eggs, one at a time, beating well. Fold in the dry ingredients alternately with the soaked fruit. Blend in almonds. Spoon mixture evenly into a 20 cm (8 inch) round or square deep cake tin, previously lined with two layers of brown paper and one of greaseproof paper. Bake in a slow oven for 3½ to 4 hours. Cool slowly in tin by wrapping in a thick cloth. Store for several weeks for best flavour. Decorate if desired with Seven Minute Frosting.

Seven minute frosting: Place ¾ cup sugar, 1 teaspoon liquid glucose (or ½ teaspoon cream of tartar), 1 egg white and 2 tablespoons water in a heatproof bowl over gently boiling water. Beat with a rotary beater for 7 minutes until mixture is thick enough to hold its shape. Cool slightly, stir in ¼ teaspoon vanilla essence and spread roughly over cake.

Spiced Carrot Cake

Cooking time: 40-45 minutes
Oven temperature: 180-190° C (350-375° F)

125 g (4 oz) butter
½ cup caster sugar
1 tablespoon honey
2 eggs
½ cup chopped walnuts
1 cup plain flour
1 teaspoon baking powder
1 teaspoon mixed spice
½ teaspoon bicarbonate of soda
1 cup finely grated carrot
walnut halves to decorate
Cream cheese frosting
90 g (3 oz) packaged cream cheese
½ teaspoon vanilla essence
1 cup icing sugar, sifted
milk to mix

Cream butter, sugar and honey until light and fluffy, add eggs one at a time, beating well after each addition. Fold in walnuts. Sift dry ingredients twice and fold into mixture with grated carrot. Grease a 20 x 10 cm (8 x 4 inch) loaf tin and line base with greased greaseproof paper. Spread mixture in tin and bake in a moderate oven for 40 to 45 minutes until cooked. Cool on a wire rack. Spread top with cream cheese frosting and decorate with walnut halves.

Cream cheese frosting: Soften cream cheese and beat with vanilla essence until creamy. Add icing sugar gradually, beating well. Add a little milk if necessary to give a spreading consistency.

Simnel Cake

Cooking time: 2½-3 hours
Oven temperature: 160-170° C (325-350° F)
reducing to 150-160° C (300-325° F)

2 cups plain flour
pinch of salt
⅓ cup ground rice
1 teaspoon baking powder
1 teaspoon mixed spice
250 g (8 oz) butter
1 cup caster sugar
5 eggs
1½ cups currants
1½ cups sultanas
⅔ cup chopped mixed peel
milk to mix
375 g (12 oz) almond paste or marzipan
apricot jam

Line and grease an 18 × 8 cm (7 × 3 inch) round cake tin. Sift the flour, salt, ground rice, baking powder and spice together. Cream the butter and sugar until light, then gradually beat in eggs. Fold in the flour mixture alternately with the fruit. Add sufficient milk to make a dropping consistency. Spoon half the mixture into prepared cake tin and smooth top. Halve almond paste. Roll out one portion to an 18 cm (7 inch) circle and lay on top of cake mixture. Cover with remaining mixture and smooth top. Bake in a moderately slow oven for 1 hour, reduce to slow and continue cooking for 1½ to 2 hours or until the cake is cooked when tested. Cool on a wire rack. Sieve the jam, warm it and brush top of cake. Roll out remaining almond paste and place on top. Make a criss cross design on the paste using the back of a knife. Brush with a little beaten egg. Grill slowly until golden brown. Decorate with confectionery eggs and toasted, shredded coconut.

SMALL CAKES & BISCUITS

Cornflake Crunches
Yield: 60
Cooking time: 10-12 minutes
Oven temperature: 180-190° C (350-375° F)

1 cup butter
¾ cup caster sugar
1 egg
2½ cups plain flour
2 teaspoons baking powder
2 cups cornflakes, lightly crushed
2 tablespoons glacé cherries

Cream butter and sugar until light and fluffy. Add the egg and beat well. Sift the flour and baking powder and fold into the mixture. Form mixture into small balls and roll in cornflakes. Place on a greased baking tray and flatten with a fork. Cut cherries into small pieces and place a piece on top of each biscuit. Bake in a moderate oven for 10 to 12 minutes. Cool on a wire rack.

Custard Creams
Yield: 30
Cooking time: 15 minutes
Oven temperature: 180-190° C (350-375° F)

250 g (8 oz) butter
1 cup caster sugar
1 egg
1 teaspoon vanilla essence
2¼ cups plain flour
½ cup custard powder
1½ teaspoons baking powder
Butter icing
1 cup icing sugar, sifted
2 tablespoons butter, softened
½ teaspoon vanilla essence
2 tablespoons condensed milk

Cream the butter and sugar until light and fluffy. Gradually beat in the egg and vanilla essence. Sift dry ingredients and fold into mixture. Break off pieces and roll into small balls. Place on ungreased baking trays and press down with a fork. Bake in a moderate oven for 15 minutes. Cool on a wire rack. When cool, join pairs together with butter icing.

Butter icing: Gradually beat half the icing sugar into the softened butter, add vanilla essence. Beat in condensed milk and add remaining icing sugar.

Meringues

Yield: 12-14
Cooking time: 1-2 hours
Oven temperature: 100° C (200° F)

4 egg whites
1 cup caster sugar
¼ teaspoon cream of tartar
few drops vanilla essence
½ pint whipped cream
½ cup crushed strawberries, raspberries or loganberries

Whisk egg whites until stiff. Add the sugar gradually, a tablespoon at a time, beating continuously. Fold in the cream of tartar and finally vanilla essence. Place a smooth piping tube into a forcing bag and pipe in small circles onto greased greaseproof paper placed on greased baking trays. Alternatively, place meringue mixture in teaspoons on the prepared trays. Place in a cool oven to dry out for 1 to 2 hours. When cool, join together with whipped cream mixed with crushed fruit.

Polka Dot Biscuits

Yield: 48
Cooking time: 10 minutes
Oven temperature: 180-190° C (350-375° F)

¾ cup butter
½ cup brown sugar
1 egg
1 teaspoon vanilla essence
1 cup plain flour
2 teaspoons baking powder
½ cup chopped cooking chocolate

Cream the butter and sugar together until light and fluffy, add the egg and vanilla essence and beat well. Sift the flour and baking powder and gently fold into the mixture. To one-third of the dough, add the chocolate and mix well. Form into two 5 x 20 cm (2 x 8 inch) rolls. Divide the plain mixture into two and roll each into 10 x 20 cm (4 x 8 inch) rectangles. Place a roll of chocolate dough in the centre of each and wrap the plain dough around firmly. Wrap in aluminium foil and place in the freezing compartment of the refrigerator. Chill for at least 3 hours. Remove from freezer, cut into 5 mm (¼ inch) slices and bake on a greased baking tray in a moderate oven for 10 minutes. Cool on a wire rack.

Coconut Tarts

Yield: 30
Cooking time: 15 minutes
Oven temperature: 200-230° C (400-450° F)

Biscuit pastry
125 g (4 oz) butter
4 tablespoons caster sugar
½ teaspoon vanilla essence
1 egg
2 cups plain flour
1 teaspoon baking powder
raspberry jam
Coconut filling
1 egg
½ cup sugar
1 cup coconut

Beat butter, sugar and vanilla essence until light. Add egg and beat well. Sift flour and baking powder and mix into butter mixture. Knead lightly on a floured board, roll out to 5 mm (¼ inch) thickness and cut into rounds to fit small tart tins. Place a scant half teaspoon of jam in the base of each tart, top with a generous teaspoon of coconut filling, spreading it over the jam. Bake in a hot oven for 15 minutes. Remove from tart tins and cool on a wire rack.

Coconut filling: Beat egg lightly and mix in sugar and coconut until blended.

Apricot Fingers

Yield: 20
Cooking time: 30 minutes
Oven temperature: 200-230° C (400-450° F)
  reducing to 180-190° C (350-375° F)

1¼ cups dried apricots
6 tablespoons caster sugar
125 g (4 oz) butter
2 cups plain flour, sifted
2 teaspoons baking powder
1 egg, beaten
1 teaspoon ground cinnamon
milk
lemon icing (see below)

Soak apricots in 1 cup hot water for 1 hour. Cook apricots with 3 tablespoons sugar until soft. Purée and cool. Rub butter into sifted flour and baking powder. Add 2 tablespoons sugar and mix to a firm dough with the egg, chill. Divide dough in half. Roll out and line a 28 x 18 cm (11 x 7 inch) greased slab cake tin with half the dough. Spread with apricot purée, sprinkle with remaining sugar and cinnamon. Cover with remaining rolled pastry, brush with milk. Bake in a hot oven for 10 minutes, lower heat to moderate and cook for a further 20 minutes. When cold, ice with lemon icing. Cut into fingers.

Lemon icing: Sift 1 cup icing sugar into a bowl, add 1 tablespoon melted butter and 2 teaspoons lemon juice. Mix to a spreading consistency with boiling water. Colour with yellow food colouring.

Butterfly Cakes

Yield: 36
Cooking time: 15 minutes
Oven temperature: 190-200° C (375-400° F)

185 g (6 oz) butter
¾ cup caster sugar
½ teaspoon vanilla essence
3 eggs
2 cups self-raising flour
½ cup milk
jam
whipped cream
extra icing sugar

Set oven temperature at hot. Butter 36 patty cake tins or line tins with paper patty cases. Cream butter, sugar and vanilla essence until light, white and fluffy. Add beaten eggs gradually, beating well after each addition. Gently stir in sifted flour and milk. Place a heaped teaspoon of the mixture into each of the patty cake tins. Reduce oven temperature to moderately hot and bake for approximately 15 minutes until tops have risen well and are evenly brown.

Cool on a wire rack. When cakes are cool cut a circle from the top of each using a small, sharp knife. Cut the circles in half. Place a small quantity of apricot or raspberry jam onto each cake. Cover the jam with 1 teaspoon of whipped cream. Replace the half circles to form butterfly wings on top of the cakes. Sprinkle the butterfly cakes lightly with sifted icing sugar.

Golden Butter Drops

Yield: 36
Cooking time: 10-12 minutes
Oven temperature: 180-190° C (350-375° F)

125 g (4 oz) butter
½ cup sugar
1 egg
1 teaspoon grated orange rind
1 teaspoon grated lemon rind
1¼ cups self-raising flour
blanched almonds or walnut pieces

Melt butter in a large saucepan and heat until it becomes light brown in colour. Cool, add the sugar and beat well. Add egg, orange and lemon rind, and beat again. Add sifted flour and mix in well. Drop in very small teaspoonfuls on to a greased baking tray, allowing room for spreading. Place half a blanched almond or a piece of walnut on top of each biscuit and bake in a moderate oven for 10 to 12 minutes. Lift off with a spatula and cool on a wire rack.

Cream Puffs

Yield: 20
Cooking time: 30-35 minutes
Oven temperature: 200-230° C (400-450° F)
  reducing to 180-190° C (350-375° F)

Choux pastry
1 cup plain flour
1 cup water
125 g (4 oz) butter
2 teaspoons sugar
4 eggs, lightly beaten
Filling
whipped sweetened cream flavoured with vanilla essence
icing sugar

Choux Pastry: Sift flour onto a square of paper. Place water, butter and sugar into a saucepan and bring to the boil. Quickly pour flour into boiling liquid, stirring rapidly with a wooden spoon. Stir over gentle heat until mixture leaves sides of pan. Cool for 2 minutes. Gradually add eggs to mixture and beat until smooth and shiny.

To finish: Spoon or pipe smooth high mounds well apart on a greased baking tray. Bake in a hot oven for 20 minutes, reduce to moderate and cook for further 10 to 15 minutes until crisp. Cool puffs on wire rack. Cut open and remove any soft dough. Fill with whipped cream and dust with icing sugar.

Chocolate éclairs: Using a pastry bag fitted with a 1 cm (½ inch) tube, pipe choux pastry onto greased baking tray in 8 cm (3 inch) lengths. Bake in hot oven for 15 minutes, reduce to moderate and cook for further 10 minutes. Cool, split and fill with whipped cream. Spread tops with melted chocolate. Makes 30.

Lamingtons

Yield: 28
Cooking time: 30-35 minutes
Oven temperature: 180-190° C (350-375° F)

½ quantity Butter Cake mixture (page 142)
Icing
3-4 tablespoons boiling water
1 tablespoon butter
2 tablespoons cocoa
2 cups icing sugar
2 cups desiccated coconut

Make the basic Butter Cake mixture using half quantities of ingredients given. Place in a greased, greaseproof paper-lined 28 x 18 cm (11 x 7 inch) lamington tin and bake in a moderate oven for 30 to 35 minutes. Cool on a wire rack. Make the butter cake at least two days before needed.

To make lamingtons: Cut the cake into 4 cm (1½ inch) squares. Make the icing by pouring the boiling water over the butter, add cocoa and mix, add sifted icing sugar and beat well. Stand the bowl of icing over a bowl of hot water. Using two forks, dip each piece of cake into the chocolate icing then roll in coconut. Place on a wire rack to set.

Ambrosia Cheese Squares

Yield: 28
Cooking time: 50-55 minutes
Oven temperature: 200-230° C (400-450° F)
* reducing to 160-170° C (325-350° F)*

90 g (3 oz) butter
½ cup sugar
½ teaspoon grated orange rind
1 egg yolk
1 cup plain flour
½ cup desiccated coconut
Ambrosia cheese topping
1 cup cottage cheese
125 g (4 oz) packaged cream cheese
½ cup caster sugar
1 teaspoon grated orange rind
2 eggs, separated
3 tablespoons orange juice
few drops orange food colouring
1 egg white
½ cup desiccated coconut

Cream butter, sugar and orange rind until light. Add egg yolk and beat well. Sift flour and add with coconut. Mix to a firm dough and press in the base of a greased 28 × 18 cm (11 x 7 inch) slab cake tin. Bake in a hot oven for 10 minutes and remove. Reduce oven temperature. Pour topping over partly cooked base and cook, one shelf above centre, in a moderately slow oven for 40 to 45 minutes until topping is set. Turn off oven heat and leave in oven for 30 minutes. Remove and cool thoroughly. Cut into squares, and top each with a swirl of whipped cream.

Ambrosia cheese topping: Sieve cottage cheese into a mixing bowl, add softened cream cheese, sugar and orange rind and beat until light. Beat in egg yolks, orange juice and food colouring. Beat egg whites until stiff and fold into cheese mixture with coconut.

Walnut Meringue Squares

Yield: 30
Cooking time: 35-40 minutes
Oven temperature: 190-200° C (375-400° F)

125 g (4 oz) butter
¾ cup firmly packed brown sugar
1 teaspoon vanilla essence
2 egg yolks
1½ cups plain flour
1 teaspoon baking powder
1-2 tablespoons milk
Meringue topping
2 egg whites
pinch salt
¾ cup firmly packed brown sugar
½ teaspoon vanilla essence
½ cup chopped walnuts

Beat butter, sugar and vanilla essence until light, add egg yolks and beat well. Sift dry ingredients and mix into creamed mixture with milk. Spread in a greased 30 x 25 cm (12 x 10 inch) Swiss Roll tin. Bake in a moderately hot oven for 10 minutes. Spread with meringue topping (see below) and return to oven to cook for further 25 to 30 minutes. Cool in tin and cut into 5 cm (2 inch) squares when cold. Lift out with a spatula.

Meringue topping: Beat egg whites with salt until stiff and gradually add brown sugar, beating well until stiff, glossy peaks form. Fold in vanilla essence and walnuts.

Strawberry Cream Tartlets

Yield: 12
Cooking time: 8-10 minutes
Oven temperature: 180-190° C (350-375° F)

½ quantity biscuit pastry (page 152)
185 g (6 oz) packaged cream cheese
3 tablespoons caster sugar
1 teaspoon kirsch
1 punnet strawberries, cleaned and hulled
½ cup redcurrant jelly

Make pastry, using 1 egg yolk in place of whole egg. Roll out thinly and cut into rounds to line 12 tartlet tins. Press well into tins and prick with a fork. Bake in a moderate oven for 8 to 10 minutes until cooked. Turn onto a wire rack and cool.

Beat cream cheese and sugar until creamy, blend in kirsch. Spread a heaped teaspoon of cream filling into tartlet cases and top with whole or halved strawberries, depending on size. Heat redcurrant jelly until melted and brush over strawberries to glaze. Leave until set before serving.

Chocolate Rum Balls

Yield: 18

½ cup mixed dried fruit
1 tablespoon caster sugar
¼ cup ground almonds
1 cup stale cake crumbs, firmly packed
3 teaspoons cocoa, sifted
2 tablespoons butter, softened
2-3 teaspoons rum
1 egg white, lightly beaten
desiccated coconut to coat
glacé cherries to decorate (optional)

Chop mixed fruit as finely as possible. Place in a bowl and mix in sugar, ground almonds, cake crumbs and sifted cocoa. Bind with softened butter and rum. Roll heaped teaspoons of the mixture into balls. Brush with lightly beaten egg white and roll in coconut to coat. Lightly press a piece of glacé cherry into centre of each ball if desired. Chill for 1 hour to firm them. Serve with after-dinner coffee.

Chocolate Walnut Creams

Yield: 30
Cooking time: 20-25 minutes
Oven temperature: 180-190° C (350-375° F)

125 g (4 oz) butter
¾ cup caster sugar
½ teaspoon vanilla essence
1½ cups plain flour
1 tablespoon cocoa
1 teaspoon baking powder
pinch of salt
½ cup chopped walnuts
¼ cup milk
Chocolate cream icing
1 cup icing sugar
2 teaspoons cocoa
1 tablespoon softened butter
1-2 tablespoons condensed milk

Cream butter, sugar and vanilla essence until light and fluffy. Sift dry ingredients and blend in with walnuts and milk. Place generous teaspoonfuls in rough mounds on greased baking trays and bake in a moderate oven for 20 to 25 minutes until cooked. Cool on a wire rack and sandwich biscuits together with the icing.

Chocolate cream icing: Sift icing sugar and cocoa into a mixing bowl. Add softened butter and blend to a spreading consistency with condensed milk.

Macaroons

Yield: 50
Cooking time: 12-15 minutes
Oven temperature: 150-160° C (300-325° F)

2 egg whites
1 cup ground almonds
1 cup caster sugar
2 tablespoons ground rice
1 teaspoon almond essence
4 tablespoons blanched almonds, split
extra egg white

Grease and cover three baking trays with rice paper. Whisk the egg whites until fairly stiff, stir in the ground almonds, caster sugar, ground rice and almond essence. Using a large plain pipe, pipe mixture on to the prepared baking trays, leaving space between each biscuit to allow them to spread. Place a split almond on each biscuit and brush with egg white. Bake in a slow oven for 12 to 15 minutes until pale golden. Cool on a wire rack.

Peanut Butter Cookies

Yield: 60
Cooking time: 12-15 minutes
Oven temperature: 190-200° C (375-400° F)

125 g (4 oz) butter
½ cup caster sugar
½ cup peanut butter
1 egg
1½ cups plain flour
½ teaspoon baking powder
peanut halves to decorate
milk to glaze

Cream butter, sugar and peanut butter in a mixing bowl. Add beaten egg and mix well. Sift flour and baking powder and mix into butter mixture to form a firm dough. Roll out on a floured board till 5 mm (¼ inch) thick. Cut into rounds with a small fluted biscuit cutter and place on greased baking trays. Press a peanut half lightly into the centre of each biscuit. Glaze with milk. Bake in a moderately hot oven for 12 to 15 minutes. Lift off with a spatula and cool on a wire rack.

Chocolate Nougat Slice

Yield: 20 slices
Cooking time: 30-35 minutes
Oven temperature: 180-190°C (350-375° F)

60 g (2 oz) cooking chocolate
1 tablespoon honey
¼ cup milk
60 g (2 oz) butter
½ cup caster sugar
1 egg
1 cup plain flour
½ teaspoon baking powder
pinch of salt
¼ teaspoon bicarbonate of soda
Chocolate Icing (page 146) to decorate
Nougat frosting
30 g (1 oz) butter
1½ cups icing sugar, sifted
1 teaspoon honey
2 tablespoons milk

Melt chocolate over hot water, add honey and milk. Stir well until combined and cool.

Beat butter and sugar until light, add egg and beat well. Fold in sifted dry ingredients alternately with chocolate mixture. Spread in a greased and lined 28 x 18 cm (11 x 7 inch) slab cake tin and bake in a moderate oven for 30 to 35 minutes until cooked. Turn onto a wire rack and cool. Spread with frosting, and pipe zig-zag lines of chocolate icing on top. (See Chocolate Layer Cake). Cut into squares to serve.

Nougat frosting: Melt butter until golden brown and pour onto sifted icing sugar. Add honey and milk and beat well until light and fluffy.

Custard Rings

Yield: 12
Cooking time: 30-35 minutes
Oven temperature: 200-230° C (400-450° F)
  reducing to 180-190° C (350-375° F)

1 quantity Choux Pastry (page 154)
double quantity Custard (page 126)
½ cup whipped cream
125 g (4 oz) chocolate
½ cup toasted, flaked almonds

To make rings: Lightly grease a baking tray. Take a 5 cm (2 inch) pastry cutter, dip the edge into flour, then mark circles on greased tray 5 cm (2 inches) apart. Using a pastry bag fitted with a 1 cm (½ inch) plain tube, pipe choux pastry around the edge of the marked rings. Bake for 20 minutes in a hot oven, reduce temperature to moderate and cook for further 10 to 15 minutes. The rings should be crisp, light and of even colour. Remove to a wire rack to cool.

Make custard according to directions in Raspberry Fool recipe, doubling ingredients. Leave until cool. Blend in whipped cream.

To finish custard rings: Slice rings through centre. Pipe custard on top of base with a 1 cm (½ inch) tube. Melt chocolate in a heatproof bowl over simmering water, dip smooth side of top of ring into the chocolate, place on top of custard and sprinkle with flaked, toasted almonds.

Refrigerator Biscuits

Yield: 4-5 dozen
Cooking time: 10-15 minutes
Oven temperature: 180-190° C (350-375° F)

250 g (8 oz) butter
250 g (8 oz) caster sugar
2 eggs
2 teaspoons vanilla essence
3½ cups plain flour
3 tablespoons baking powder
½ teaspoon salt

Cream butter and sugar in a mixing bowl, add eggs, vanilla essence and beat well. Sift flour, baking powder and salt and mix in well. Divide into four portions and use as follows.

Coffee: Add 2 teaspoons instant coffee and shape into a triangular roll, wrap in waxed paper and chill. Slice thinly and top with an almond.

Coconut and Orange: Add ⅓ cup desiccated coconut and ½ teaspoon orange essence. Shape into a roll. Wrap, chill and slice thinly.

Ginger: Roll, wrap, chill and slice, topping with a piece of preserved ginger.

Chocolate pinwheels: Divide mixture in half. Add 2 teaspoons cocoa, ½ teaspoon ground cinnamon to half mixture. Shape into a rectangle 5 mm (¼ inch) thick. Shape remaining half into a rectangle 5 mm (¼ inch) thick. Put one on top of the other, roll up tightly, wrap in waxed paper, chill and slice thinly.

To Cook: Place sliced biscuits on a greased baking tray and cook in a moderate oven for 10 to 15 minutes.
Note: This biscuit dough will keep for months in the freezer if wrapped securely in aluminium foil or plastic. Slice and bake whenever required for unexpected visitors.

SCONES & QUICK BREADS

When the need arises for something quick to prepare for baking, you'll find the recipes following are just right. For those who like to add fibre and extra nourishment to breads and scones, there are recipes using bran, wholemeal flour, nuts and dried fruits.

For all these recipes, use a light hand in the mixing and kneading.

Wholemeal Rock Cakes
Yield: 20
Cooking time: 12-15 minutes
Oven temperature: 200-230° C (400-450° F)

1 cup self-raising flour
1 cup wholemeal self-raising flour
½ teaspoon mixed spice
¼ teaspoon ground nutmeg
½ cup raw or white sugar
90 g (3 oz) butter
½ cup dried mixed fruit
1 egg
¼ cup milk

Sift flours and spices into a mixing bowl, adding any grist remaining in sifter. Blend in sugar. Rub butter into flour mixture until crumbly. Stir in dried fruit. Beat egg and add with milk. Mix quickly to a soft dough using a round-bladed knife. Place rough tablespoons of the dough onto a greased baking tray and bake in a hot oven for 12 to 15 minutes until golden brown. Serve warm or cold with butter.

Drop Scones
Yield: 20-24
Cooking time: 2-3 minutes

1 cup self-raising flour
1 tablespoon caster sugar
1 egg
½ cup milk
1 tablespoon melted butter

Sift flour into a mixing bowl and add sugar. Make a well in the centre and add the egg. Add the milk gradually with melted butter while stirring rapidly with a wooden spoon. Beat until smooth. Drop from a dessertspoon onto a lightly greased, heated griddle or frypan. When small bubbles appear on surface and underneath is lightly browned, turn over and cook other side. Cool on a clean tea towel on a wire rack.

Serve when cold with butter or whipped cream and jam.

Damper

Cooking time: 25-30 minutes
Oven temperature: 200-230° C (400-450° F)

2 cups self-raising flour
½ teaspoon salt
2 tablespoons melted butter
¾ cup milk

Sift flour and salt into a mixing bowl. Make a well in the centre and add the melted butter and milk while mixing with a knife to form a fairly moist dough. Turn immediately onto a lightly floured board, dust top with flour and knead lightly. With floured hands shape into an 18 cm (7 inch) round and place on a greased baking tray. Bake in a hot oven for 25 to 30 minutes. Turn onto a wire rack and while warm, slice and butter.

Cheese damper: Add ½ cup grated cheese and a pinch of cayenne pepper to the sifted flour and salt before adding the liquid and sprinkle the damper with a little more grated cheese before baking.

Fruit damper: Add ½ cup mixed dried fruit and 1 tablespoon sugar to the sifted flour and salt before adding liquid.

Orange damper: Add the finely grated rind of an orange and 1 tablespoon caster sugar to the sifted flour and salt before adding liquid. Sprinkle the top of the damper with a little sugar before baking.

Gem Scones

Yield: 24
Cooking time: 10-15 minutes
Oven temperature: 200-230° C (400-450° F)

60 g (2 oz) butter
½ cup caster sugar
2 eggs
1½ cups self-raising flour
pinch salt
¾ cup milk

While the oven is preheating, place the ungreased gem irons in it to heat.

Cream the butter and sugar together, add beaten eggs gradually, beating well between each addition. Sift flour and salt together and add alternately with the milk, folding gently until the batter is an even consistency. Remove heated gem irons from oven, brush them with butter and half fill them with the batter. Bake in a hot oven for 10 to 15 minutes. Turn onto a wire rack and when cold split and spread with butter.

Plain Scones
Yield: 12-14
Cooking time: 12-15 minutes
Oven temperature: 230-250° C (450-500° F)

2 cups self-raising flour
½ teaspoon salt
30 g (1 oz) butter or margarine
¾ cup milk

Sift flour and salt into a mixing bowl. Rub butter into flour with fingertips until the mixture resembles fine breadcrumbs. Using a round-bladed knife, quickly mix in milk to make a soft dough. Turn dough onto a lightly floured board, sprinkle top of dough with flour and knead lightly until smooth. Roll out to 2 cm (¾ inch) thick and cut into rounds with a floured cutter. Place scones onto a greased baking tray. Glaze with a little milk and bake in a very hot oven for 12 to 15 minutes. Place scones on a wire rack. When cool break in halves and spread with butter or serve with strawberry jam and whipped cream.

Sultana scones: Before adding the milk add ½ cup sultanas and 1 tablespoon caster sugar.

Cheese scones: Before adding the milk add ½ cup grated cheese.

Wholemeal scones: Substitute 1 cup wholemeal self-raising flour for 1 cup self-raising flour.
Note: The scone dough may also be shaped into a circle, marked into 6 or 8 wedges and baked in a very hot oven for 20 to 30 minutes.

Cooking tip: Instead of rubbing butter into flour, heat butter with 1 teaspoon water until frothy and pour onto flour with milk. The result is just as good.

Marmalade Scones
Yield: 18-20
Cooking time: 15-20 minutes
Oven temperature: 200-230° C (400-450° F)

1½ cups self-raising flour
1½ cups wholemeal self-raising flour
½ teaspoon salt
60 g (2 oz) butter
1 egg
½ cup marmalade
¼ cup milk
extra milk for glazing

Sift flours and salt together twice. Cut butter into mixture with a round-bladed knife then rub in with fingertips. Beat egg and combine with marmalade, then add milk. Combine with dry ingredients and mix to a soft dough with the knife.

Knead lightly on a floured board and roll out to 2 cm (¾ inch) thickness. Cut into rounds with a floured scone cutter. Place scones on a greased baking tray. Brush tops with milk to glaze. Bake in a hot oven for approximately 15 to 20 minutes or until golden brown.

Serve warm with butter.

Caramel Walnut Pinwheels

Yield: 12
Cooking time: 20-25 minutes
Oven temperature: 200-230° C (400-450° F)

2 cups self-raising flour
4 tablespoons caster sugar
1 egg
milk
4 tablespoons melted butter
1 teaspoon ground cinnamon
3 tablespoons brown sugar
2 tablespoons butter
1 cup chopped walnuts

Sift flour into a mixing bowl, stir in 2 tablespoons of the caster sugar. Beat egg lightly in measuring cup and make up to ¾ cup liquid with milk. Pour into flour with 3 tablespoons of the melted butter. Mix with a round-bladed knife to a soft dough. Turn onto a floured board and knead lightly. Roll out to a 30 x 25 cm (12 x 10 inch) rectangle. Brush with remaining melted butter, and sprinkle with remaining caster sugar and the cinnamon. Roll up tightly from longer side and cut into 12 equal slices.

Grease a 23 cm (9 inch) round layer cake tin and line base with greaseproof paper. Blend brown sugar with butter, spread in the base of tin and sprinkle walnuts on top. Place pinwheels cut side down in tin and bake in a hot oven for 20 to 25 minutes until cooked. Invert onto wire rack, leave a few seconds and remove tin and paper. Serve warm or cold, with butter if desired.

Pumpkin Scones

Yield: 18
Cooking time: 15-20 minutes
Oven temperature: 200-230° C (400-450° F)

60 g (2 oz) butter
2 tablespoons caster sugar
½ cup cooked mashed pumpkin
1 egg
½ cup milk
2½ cups self-raising flour

Cream butter and sugar. Add the pumpkin and mix well. Add egg and mix in milk a little at a time. Add the sifted flour and mix to a soft dough. Turn onto a floured board and knead lightly. Roll out to 2 cm (¾ inch) thick and cut into rounds with a floured cutter. Place rounds onto a greased baking tray. Glaze with milk and bake in a hot oven for 15 to 20 minutes. Turn onto a wire rack and when cool break open and spread with butter.

Doughnuts

Yield: 12-15
Cooking time: 3-4 minutes

2 cups plain flour
¼ teaspoon bicarbonate of soda
½ teaspoon cream of tartar
¼ teaspoon ground nutmeg
½ teaspoon ground cinnamon
¼ cup caster sugar
1 egg
½ cup sour milk
1 tablespoon melted butter
oil for frying
cinnamon sugar for coating

Sift dry ingredients into a bowl. Beat egg lightly and add with sour milk and melted butter to flour. Mix to a soft dough. Turn onto a floured board and knead lightly. Roll out till about 5 mm (¼ inch) thick and cut into rings with a floured doughnut cutter or a large and a very small biscuit cutter.

Fry 3 or 4 at a time in deep, hot oil, 190°C (375°F), for 3 to 4 minutes, turning them to brown evenly. Drain on absorbent paper and coat with cinnamon sugar (i.e., caster sugar mixed with ground cinnamon).

Note: To sour milk, add 2 teaspoons vinegar or lemon juice to ½ cup fresh milk. Leave at room temperature for 10 to 15 minutes if milk is icy cold.

Peanut Butter Bread

Cooking time: 1 hour
Oven temperature: 190-200°C (375-400°F)

1 cup self-raising flour
1 cup wholemeal self-raising flour
¾ cup brown sugar
½ cup smooth peanut butter
60 g (2 oz) butter
1 egg
¾ cup milk
Nut topping
1 tablespoon butter
1 tablespoon honey
1 tablespoon brown sugar
3 tablespoons chopped peanuts

Sift flours into a mixing bowl, adding any grist to bowl which doesn't pass through sifter. Add brown sugar and blend in with fingers to break up sugar lumps. Blend peanut butter with butter, cut into flour with a knife, then rub in lightly with fingertips. Beat egg lightly and combine with milk. Pour into flour mixture and mix until thoroughly combined without over-mixing. Turn into a greased and floured 20 x 10 cm (8 x 4 inch) loaf tin and bake in a moderately hot oven for 45 minutes. Spread topping on loaf and cook for further 15 minutes. Invert onto a wire rack covered with foil, turn right side up on rack to cool. Replace any topping from foil onto loaf if necessary. Serve sliced, spread with cream cheese or butter and honey.

Nut topping: Blend ingredients in a saucepan and heat just long enough to combine.

Date and Walnut Roll

Cooking time: 35-40 minutes
Oven temperature: 180-190° C (350-375° F)

125 g (4 oz) butter
2 cups plain flour
¼ teaspoon ground cloves
1⅓ cups dates, chopped
½ cup caster sugar
½ cup chopped walnuts
1 teaspoon baking powder
1 teaspoon bicarbonate of soda
½ cup milk
1 egg, beaten

Rub butter into the sifted flour and ground cloves until the mixture resembles breadcrumbs. Mix in the dates, sugar and walnuts. Dissolve baking powder and bicarbonate of soda in milk. Stir into the dry ingredients with egg. Spoon into 2 well greased nut roll tins. Bake in a moderate oven for 35 to 40 minutes. Leave in tins for a few minutes before turning out onto a wire rack to cool. Serve sliced with butter.

Ginger Coffee Cake

Cooking time: 30-35 minutes
Oven temperature: 180-190° C (350-375° F)

1½ cups self-raising flour
pinch salt
½ teaspoon ground cinnamon
½ cup caster sugar
60 g (2 oz) butter
1 egg, beaten
½ cup dry ginger ale
3 tablespoons sultanas
1 tablespoon chopped mixed peel
1 tablespoon chopped preserved ginger
Topping
2 tablespoons plain flour
2 tablespoons brown sugar
1 tablespoon butter
¼ teaspoon ground ginger

Sift flour, salt and cinnamon into a bowl, mix in sugar, rub in butter with fingertips. Add beaten egg with dry ginger ale, stirring mixture with a knife. Lastly add sultanas, peel and ginger. Spoon batter into an 18 cm (7 inch) square cake tin greased and lined with greased greaseproof paper. Spread top evenly.

Mix the topping ingredients to a crumbly consistency and sprinkle over the batter. Bake in a moderate oven for 30 to 35 minutes. Leave in the tin for a few minutes before turning out onto paper-covered cooling rack, then turning back so that the crumbly topping is uppermost. Serve warm, cut in slices.

Spread with butter if desired.

German Coffee Cake

Cooking time: 25-30 minutes
Oven temperature: 200-230° C (400-450° F)

1½ cups self-raising flour
½ teaspoon mixed spice
¼ cup caster sugar
60 g (2 oz) butter
¾ cup mixed dried fruit
1 egg
milk
Streusel topping
2 tablespoons caster sugar
2 tablespoons butter
2 tablespoons flour
1 teaspoon ground cinnamon

Sift flour, spice and sugar into a mixing bowl. Rub butter in lightly with fingertips until mixture resembles fine bread-crumbs. Stir in mixed fruit. Beat egg lightly in measuring cup and add milk to make ¾ cup liquid. Stir into flour mixture with a round-bladed knife. Blend thoroughly and turn into a greased and floured 20 cm (8 inch) layer cake tin. Level top with a spatula and sprinkle with streusel topping (see below). Bake in a hot oven for 25 to 30 minutes until cake shrinks away from sides of tin. Turn out onto a wire rack covered with a piece of greaseproof paper. Place another rack on top and turn cake right side up. Serve warm or cold with butter if desired.

Streusel topping: Blend ingredients together until crumbly.

Banana Bread

Cooking time: 50-60 minutes
Oven temperature: 180-190° C (350-375° F)

2 cups self-raising flour
pinch salt
½ cup caster sugar
90 g (3 oz) butter
½ teaspoon bicarbonate of soda
½ cup milk
1 egg
2 large or 3 small ripe bananas, mashed

Sift flour and salt into mixing bowl, stir in sugar. Rub butter into flour with fingertips until well combined. Dissolve bicarbonate of soda in milk and add to flour mixture with lightly beaten egg and mashed banana. Stir until thoroughly blended and spread in a greased and floured 25 x 15 cm (10 x 6 inch) loaf tin. Bake in a moderate oven for 50 to 60 minutes until cooked when tested. Turn onto wire rack to cool. Serve sliced with butter.

Note: This is a quick method of making this old favourite. The texture may not be as fine as the traditional creaming method, but if you do not over-beat the mixture once the liquid ingredients are added, the difference will be minimal.

Spiced Apple Teacake

Cooking time: 40-50 minutes
Oven temperature: 180-190° C (350-375° F)

2½ cups self-raising flour
pinch of salt
¾ cup caster sugar
90 g (3 oz) butter
1 egg
½ cup milk
1 cup apple pulp
125 g (4 oz) sultanas
2 teaspoons ground cinnamon
melted butter
extra caster sugar

Sift the flour and salt with ½ cup of the sugar. Rub in the butter with the fingertips and mix to a soft dough with the beaten egg and milk. Turn onto a floured board, knead lightly and cut into two. Line a greased 23 cm (9 inch) sandwich tin with half the mixture, spread with apple pulp. Sprinkle with the sultanas, half the cinnamon and the remaining ¼ cup sugar. Cover with the remainder of the dough. Glaze with melted butter and sprinkle with the remaining cinnamon and extra caster sugar (about 2 teaspoons). Bake in a moderate oven for 40 to 50 minutes. Serve warm or cold.

Apricot Bran Bread

Cooking time: 1-1¼ hours
Oven temperature: 180-190° C (350-375° F)

1½ cups bran cereal
¾ cup raw sugar
1 cup chopped, dried apricots
¾ cup boiling water
½ cup orange juice
1½ cups self-raising flour
¼ teaspoon bicarbonate of soda
½ teaspoon salt
3 tablespoons melted butter
2 eggs, beaten

Place bran cereal, sugar and chopped apricots into a mixing bowl. Pour on boiling water and orange juice, stir and leave for 10 minutes. Sift dry ingredients and stir into bran mixture with melted butter and beaten eggs. Blend well and turn into a greased 25 x 15 cm (10 x 6 inch) loaf tin lined on base with greased greaseproof paper. Bake in a moderate oven for 1 hour or until cooked when tested. Turn onto a wire rack to cool. Serve sliced with butter or cream cheese.
Note: This bread keeps moist for a few days. Store in an airtight container.

YEAST BREADS

The aroma of freshly baked bread is sufficient incentive for the cook to try her hand at yeast cookery. Working with yeast is both fascinating and satisfying.

When substituting compressed yeast for active dry yeast, use 30 g (1 oz) for each 2 teaspoons (1 sachet, i.e., 7 g or ¼ oz) active dry yeast. Compressed yeast should be creamed with a little sugar before being added to the liquid.

Wholemeal Bread

Yield: 2 loaves
Cooking time: 35-40 minutes
Oven temperature: 190-200° C (375-400° F)

4 cups plain white flour
4 cups wholemeal plain flour
1 teaspoon salt
1 tablespoon sugar
4 teaspoons active dry yeast
2½ cups water
1 tablespoon butter or lard
milk
2 tablespoons cracked wheat (optional)

Blend the two flours and sift. Add any grist left in sifter to flour. Mix half the flour, the salt and sugar in a warm mixing bowl, stir in yeast. Heat butter or lard with 1 cup water, add remaining water and cool to lukewarm. Add to dry ingredients. Beat 2 minutes on mixer or 300 strokes by hand. Blend in remaining flour and knead to a soft, elastic dough. Follow Milk Bread recipe for proving, shaping and proving a second time. When loaves have risen brush tops with milk and sprinkle on cracked wheat if used. Bake in a moderately hot oven for 35 to 40 minutes.

Wholemeal bread rolls: Divide half the dough into 20 pieces after first proving. Roll each into a ball and place on greased baking trays. Cover and leave in a warm place until doubled in size. Brush with milk and sprinkle with cracked wheat. Bake in a moderately hot oven for 15 to 20 minutes.

Milk Bread

Yield: 2 loaves
Cooking time: 35-40 minutes
Oven temperature: 190-200° C (375-400° F)

8 cups plain flour (warmed)
2 teaspoons salt
1 tablespoon sugar
4 tablespoons full cream powdered milk
4 teaspoons active dry yeast
90 g (3 oz) butter
2¼ cups water

Sift half the flour, the salt, sugar and powdered milk into a warm bowl, stir in yeast. Melt butter in 1 cup water over heat. Add remaining water and cool to lukewarm (blood heat). Add to dry ingredients and beat about 2 minutes on mixer or by hand (about 300 strokes). Add remaining flour and knead to a soft, elastic dough. Butter bowl, turn dough in it to coat top, cover with plastic film and leave in a warm, draught-free place until doubled in bulk. Punch down. Divide dough in half, shape into two loaves and place in greased 23 × 12 × 8 cm (9 × 5 × 3 inch) loaf tins. Cover with cloth and let rise in a warm place until dough doubles in bulk again. Bake in a moderately hot oven for approximately 35 to 40 minutes. When cooked remove one loaf from tin — it should sound hollow when rapped on the base with the knuckles. Cool loaves on a wire rack.

Cottage loaf: After first rising, divide one half of the dough into 2, one piece two-thirds larger than other. Shape larger piece into a 15 cm (6 inch) round, roll smaller piece into a ball and place on top. Place on greased baking tray. Press a floured finger through centre of loaf to base. Cover, prove and bake as above.

Pizza

Serves: 8-10
Cooking time: 20-25 minutes
Oven temperature: 190-200° C (375-400° F)

2 cups plain flour
¼ teaspoon dried oregano
½ teaspoon salt
1 teaspoon sugar
2 teaspoons active dry yeast
½ cup warm water
1 tablespoon olive oil
Filling
½ cup tomato paste or 3-4 tomatoes, sliced
salt and pepper
pinch sugar
125 g (4 oz) cabana sausage, sliced
¼ cup finely chopped onion
1 × 210 g (6¾ oz) can champignons, drained
2 tablespoons sliced black olives
½ cup chopped green capsicum
¼ teaspoon dried oregano
1½ cups grated Mozzarella cheese

Sift 1 cup flour, oregano, salt and sugar into a bowl. Stir in yeast. Add warm water and oil and beat for 2 minutes in a mixer or 300 strokes by hand. Add remaining sifted flour and blend in with a spoon. Knead on floured board until smooth. Cover and stand for 10 minutes. Spread dough evenly with a spoon or oiled fingers into a greased 30 cm (12 inch) pizza tin.

Cover dough with a thick layer of tomato paste or sliced tomatoes and season with salt, pepper and sugar. Arrange layers of sliced cabana, onion, champignons, olives and capsicum on top. Sprinkle with oregano and grated cheese.

Bake in a moderately hot oven for 20 to 25 minutes. Cut into wedges and serve hot.

Bread Rolls

Yield: 36 rolls
Cooking time: 10-15 minutes
Oven temperature: 200-230° C (400-450° F)

1 quantity Milk Bread dough (page 168)
melted butter
beaten egg or milk to glaze
sesame and poppy seads

Make milk bread as directed. After first rising divide into 4.

Crescent rolls: Roll out 2 portions of dough into 2 circles 5 mm (¼ inch) thick. Brush with melted butter and cut each circle into 8 wedges. Roll each wedge from wider edge to point. Stretch slightly and shape into a crescent. Place well apart on a greased baking tray. Cover and let rolls rise until doubled in size. Glaze with beaten egg and sprinkle with sesame seeds. Bake in a hot oven for 15 minutes.

Knots: Divide 1 portion of the dough into 10 equal pieces. Roll each into a rope and tie in a knot. Place on a greased baking tray, cover and prove as above. Brush with egg or milk and sprinkle with sesame or poppy seeds. Bake as for crescent rolls.

Snails: Divide 1 portion of the dough into 10 equal pieces. Roll each into a rope, place one end on greased tray and twist rope round into a snail shape. Press end of rope into side of roll. Cover and prove as above. Brush with egg or milk and sprinkle with sesame or poppy seeds. Bake as for crescent rolls.

Garlic Bread

Serves: 4-6
Cooking time: 20 minutes
Oven temperature: 190-200° C (375-400° F)

1 loaf French bread
125 g (4 oz) butter
1 tablespoon chopped parsley
1 garlic clove, crushed
salt to taste

Slice bread diagonally into 2 cm (¾ inch) slices, cutting to, but not through, the bottom crust.

Cream butter with parsley, garlic and salt to taste. Spread butter mixture on both sides of each slice, pressing together to re-form loaf. Wrap in aluminium foil. Bake in a moderately hot oven for 15 minutes. Open foil and cook 5 minutes longer to crisp the bread. Cut through bottom crust and serve warm.

Cheese bread: Add 1 tablespoon fresh or ½ teaspoon dried oregano, omit salt and blend in ¼ cup grated Parmesan cheese.

Onion bread: Omit garlic and blend in 2 tablespoons grated onion.

Cooking tip: Make your own French bread using the Milk Bread recipe. After first rising, divide dough in two, roll each portion to a rectangle. Brush lightly with melted butter and roll up, sealing ends. Place on greased baking tray, slash tops diagonally in 3 or 4 places, cover and leave to prove. Bake at same temperature for 30 minutes with a baking dish of boiling water placed on the oven shelf below the bread. This crisps the crust.

Hot Cross Buns

Yield: 20
Cooking time: 25-30 minutes
Oven temperature: 200-230° C (400-450° F)

4 cups plain flour
½ teaspoon salt
1 teaspoon ground cinnamon
½ teaspoon mixed spice
1 cup dried fruit (sultanas, currants and mixed peel)
30 g (1 oz) compressed yeast
3 tablespoons caster sugar
1 cup lukewarm milk
3 tablespoons melted butter
1 egg yolk, beaten
Sugar Glaze (page 172)

Sift flour, salt and spices into a warm mixing bowl, add fruit and make a well in the centre. Cream yeast with 1 tablespoon of the sugar. Combine milk, butter and egg yolk and mix with yeast. Pour into flour mixture and beat with a wooden spoon until combined. Use a little more warm milk if necessary. Knead in the bowl till dough is smooth, elastic and the fruit starts popping out. Lift out dough, grease bowl with butter, return dough to bowl and turn it to coat top with butter. Cover bowl and stand in a warm place till dough is doubled in bulk. Punch down, knead lightly and turn onto a floured board. Divide into 20 equal pieces and roll each into a smooth ball. Place balls in a greased baking tin 30 x 25 cm (12 x 10 inches) four across and five down. Cover with a cloth and allow to rise in a warm place till the buns are doubled in size and almost touching. Bake in a hot oven for 25 minutes or until golden brown. Turn out onto a wire rack and brush while hot with Sugar Glaze (see Swedish Tea Ring). Pipe a white icing cross on top of each bun when cool.

Latvian Birthday Cake

Cooking time: 50 minutes
Oven temperature: 200-230° C (400-450° F)
  reducing to 180-190° C (350-375° F)

1 quantity Hot Cross Bun dough (page 170)
½ teaspoon ground cardamom
½ teaspoon powdered saffron
⅓ cup sultanas
⅓ cup currants
1 slice glacé pineapple, finely chopped
½ cup blanched, chopped almonds
finely grated rind of 1 lemon
beaten egg for glazing
1 tablespoon blanched whole almonds, split in halves
icing sugar

Make hot cross bun dough according to directions, substituting cardamom and saffron for spices, and sultanas, currants, pineapple and almonds for dried fruit listed. Add lemon rind to dough with fruit. Mix, knead, cover and prove as directed in recipe.

Punch down dough and knead for about 10 minutes. Cover and let it rise a second time. Turn out onto a floured board and knead lightly. Pull and twist the dough into a long cylinder. Place on a large greased baking tray and form into a letter 'B' shape. Press joins firmly together. Cover with a cloth and prove again until doubled in size. Glaze with beaten egg and press split almonds on top. Bake in a hot oven for 20 minutes, reduce to moderate and bake for further 30 minutes or until cake is golden brown. If top browns too quickly, cover loosely with aluminium foil. When cooked, slide onto wire rack, cook slightly and dust with icing sugar. Serve warm or cold.

Hazelnut and Strawberry Cake

Cooking time: 40 minutes
Oven temperature: 200-230° C (400-450° F)
  reducing to 180-190° C (350-375° F)

2 cups plain flour
¼ teaspoon salt
¼ teaspoon ground cardamom
15 g (½ oz) compressed yeast
1 tablespoon caster sugar
½ cup lukewarm milk
125 g (4 oz) melted butter
4 tablespoons sugar mixed with 1 teaspoon ground cinnamon
strawberry jam
¾ cup finely chopped hazelnuts

Sift flour, salt and cardamom into a warm bowl and make a well in the centre. Cream yeast and caster sugar. Combine milk with half the butter and add to yeast. Pour into flour and hand mix to a soft dough, using extra warm milk, if required. Knead till the dough is smooth, elastic and leaves sides of bowl cleanly. Lift out dough, butter bowl, return dough and turn to coat with butter. Cover bowl and stand in a warm place till doubled in bulk. Punch down and knead lightly. Turn onto a floured board and divide into 15 pieces. Shape each into a smooth ball. Roll each ball in remaining melted butter, then in sugar and cinnamon mixture. Arrange some of the balls on the bottom of a greased baba tin. Place 1 teaspoon of strawberry jam between each ball, sprinkle with hazelnuts. Repeat until all the dough has been used. Finish with a sprinkling of hazelnuts. Stand covered in a warm place till the cake rises almost to the top of the tin. Bake in a hot oven for 20 minutes, reduce to moderate and bake for a further 20 minutes. Turn onto a wire rack to cool.

Swedish Tea Ring

Cooking time: 30-35 minutes
Oven temperature: 200-230° C (400-450° F)
  reducing to 180-190° C (350-375° F)

½ quantity plain Milk Bread dough (page 168)
60 g (2 oz) butter
1 cup raisins or a mixture of dried fruits (larger ones should
  be coarsely chopped)
½ cup caster sugar
2 teaspoons ground cinnamon
Sugar glaze
2 tablespoons water
2 tablespoons sugar

Roll the dough into a long, narrow rectangle 1 cm (½ inch)
thick. Brush with melted butter, sprinkle with a mixture of
raisins, caster sugar and cinnamon. Starting at one of the
long edges, roll the dough up tightly. Stretch slightly and
shape into a circle. Tuck one end into the other. Make deep
slanting slashes on the outer side of the circle about 4 cm
(1½ inches) apart. Gently twist each slice to show the filling.
Cover with a cloth and allow to rise in warm place until
doubled in size. Bake in a hot oven for 15 minutes, reduce
temperature to moderate and bake for another 15 to 20
minutes or until the ring is golden brown top and bottom.
While hot, glaze with sugar glaze. Cool on wire rack and
serve with butter.

Sugar glaze: Combine water and sugar in a small pan, stir
over heat until sugar dissolves, bring to the boil and boil 1
minute.

Herbed Buns

Yield: 12
Cooking time: 15-20 minutes
Oven temperature: 190-200° C (375-400° F)

½ cup milk
2 teaspoons sugar
2 teaspoons salt
2 tablespoons butter
1½ cups lukewarm water
2 teaspoons active dry yeast
5½ cups plain flour
1 cup finely grated sharp Cheddar cheese
2 tablespoons chopped chives
2 tablespoons chopped parsley
milk for glazing

In a saucepan heat together milk, sugar, salt and butter. Cool
to lukewarm. Place lukewarm water in a large mixing bowl
and sprinkle over yeast, stirring until dissolved. Add milk
mixture and half the flour. Beat until smooth. Add cheese
and herbs. Stir in rest of flour by hand, adding enough to
form a stiff dough. Knead on a floured board until smooth
and elastic. Place in a buttered bowl, turn dough to coat top
with butter and cover bowl with plastic film. Leave to rise in
a warm place, free from draught, until doubled in bulk (30 to
40 minutes). Knock down dough and knead until smooth.

Divide into 12 equal portions. Roll each piece into a round
and place on a greased baking tray. Cover with a dry cloth
and leave to rise until doubled in size. Glaze buns with milk.
Bake in a moderately hot oven for 15 to 20 minutes or until
buns sound hollow when tapped on bottom.

GLOSSARY

Bake: To cook by dry heat in the oven. Usually refers to breads, cakes etc.

Baste: To spoon or pour liquid over food as it cooks to flavour it and keep it moist.

Batter: A mixture of flour and liquid, beaten together, used to coat foods or for making pancakes; the term used for cake and pudding mixtures before they are cooked.

Beat: To mix with a spoon, whisk, rotary beater or electric mixer so that air may be enclosed in the mixture to make it light.

Beurre manié: Equal quantities of plain flour and butter blended together then added a little at a time to a stew or casserole to thicken it. May be made ahead and stored in refrigerator for use as required.

Blanch: To heat in boiling water or steam. This can be done for several reasons: (1) to loosen outer skins of fruit, nuts or vegetables; (2) to whiten sweetbreads, veal or chicken; (3) to remove excess salt or bitter flavour from bacon, cured meats and strong flavoured vegetables; (4) to prepare fruits and vegetables for freezing and preserving.

Blend: To mix two or more ingredients thoroughly.

Boil: To cook in any liquid at boiling point.

Bone: To remove bones from meat, poultry, game and fish.

Bouquet garni: A bunch of culinary herbs used to flavour stocks, casseroles, stews and sauces. Tie together 2 sprigs each parsley and thyme, 1 bay leaf and the leafy top of a celery stalk, using white string or thread. Make up a number of bunches and store in a polythene bag in refrigerator. When fresh thyme is not available, add ½ teaspoon dried thyme to the dish being prepared.

Bruise: To soften a food such as root ginger to release flavour in cooking; place on a board, put knife blade on top and hit blade with side of hand.

Chill: To place in refrigerator until cold.

Clarify: (1) To clear stock or broth: add slightly beaten egg whites and crushed egg shells and bring to the boil. Cool and strain through a muslin-lined sieve before using. (2) to cleanse fat for deep frying by adding water and melting gently. Cool and when fat sets, remove, scrape sediment from bottom of fat and store in refrigerator. (3) To melt butter gently, skim salty froth and pour off oil, leaving sediment behind. Clarified butter has a high fuming point and is an ideal cooking medium. Use-skimmed froth and sediment for flavouring vegetables.

Coat: To cover entire surface of food with flour, breadcrumbs or batter.

Cream: To combine butter or other shortening with sugar, using a wooden spoon or electric mixer, until light, white and fluffy.

Crêpe: A very thin pancake served with a savoury or sweet filling.

Croûte: Large slices of stale, crustless white bread, often cut into fancy shapes, fried in oil or butter until crisp. Used as a garnish for savoury dishes or as a base for grilled or fried steaks.

Crouton: Small cubes of stale white bread, fried until crisp in butter or oil and used as a garnish or topping.

Cut in: To combine fat and dry ingredients with two knives, scissors fashion, or with a pastry blender, when making pastry.

Deep fry: To cook in deep hot fat or oil which covers the food, until crisp and golden.

Dripping: The residue left in the dish after meat or poultry is cooked, usually including fat.

Flake: To break into small pieces with a fork.

Flame: To spoon alcoholic liquid over food and ignite; to warm alcoholic liquid, ignite and pour flaming over food. Flambé is another term used for this procedure.

Fold in: To add other ingredients to a beaten mixture, using a plastic spatula or tablespoon with a light cut-and-fold movement so that air is not lost.

Fry: To cook in a little fat or oil in a frying pan using moderate to high heat.

Ghee: Clarified butter fat obtainable commercially. Used in curries, but may replace butter in meat and chicken dishes.

Glaze: A thin coating of beaten egg, milk, syrup or aspic which is brushed over pastry (egg or milk), fruits and sweet breads (syrup) or cooked fish, ham, chicken, etc. (aspic).

Grate: To rub food against a grater to form small particles.

Grease: To rub lightly with butter or margarine. For cakes, brush melted shortening onto inner surfaces of tin, covering completely. Place in refrigerator to set. A dusting of flour will ensure that cake comes out cleanly.

Grill: To cook by direct heat, either over a glowing charcoal fire (barbecue), or under a gas or electric grill unit.

Julienne: Cut into fine strips the length of a matchstick.

Knead: To work dough with hands until it is of the desired elasticity or consistency.

Marinade: Usually a mixture of oil, acid (wine, fruit juice) and seasonings in which food is steeped to give it more flavour and to soften fibres of tough foods.

Marinate: To let food stand in a marinade.

Monosodium glutamate: A crystalline chemical product added to food to intensify the natural flavours.

Mince: To reduce to very small particles with a mincer, chopper or knife.

Parboil: To boil until partly cooked.

Pâté: A highly seasoned meat paste, usually served as an hors d'oeuvre.

Pit: To remove pit, stone or seed, as from cherries.

Poach: To cook gently in simmering liquid.

Pound: To reduce to very small particles, or a paste, with a pestle and mortar.

Preheat: To have oven or cooking appliance at desired temperature before putting in food.

Prove: To let yeast dough rise in a warm place until doubled in bulk.

Purée: To press through a fine sieve or put in a food blender to produce a smooth mixture.

Reduce: To cook a liquid over a high heat, uncovered, until it is reduced by evaporation to desired consistency.

Roast: To cook meat by dry heat on a spit. Today it is applied to cooking meats etc. by dry heat in the oven.

Roux: A mixture of fat and flour cooked slowly over a low heat as a foundation for sauces, soups etc.

Sauté: To fry lightly in a small amount of hot fat or oil, moving food frequently by shaking pan, turning or stirring.

Scald: To heat to temperature just below boiling point, with small bubbles rising occasionally to the surface.

Score: To make evenly spaced, shallow slits or cuts with a knife on the surface of food.

Shred: To cut into fine strips.

Simmer: To cook in liquid just below boiling point, with small bubbles rising occasionally to the surface.

Skim: To remove foam, fat or solid substance from the surface of a cooking, or cooked mixture.

Sliver: To cut into long, thin strips.

Steam: To cook food in vapour rising from boiling water.

Stew: A long slow method of cooking in a liquid in a covered pan to tenderise tough meats etc.

Stir: To mix with a spoon with a circular motion.

Stir-fry: To fry food in oil, stirring and tossing food constantly with a wooden or slotted spoon (oriental cooking).

Stock: A liquid containing the flavours, extracts and nutrients of bones, meat, fish or vegetables in which they were cooked.

Toss: To mix lightly, using a fork and spoon.

INDEX

A

Aioli, *see* garlic mayonnaise 16
Ambrosia cheese squares 155
Anchovied vegetable salad 66
Antipasto 25
Apple dumplings, baked 125
Apple pie, latticed 139
Apples, baked 121
Apricot and orange pancakes 124
Apricot apple cobbler 119
Apricot bran bread 167
Apricot fingers 84
Apricot shortcake 122
Asparagus and ham casserole 56
Asparagus flan 48
Asparagus rolls supreme 59
Avocado pears with orange 29
Avocado salad mould 73

B

Baked apple dumplings 125
Baked apples 121
Baked cheesecake 138
Banana bread 166
Barbecue, bush 92
Barbecued chicken 115
Barbecued hamburgers 94
Batter 35
Batter, fritter 87, 120
Bean and egg salad 69
Bean and frank pot 86
Bean salad, Italian 68
Beans amandine 56
Béarnaise sauce 19
Béchamel sauce 16
Beef, *see also* Steak
  and mushroom rolls 85
  bourguignonne 105
  cabbage rolls 83
  carbonnade 101
  chilli con carne 93
  corned, crusted 97
  devilled meat balls 90
  enchiladas 80
  family meat pie 76
  fondue bourguignonne 98
  goulash with noodles 85
  kofta curry 88
  meat loaf 91
  Mexican medley 91
  orange cheeseburgers 86
  oxtail ragoût 74
  pot roast 76
  ragoût 78
  roast Scotch fillet 103
  sauerbraten 104
  spiced apricot short ribs 84
  strips in sour cream 82
  stuffed capsicums 79
  Wellington 105
Beef stock 8
Belgian Parmesan cakes 49
Biscuits 150-159
  apricot fingers 152
  chocolate pinwheels 159
  chocolate walnut creams 157
  coconut orange 159
  coffee 159
  cornflake crunches 150
  custard creams 150
  ginger 159
  golden butter drops 153
  macaroons 157
  peanut butter cookies 158

polka dot 151
refrigerator 159
Blanquette of veal 103
Blender hollandaise sauce 17
Blushing duckling 116
Boiled fruit cake, rich 143
Boiling eggs 69
Bolognese, spaghetti 53
Bortsch 14
Bourguignonne, beef 105
Bourguignonne, fondue 98
Brains, fricassee 90
Braised chicken and potatoes 113
Braised red cabbage 60
Brandied tomatoes 23
Brandied yule cake 145
Brazilian salad 70
Bread
  apricot bran 167
  banana 166
  cheese 170
  garlic 170
  milk 168
  onion 170
  peanut butter 164
  wholemeal 168
Bread and butter custard 123
Bread rolls 169
Brussels sprouts polonaise 57
Buns, herbed 172
Buns, hot cross 170
Bush barbecue 92
Butter cake 142
Butterfly cakes 153

C

Cabbage, braised red 60
Cabbage rolls 83
Caesar salad 65
Cakes, large 140-149
  brandied yule 145
  butter 142
  cherry yoghurt 142
  chocolate layer 146
  chocolate, Swiss roll 141
  Christmas 148
  coffee layer 143
  date and walnut roll 165
  festive frozen 133
  gala fruit ring 147
  German coffee 166
  ginger coffee 165
  hazelnut and strawberry 171
  Jaffa 140
  Latvian birthday 171
  light fruit 148
  linzertorte 147
  marble 145
  mocha torte 144
  orange gâteau 146
  passionfruit sponge 144
  quick mix chocolate 141
  rich boiled fruit 143
  rippled coffee liqueur 140
  simnel 149
  spiced apple teacake 167
  spiced carrot 149
Cakes, small 150-159
  ambrosia cheese squares 155
  butterfly 153
  chocolate éclairs 154
  chocolate nougat slice 158
  chocolate rum balls 156
  cream puffs 154
  custard rings 159
  lamingtons 154

meringues 151
walnut meringue squares 155
wholemeal rock 160
Cannelloni, stuffed 51
Capsicums, stuffed 79
Caramel banana tart 136
Caramel walnut pinwheels 163
Carbonnade of beef 101
Carpetbag steak 99
Carrots, curried 63
Casserole
  asparagus and ham 56
  cider cheese 49
  Dutch egg 45
  eggplant 61
  Georgian lamb 75
  instant steak 88
  macaroni 53
  veal and pork 74
Cassoulet, lamb 81
Cauliflower salad, German 66
Caviare butter 35
Cheese 40-49
Cheese and pineapple refresher 28
Cheese bread 170
Cheese damper 161
Cheese fondue 44
Cheese scones 162
Cheese soufflé 47
Cheeseburgers, orange 86
Cheesecake, baked 138
Cheesecake, citrus 135
Cherry cake 142
Cherry strudel, quick 119
Cherry yoghurt cake 142
Chicken 106-117
  à la king 110
  and ham pancakes 41
  and mushroom vols-au-vent 21
  and orange kebabs 26
  and potatoes, braised 113
  barbecued 115
  breasts, spiced 112
  coq au vin 108
  curried 111
  French colonial style 114
  grand-mère 108
  kebabs teriyaki 117
  liver pâté 22
  livers bordelaise 106
  Maryland 112
  paprika 106
  pie 109
  roast with rice stuffing 117
  salad, tangy 71
  soup, Venetian 14
  with cashews 110
Chicken stock 8
Chilli con carne 93
Chinese egg noodle soup 15
Chocolate cake, quick mix 141
Chocolate éclairs 154
Chocolate fondue 122
Chocolate ice cream 129
Chocolate layer cake 146
Chocolate mousse 129
Chocolate nougat slice 158
Chocolate rum balls 156
Chocolate rum pie 134
Chocolate soufflé 118
Chocolate Swiss roll 141
Chocolate walnut creams 157
Chops, orange glazed lamb 89
Chops, pork with apple pancakes 97

Chowder, egg and prawn 11
Chowder, scallop 13
Christmas cake 148
Christmas pudding 123
Cider cheese casserole 49
Citrus cheesecake 135
Clam sauce, pasta with red 50
Coconut milk 69, 82
Coconut tarts 152
Cod fingers, crunchy 37
Coffee gâteau 133
Coffee ice cream 129
Coffee layer cake 143
Coffee liqueur cake, rippled 140
Cold desserts 126-133
Continental rolled steak 81
Coq au vin 108
Coquilles St Jacques 39
Corned beef, crusted 97
Cornflake crunches 150
Cottage loaf 168
Crab crêpes 24
Cream of carrot soup 10
Cream of cauliflower soup 9
Cream of celery soup 9
Cream of lettuce soup 9
Cream of mushroom soup 10
Cream puffs 154
Creamy lemon soufflé 130
Creamy mushroom sauce 18
Crêpes 41
Crêpes, crab 24
Crescent rolls 169
Croutons 11
Crown roast of pork 98
Crunchy cod fingers 37
Crusted corned beef 97
Crusted pineapple slices 118
Cucumber mayonnaise 16
Curried carrots 63
Curried chicken 111
Curried lamb 82
Curried rice salad 73
Curry, kofta 88
Custard 126
Custard, bread and butter 123
Custard creams 150
Custard rings 159

D

Damper 161
Date and walnut roll 165
Desserts, cold 126-133
Devilled meat balls 90
Doughnuts 164
Dressings
  anchovy 66
  French 28, 29, 32, 70
  herb 71
  pickle 72
  salad 68
Drop scones 160
Duck in red wine 114
Duck, roast wild 111
Duck with sour cherries 107
Duckling, blushing 116
Dumplings, orange 75
Dutch egg casserole 45
Dutch pea soup 9

E

Egg and prawn chowder 11
Egg and tuna croquettes 34
Eggplant casserole 61
Eggplants, stuffed 20
Eggs 40-49
Eggs and cheese en cocotte 46

Eggs Florentine 43
Eggs, Scotch 92
Eggs, scrambled cheese 40
Eggs, stuffed, with mushrooms 24
Enchiladas 80
Entrées 20-29
Espagnole sauce 18

F
Family meat pie 76
Festive frozen cake 133
Fish and shellfish 30-39
Fish and spinach soup 12
Fish'n'chips 35
Fish, oven poached 31
Fish pie, old fashioned 39
Fish salad, marinated 69
Fish, stuffed baked 38
Fish, sweet and sour 31
Flan, asparagus 48
Flan, ham and mushroom 45
Flan, no bake strawberry 135
Flan, onion and cheese 48
Flan, rhubarb 138
Flan, smoked salmon 42
Flan, strawberry 137
Fondue bourguignonne 98
Fondue, cheese 44
Fondue, chocolate 122
Fondue, mushroom 42
Fool, raspberry 126
Frankfurters and rice 87
French colonial style chicken 114
French dressing 28, 29, 32, 70
French onion soup gratinée 12
Fricassee of brains 90
Fried rice 50
Fried vegetables oriental 58
Frozen plum pudding 126
Fruit bowl, summer 132
Fruit damper 161
Fruit desserts, see under names of individual fruit

G
Gala fruit ring 147
Garlic bread 170
Garlic mayonnaise (aioli) 16
Garlic prawns 25
Gâteau, coffee 133
Gâteau, orange 146
Gazpacho 11
Gem scones 161
Georgian lamb casserole 75
German cauliflower salad 66
German coffee cake 166
Ginger coffee cake 165
Ginger orange pumpkin 60
Glazed pork spareribs 94
Golden butter drops 153
Goose, roast 107
Goulash and noodles 85
Grapefruit prawns 27
Grapes, honeyed 127

H
Ham and asparagus flan 45
Ham and corn omelette 44
Ham and rice salad 67
Ham casserole, asparagus and 56
Ham pancakes, chicken and 41
Ham, peach baked 96
Ham, smoked, with fruit 20
Hamburgers, barbecued 94

Hamburgers, Hawaiian 94
Hard sauce 123
Hare hunter style 115
Hasselback potatoes 61
Hazelnut and strawberry cake 171
Herbed buns 172
Herring salad, Swedish 67
Herrings, Russian 22
Hollandaise sauce 17
Honey fruit pie 137
Honey tart 136
Honeyed grapes 127
Hors d'oeuvre, sardine 27
Hors d'oeuvre, vegetable 28
Hot cross buns 170
Hot herbed tomatoes 58
Hot puddings 118-125

I
Ice cream 129
Ice, raspberry mallow 131
Icings and frostings
    butter 141, 150
    chocolate 146
    chocolate cream 157
    chocolate glacé 140
    coffee 143
    coffee glacé 144
    cream cheese 149
    lemon 152
    nougat 158
    seven-minute 148
Indian ghee rice 55
Instant steak casserole 88
Island tuna 30
Italian bean salad 68

J
Jaffa cake 140
Jelly, mandarin layer 128

K
Kebabs, chicken and orange 26
Kebabs, chicken teriyaki 117
Kebabs, minted lamb 95
Kebabs, shish 93
Kidneys, sauté turbigo 80
Knots (bread rolls) 169
Kofta curry 88
Koulibiaka, salmon 38
Kromeskies 87

L
Lamb
    apricot roll 84
    boulangère 104
    cassoulet 81
    chops, orange glazed 89
    curried 82
    Georgian casserole 75
    kebabs, minted 95
    loin provençale 99
    navarin 78
    pie 83
    shish kebabs 93
Lamingtons 154
Latticed apple pie 139
Latvian birthday cake 171
Lemon cake 142
Lemon delicious, sultana 125
Lemon meringue pie 139
Lemon soufflé, creamy 130
Lemons, stuffed 23
Light fruit cake 148
Linzertorte 147
Lobster en brochette 32

Lobster tails marinière 30
Lobster, west coast 33
Loganberry soufflé 131
Loin of lamb provençale 99
Loin of pork with prunes 102

M
Macaroni casserole 53
Macaroni salad 64
Macaroons 157
Mandarin layer jelly 128
Marble cake 145
Marinades for beef, lamb, pork 92, 93, 95
Marinades for chicken 114, 115, 117
Marinated fish salad 69
Marmalade scones 162
Mayonnaise 16
Meat balls, devilled 90
Meat loaf 91
Meringues 151
Mexican beef medley 91
Milk bread 168
Minted lamb kebabs 95
Mocha torte 144
Mousse, chocolate 129
Mousse, salmon 37
Mulligatawny 15
Mushroom fondue 42
Mushroom salad 68
Mushroom sauce 18
Mushroom sauce, creamy 18
Mushroom soup, cream of 10
Mushrooms à la Grecque 26
Mushrooms, stuffed 59
Mushrooms, stuffed eggs with 24
Mussels marinière 36

N
Navarin of lamb 78
Niçoise, salad 71
Niçoise, tarte 46
No bake strawberry flan 135

O
Old fashioned fish pie 39
Omelette, ham and corn 44
Omelette, rice 47
Onion bread 170
Onion soup gratinée, French 12
Orange cake 142
Orange cheeseburgers 86
Orange damper 161
Orange dumplings, steak with 75
Orange gâteau 146
Orange glazed lamb chops 89
Oven poached fish 31
Oxtail ragoût 74
Oyster soup vert 13
Oysters, Russian 21

P
Paella Barcelona 54
Pancakes 41
Pancakes, apricot and orange 124
Pancakes, chicken and ham 41
Pancakes, spinach 43
Paprika, chicken 106
Parmigiana, veal 101
Passionfruit sponge 144
Pasta 50-55
Pasta with red clam sauce 50
Pastry, biscuit 136, 152

Pastry, choux 154
Pastry for savoury flans 42
Pastry, rich short crust 134
Pastry, short crust 125
Pastry, suet crust 77
Pâté, chicken liver 22
Pavlova 130
Pea soup 9
Peach baked ham 96
Peanut butter bread 164
Peanut butter cookies 158
Pepper steak 96
Pesto sauce, spaghetti with quick 55
Pickle dressing 72
Pies, sweet 134-139
    chicken 109
    chocolate rum 76
    family meat 76
    lamb 83
    old fashioned fish 39
    salmon koulibiaka 38
    steak and mushroom 79
Pilaf, rice 52
Pineapple mint sherbet 128
Pineapple refresher, cheese and 28
Pineapple slices, crusted 118
Pizza 169
Plain scones 162
Plum pudding, frozen 126
Poached trout 35
Polka dot biscuits 151
Polynesian pork saté 95
Pork
    casserole, veal and 74
    chops with apple pancakes 97
    crown roast 98
    fillet, stuffed 102
    loin with prunes 102
    Polynesian saté 95
    spareribs, glazed 94
    sweet and sour 89
Pot roast 76
Potato frosted meat loaf 91
Potato salad 72
Potatoes Anna 63
Potatoes, hasselback 61
Poultry and game 106-117
Prawn chef's salad 72
Prawn Créole 33
Prawns, garlic 25
Prawns, grapefruit 27
Pudding, Christmas 123
Pudding, steak and kidney 77
Pudding, steamed jam 121
Pudding, summer 127
Puddings, hot 118-125
Pumpkin, ginger orange 60
Pumpkin scones 163
Pumpkin soup 8

Q
Quick breads 160-167
Quick cherry strudel 119
Quick creamed rice 124
Quick meat dishes 86-91
Quick mix chocolate cake 141

R
Rabbit with prunes and pinenuts 109
Ragoût of beef 78
Ragoût, oxtail 74
Raspberry fool 126
Raspberry mallow ice 131
Ratatouille 62

Red cabbage, braised 60
Refrigerator biscuits 159
Rhubarb flan 138
Rice 50-55
    frankfurters and 87
    fried 50
    Indian ghee 55
    omelette 47
    pilaf 52
    quick creamed 124
    rissoles 52
    salad, curried 73
    salad, ham and 67
Rich boiled fruit cake 143
Rich short crust pastry 134
Rippled coffee liqueur cake 140
Rissoles, rice 52
Roast chicken with rice stuffing
    117
Roast crown of pork 98
Roast goose 107
Roast, pot 76
Roast Scotch fillet 103
Roast turkey 113
Roast wild duck 111
Rock cakes, wholemeal 160
Rolls, bread 169
Rolls, wholemeal bread 168
Rosti, Swiss bread 40
Russian herrings 22
Russian oysters 21

S
Salad dressings *see* Dressings
Salads 64-73
    anchovied vegetable 66
    avocado mould 73
    bean and egg 69
    Brazilian 70
    Caesar 65
    curried rice 73
    German cauliflower 66
    ham and rice 67
    Italian bean 68
    macaroni 64
    marinated fish 69
    mushroom 68
    niçoise 71
    potato 72
    prawn chef's 72
    spinach 67
    Swedish herring 67
    tangy chicken 71
    waldorf 65
    zucchini 64
Salmon flan, smoked 42
Salmon koulibiaka 38
Salmon mousse 37
Sardine hors d'oeuvre 27
Saté, Polynesian pork 95
Sauces 16-19
    barbecue 94
    béarnaise 19
    béchamel 16
    cocktail (for seafood) 29
    creamy mushroom 18
    curry 88
    espagnole 18
    hollandaise 17
    mayonnaise 16
    mushroom 18
    sweet and sour 19
    tartare 37
    tomato 17, 51, 101
    white 16
    wine 97
Sauerbraten 104

Sauté of kidneys turbigo 80
Scallop chowder 13
Scallops en brochette 36
Scallops with cream 39
Schnitzel, wiener 100
Scones 160-167
    cheese 162
    drop 160
    gem 161
    marmalade 162
    plain 162
    pumpkin 163
    sultana 162
    wholemeal 162
Scotch eggs 92
Scrambled cheese eggs 40
Seafood cocktail 29
Shellfish 30-39
Sherbet, pineapple mint 128
Shish kebabs 93
Shortcake, apricot 122
Simnel cake 149
Small cakes 150-159
Smoked ham with fruit 20
Smoked salmon flan 42
Snails (bread rolls) 169
Solid syllabub 132
Soufflé, cheese 47
Soufflé, chocolate 118
Soufflé, creamy lemon 130
Soufflé, loganberry 131
Soufflé, vanilla 118
Soups 8-15
    bortsch 14
    Chinese egg noodle 15
    cream of carrot 10
    cream of cauliflower 9
    cream of celery 9
    cream of lettuce 9
    cream of mushroom 10
    Dutch pea 9
    egg and prawn chowder 11
    fish and spinach 12
    French onion gratinée 12
    gazpacho 11
    mulligatawny 15
    oyster vert 13
    pea 9
    pumpkin 8
    scallop chowder 13
    Venetian chicken 14
Sour cherries, duck with 107
Spaghetti bolognese 53
Spaghetti marinara 54
Spaghetti springtime 51
Spaghetti with quick pesto
    sauce 55
Special occasion meat dishes
    96-105
Spiced apple teacake 167
Spiced apricot short ribs 84
Spiced carrot cake 149
Spiced chicken breasts 112
Spinach pancakes 43
Spinach salad 70
Spinach soup, fish and 12
Sponge, passionfruit 144
Steak
    and kidney pudding 77
    and mushroom pie 79
    bush barbecue 92
    carpetbag 99
    casserole, instant 88
    continental rolled 81
    pepper 96
    with orange dumplings 75
Steamed jam pudding 121

Stock, beef 8
Stock, chicken 8
Strawberry cream tartlets 156
Strawberry flan 137
Strawberry flan, no bake 135
Strawberry sabayon 120
Strudel, quick cherry 119
Stuffed baked fish 38
Stuffed cannelloni 51
Stuffed capsicums 79
Stuffed eggplants 20
Stuffed eggs with mushrooms
    24
Stuffed lemons 23
Stuffed mushrooms 59
Stuffed pork fillet 102
Stuffings
    chestnut 107
    rice 117
    sage and onion 98
    sausage 108
Sultana lemon delicious 125
Sultana scones 162
Summer fruit bowl 132
Summer pudding 127
Swedish herring salad 67
Swedish tea ring 172
Sweet and sour fish 31
Sweet and sour pork 89
Sweet and sour sauce 19
Swiss bread rosti 40
Swiss roll, chocolate 141
Syllabub, solid 132

T
Tangy chicken salad 71
Tart, caramel banana 136
Tart, honey 136
Tartare sauce 37
Tarte niçoise 46
Tartlets, strawberry cream 156
Tarts, coconut 152
Teriyaki, chicken kebabs 117
Tomato-cheese meat loaf 91
Tomato sauce 17, 51, 101
Tomatoes, brandied 23
Tomatoes, hot herbed 58
Trout, poached 35
Tuna almond sauté 34
Tuna croquettes, egg and 34
Tuna, island 30
Turkey, roast 113
Turkey tetrazzina 116

V
Vanilla ice cream 129
Vanilla soufflé 118
Veal
    and pork casserole 74
    birds 77
    blanquette 103
    parmigiana 101
    reboux 100
    wiener schnitzel 100
Vegetable hors d'oeuvre 28
Vegetables 56-63
Vegetables oriental, fried 58
Venetian chicken soup 14
Vols-au-vent, chicken and
    mushroom 21

W
Waldorf salad 65
Walnut meringue squares 155
West coast lobster 33
Whiting with almonds 32
Wholemeal bread 168

Wholemeal bread rolls 168
Wholemeal rock cakes 160
Wholemeal scones 162
Wiener schnitzel 100
Wine sauce 97

Y
Yeast breads 168-172

Z
Zabaglione 120
Zucchini provençale 57
Zucchini salad 64
Zucchini with sour cream 62